# Nope, that's not in †here

A guide to reading
the Bible for yourself

By Norman Snell

NOPE THAT'S NOT IN THERE
Copyright © 2025 by Norman Snell

All rights reserved. No portion of this book may be reproduced, stored in a retrieval system, or transmitted in any form or by any means—electronic, mechanical, photocopy, recording, scanning, or other—except for brief quotations in critical reviews or articles, without the prior written permission of the publisher.

Published in Northfield, New Jersey
First Edition: 2025

ISBN: 979-8-9992938-1-7 (print)
ISBN: 979-8-9992938-0-0 (ebook)

Unless otherwise noted, Scripture quotations are taken from the Holy Bible, New International Version®, NIV®. Copyright © 1973, 1978, 1984, 2011 by Biblica, Inc.™ Used by permission of Zondervan. All rights reserved worldwide. www.zondervan.com. The "NIV" and "New International Version" are trademarks registered in the United States Patent and Trademark Office by Biblica, Inc.™

Scripture quotations marked ESV are from the ESV® Bible (The Holy Bible, English Standard Version®), copyright © 2001 by Crossway, a publishing ministry of Good News Publishers. Used by permission. All rights reserved. Scripture quotations marked NLT are taken from the Holy Bible, New Living Translation, copyright © 1996, 2004, 2015 by Tyndale House Foundation. Used by permission of Tyndale House Publishers, Carol Stream, Illinois 60188. All rights reserved. Scripture quotations marked KJV are from the King James Version of the Bible, which is in the public domain.

Cover Design by Brian Niemann
Interior Design by Najdan Mancic

Printed in the United States of America

# DEDICATION

To Jesus,
who deserves to have His story told without agenda.

*"The Bible shows the way to go to heaven,
not the way the heavens go."*
—Galileo Galilei

INTRODUCTION

# Why Nobody Reads the Bible

*(and Why That's About to Change)*

Let's start with something honest: Most people don't read the Bible.

Not deeply. Not consistently. Not with clarity or hunger or any real expectation that something might actually happen when they do.

And here's the tension: Many of those same people would still say they *believe* the Bible.

Some even know it well.

We quote it. Defend it. Build frameworks around it. But often, we relate to it by reflex—repeating what we've heard, rarely stopping to ask if we've truly *seen* it for ourselves.

This isn't just about neglect. It's about overconfidence. We confuse familiarity with faithfulness.

We treat what we've already learned as the final word. And slowly—without realizing it—what began as reverence for the Bible becomes something else.

There's a thin line between reverence and ego.

Between honoring God's Word and using it to validate what we already think.

And while misinterpretation is dangerous, there's something even more subtle:

The assumption that we already see clearly. That the Bible is done speaking because we've stopped listening.

This book exists to interrupt that. Not with guilt—but with invitation.

Because whether you're skeptical, stale, stuck, or just spiritually tired, there's a deeper way to approach Scripture. One that's rooted not in performance, but in encounter.

The goal of this book isn't to get you to read the Bible more often. It's to help you read it **differently**—with openness, expectancy, and honesty.

Not to "get something out of it," but to meet someone in it.

The Bible is not a tool for self-help, a weapon for debate, or a checklist for spiritual maturity. It's a living record of God's self-revelation. And at the center of that revelation is not a principle—but a Person.

That Person isn't waiting for you to be more consistent. He's waiting to be known. If you're willing to be surprised, challenged, humbled, and led—this book is for you.

Let's start again.

Let's read like it's the first time.

Let's let the Bible speak.

And let's listen well enough to be changed.

PREFACE

# How to Use This Book

Welcome to *Nope That's Not in There*. This book is designed as a menu of biblical insights rather than a linear read. You don't need to start at page one and read straight through—although you certainly can!

Think of it like your very own Menu, offering a wide selection of "dishes" to suit every taste and stage of your journey. Whether you're:

- A skeptic curious about common misconceptions,
- A seeker looking to develop practical Bible engagement habits,
- Or a student hungry for deeper, intellectual Bible study...

You're free to jump around and "order" what resonates with you at any moment.

Each section represents a different "course" in your spiritual meal:

- **Section 1: Clearing Up Misconceptions** — For addressing common misunderstandings about Scripture

- **Section 2: Practical Bible Engagement** — For developing consistent, meaningful reading habits

- **Section 3: Theological Depth & Transformation** — For deepening your faith beyond the basics

- **Section 4: Bible Study—Learning the Mechanics** — For improving your interpretive skills

▸ **Section 5: Seeing the Big Picture** — For connecting individual passages to God's grand narrative

The Menu doesn't mean you have to read in a strict linear order. Each section is interconnected, and every "dish" contributes to a richer, fuller understanding of God's Word. Use it as a guide but always remember—the true transformation comes from encountering Jesus for yourself.

Bon appétit! May you discover the freedom and joy of engaging with the Bible on your own terms.

A WORD FROM THE AUTHOR

# When the Temple No Longer Makes the Gold Sacred

Like a thoughtfully prepared menu at a fine restaurant, Scripture offers various "courses" that nourish different aspects of our spiritual life. Some passages challenge our misconceptions, others establish practical habits, while still others transform our hearts at the deepest level. Yet too often, we focus on individual verses or rules—the "gold"—while missing the greater reality—the "temple"—that gives them meaning.

This book is structured as a menu because your spiritual journey isn't linear. Sometimes you need clarity about a misconception. Other times you need practical guidance for Bible reading. And occasionally, you need the deeper nourishment of theological transformation. Whatever your current need, you're free to choose from this menu according to your spiritual appetite.

I want to share something that has troubled me for years—a pattern I've observed throughout Scripture and church history that continues to play out today. It's a subtle inversion that Jesus identified with piercing clarity, one that explains so much about why sincere believers can know the Bible intimately yet miss its Author entirely.

The pattern begins with something sacred, something established by God. Over time, we gradually elevate the derivative elements of that sacred thing while diminishing or forgetting the foundation that gave it meaning in the first place. Eventually, we find ourselves defending the gold while forgetting the temple that made it sacred.

## JESUS EXPOSES THE INVERSION

In Matthew 23:16-19, Jesus confronts the religious leaders with a startling rebuke:

"Woe to you, blind guides! You say, 'If anyone swears by the temple, it means nothing; but anyone who swears by the gold of the temple is bound by that oath.' You blind fools! Which is greater: the gold, or the temple that makes the gold sacred?"

On the surface, this might seem like an obscure debate about oath-taking. But Jesus is exposing something far more significant—a fundamental confusion about what gives what its meaning.

The temple makes the gold sacred, not vice versa. The altar sanctifies the gift, not the other way around.

This inversion doesn't just apply to ancient oath formulas. It reveals a human tendency that has manifested throughout biblical history and continues to shape our approach to Scripture today.

**The Pattern Repeats Throughout Scripture**

This same distortion appears again and again in Scripture, taking different forms but always revealing the same fundamental error—elevating the derivative above its source.

## THE TEMPLE'S DESTRUCTION: CLINGING TO STONES WHILE REJECTING THE PRESENCE

Long before Jesus confronted the Pharisees, this pattern emerged in Jeremiah's day. The people of Judah were convinced God would never allow His temple to be destroyed. After all, wasn't it the place where He had put His name?

In Jeremiah 7, the prophet confronts this misplaced confidence: **"Do not trust in deceptive words and say, 'This is the temple of the LORD!'... Will you steal and murder...and then come and stand before me in this house, which bears my Name, and say, 'We are safe'?"**

The people had the doctrinal facts correct—God had indeed declared the temple as the place where He would put His name. But they were theologically blind to the more fundamental reality: the temple's meaning existed only in relationship to God Himself. They clung to the promise about the temple while violating their relationship with the Promise-Giver.

## THE FESTIVALS GOD HATED: FORM WITHOUT RELATIONSHIP

Moving from buildings to practices, we see the pattern continue in how Israel approached worship. In Amos 5:21, God declares something that should shock us: "I hate, I despise your religious festivals; your assemblies are a stench to me."

How can God hate the very festivals and worship practices He commanded? The answer lies in this same inversion. God established these practices as ways to connect with Him, to express devotion to Him. But when the people continued the external observances while abandoning the relationship those observances were meant to nurture, the practices became not just meaningless but offensive. It's like a husband giving his wife a wedding ring as a symbol of their covenant relationship. If she later begins an affair but continues wearing the ring, that same symbol becomes not just meaningless but offensive. The ring (doctrine) remains unchanged in its physical form, but its meaning (theology) is completely altered by the state of the relationship.

They kept the gift but abandoned the altar that made it sacred.

## JESUS AND THE SABBATH: THE LORD OF REST

This pattern clarifies Jesus' approach to the Sabbath—one of the most contentious issues in His ministry. The religious leaders were incensed when Jesus healed on the Sabbath or when His disciples plucked grain on the day of rest.

But Jesus reminded them, "The Sabbath was made for man, not man for the Sabbath. So, the Son of Man is Lord even of the Sabbath" (Mark 2:27-28).

The Sabbath was established as a gift of rest, meant to benefit humanity and honor God. But over time, the religious leaders had created such elaborate restrictions that they lost sight of its purpose. They elevated the rules about the Sabbath above the rest the Sabbath was meant to provide.

When Jesus healed on the Sabbath, He wasn't breaking God's law; He was fulfilling its deepest intention. He was restoring the proper order: The Lord of the Sabbath determines the Sabbath's meaning, not vice versa.

## THE WOMAN WITH THE ISSUE OF BLOOD: WHEN TOUCHING BRINGS HEALING

Consider the woman with the issue of blood in Mark 5. According to Levitical law, this woman was ritually unclean. Anyone she touched would become unclean. By approaching Jesus in a crowd and touching His garment, she was violating religious protocol in multiple ways.

Yet Jesus doesn't rebuke her. Instead, He calls her "Daughter" and commends her faith.

Why? Because she understood something profound—something the religious experts with all their doctrinal precision often missed. She recognized that Jesus Himself was greater than the purity laws. She grasped that the God who established those laws could transcend them for the purpose of healing and restoration.

When she touched Jesus, He didn't become unclean; she became clean.

This doesn't mean the purity laws were wrong or unnecessary. It means that the One who established those laws can't be bound or limited by them. The lawgiver transcends the law. The temple makes the gold sacred, not the other way around. This illustrates how true faithfulness sometimes requires moving beyond surface-level doctrinal adherence to a deeper theological understanding of God's heart and purpose. The religious experts knew what the law said, but this woman understood what it meant in the presence of the One who gave it.

## THE MODERN PARALLEL: DEFENDING THE GOLD, FORGETTING THE TEMPLE

This pattern of inversion continues today. I've observed it throughout my years in ministry, and perhaps you've seen it too:

We quote Scripture meticulously while resisting its transformative power. We debate theological points vigorously while neglecting justice and mercy. We defend the Bible passionately while missing the God it reveals.

I witnessed this firsthand during a church Bible study where an elderly woman shared a profound insight about God's grace that didn't fit neatly into the group's doctrinal framework. Rather than exploring her perspective, several members immediately jumped in with proof texts to "correct" her, citing chapter and verse with precision. The woman never spoke up again. In their rush to defend doctrinal accuracy, they shut down what might have been a fresh work of the Spirit in their midst. They protected the gold but forgot the temple that made it sacred.

This is particularly evident in our approach to apologetics. Don't misunderstand me—defending the faith is biblical and necessary. But there's a subtle yet crucial distinction between defending faith and becoming so entrenched in defensive postures that we lose the capacity for genuine revelation.

Sometimes, certainty becomes the enemy of understanding. When we believe we must have all the answers and defend them at all costs, we inadvertently close ourselves to the very voice we claim to champion.

In our eagerness to have answers for everything, we can create closed systems that leave no room for the Spirit to speak in ways that might surprise or challenge us. **We defend God so vigorously that we stop listening to Him.**

This is the modern manifestation of elevating the gold above the temple—valuing our understanding of Scripture more than the God it reveals.

## THE CALCIFIED WAY OF PROCESSING TRUTH

By a "calcified way of processing truth," I mean a mindset that has become so rigid and self-assured that it leaves no room for God's ongoing revelation. Like calcium deposits that harden over time, our theological frameworks can solidify to the point where they no longer flex or grow. We stop approaching Scripture expecting to be surprised or challenged. Instead, we read only to confirm what we already "know."

What makes this pattern so persistent is that it often emerges from good intentions. The religious leaders Jesus confronted weren't trying to dishonor God; they were trying to preserve what they believed was sacred. The people in Jeremiah's day weren't attempting to delude themselves; they genuinely believed the temple's presence guaranteed their safety.

Similarly, when we become rigid in our approach to Scripture today, it's usually born from a desire to honor God's Word and protect the faith "once for all delivered to the saints" (Jude 1:3).

**But good intentions don't prevent the inversion from happening.** Over time, our understanding becomes calcified. We stop approaching Scripture with the expectation of fresh revelation. We no longer read with the humility that recognizes there's always more to discover. Instead, we come to confirm what we already know, to reinforce the systems we've already built.

This calcification creates the illusion of spiritual productivity while hindering genuine growth. **We become spiritually busy but spiritually unproductive.** We might engage in Bible studies, theological discussions, and apologetic defenses—all good activities in themselves—while missing the transformation that comes from encountering the living God through His Word.

It's like the difference between studying a map and taking the journey. The map is essential, but it's not the destination. When we mistake the map for the journey, we end up knowing about places we've never actually visited.

## THE TEMPLE STILL MAKES THE GOLD SACRED

The core truth Jesus emphasized in Matthew 23 remains just as vital today: the temple makes the gold sacred, not vice versa. Applied to our approach to Scripture, this means:

- God gives the Bible its authority; the Bible doesn't give God His authority
- Divine revelation is about relationship, not just information

- Scripture's purpose is to lead us to God, not substitute for Him
- Biblical knowledge should serve transformation, not just accumulation

This isn't to diminish Scripture's importance. On the contrary, recognizing the proper order enhances our view of the Bible by restoring it to its intended function—revealing the living God who wants to be known.

When we understand that "good doctrine is good personal revelation," we see that authentic doctrine flows from and leads back to relationship. Doctrine becomes lifeless when separated from the Person it's meant to reveal.

## A CALL TO RECEPTIVE READING

Scripture repeatedly shows us that the most mature believers maintain a posture of openness and childlike receptivity—not because they're uncertain about God's character, but because they're certain He's greater than their current understanding.

I believe the sign of true spiritual maturity isn't having more answers but becoming more teachable. It isn't accumulating certainty but developing deeper capacity to receive. The greatest saints throughout history weren't those who claimed to have God figured out, but those who remained in perpetual wonder at His unfolding revelation.

The same Jesus who confronted the inverted priorities of religious leaders extends this invitation to us today: "Receive the kingdom of God like a little child" (Mark 10:15). Children approach life with curiosity, receptivity, and the expectation of discovery. They haven't yet developed the calcified patterns that prevent genuine learning.

What would happen if we approached Scripture with this same childlike openness? What if we read expecting to be surprised, challenged, and transformed? What if we valued relationship with the Author above mastery of the text?

## MY HEART FOR THIS BOOK

This brings me to my purpose in writing this book. My deepest hope isn't that you'll simply gain more biblical knowledge—though that will certainly happen. My prayer is that through these pages, you'll discover (or rediscover) the joy of encountering the living God through His Word.

I want to help you clear away the misconceptions and obstacles that prevent genuine engagement with Scripture. I want to give you practical tools for reading the Bible effectively. I want to show you how to see both the individual trees and the magnificent forest of God's redemptive story.

But most of all, I want to invite you into a relationship with the God who speaks through these pages—the God who is greater than our systems, larger than our categories, and more wonderful than our most profound understandings.

In short, I want to help you remember that the temple makes the gold sacred, not the other way around.

In the following chapters, we'll explore practical strategies for reading Scripture with this receptive mindset. We'll clear away common misconceptions, learn effective Bible study techniques, and discover how to see the big picture of God's redemptive plan. Throughout, our goal will remain the same: not just to know about God, but to truly know Him.

So, as we journey through this book together, let's commit to approaching Scripture with both reverence for its authority and openness to its Author. Let's honor the gold by remembering the temple that makes it sacred.

**May our reading lead not just to knowing about God, but to truly knowing Him.**

# TABLE OF CONTENTS

Why Nobody Reads the Bible ................................................................. 1
How to Use This Book ........................................................................... 3
When the Temple No Longer Makes the Gold Sacred ....................... 5
For the Skimmers .................................................................................. 18

## SECTION ONE: Clearing Up Misconceptions ........................... 21
1. Why Christians Can Be the Worst Bible Readers ...................... 23
2. Did the Bible Copy Other Ancient Texts? ................................. 31
3. One Verse Doesn't Topple the Whole ........................................ 35
4. The Bible's Historical Reliability ................................................ 41
5. The Bible's Incredible Journey .................................................... 46
6. Who Decided What's in the Bible? ............................................ 51
7. Why Does God Seem Different in the Old and New Testaments? .... 57
8. Why Doesn't God Just Show Up on TikTok? ........................... 63
9. Wait... Can We Curse Our Enemies or Not? ............................. 67
10. Did Jesus Claim to Be God? ........................................................ 71
11. All or Nothing .............................................................................. 76
12. Can the Bible Be Biased and Truthful? ...................................... 79
13. Do Christians Still Need the Ten Commandments? ................. 83
14. Modern Navigational Tools: Chapters, Verses, and Subheadings ... 86
15. "Paul Preached a Different Message Than Jesus" ...................... 90
16. Dividing the Word: The Sermon on the Mount and the Old Covenant .... 93
17. Even Jesus Interpreted ................................................................. 96

**SECTION TWO: Practical Bible Engagement ......................... 101**

18. You Need to Actually Like Reading the Bible ........................... 103
19. Stop Overthinking It: Just Open the Book! ............................... 109
20. Bible Reading for Beginners: Where to Start ............................ 112
21. Holy Habits: Embrace the Routine ............................................ 117
22. DIY But Not Alone: Balancing Personal Study and Community ... 120
23. Clear the Noise: Hearing God in a Cluttered World ................. 123
24. Remember what you read: Write it down ................................. 126
25. Meditate on the Word—Hearing What God Is Saying to You .... 128
26. Your Soul is Hungry—Give It the Right Food .......................... 131
27. "If I Don't Feel It, Is It Even Working?" ..................................... 133
28. When You're Too Sad to Read the Bible ................................... 137
29. Don't Spoil the Story—Read with Fresh Eyes .......................... 139
30. "The Bible is a Mirror, Not a Microphone" ............................... 142
31. Healthy Fear: The Weapon You Didn't Know You Needed ...... 143
32. It Really Is the Phone: Dealing with distraction ....................... 146
33. The Enemy of the Word ............................................................. 149
34. "Stop Treating the Bible Like a Self-Help Book ....................... 151

**SECTION THREE: From Reading to Becoming ..................... 157**

35. "Eyes on Jesus, Not Yourself" ..................................................... 159
36. Seeing is Believing: How to Deepen Your Trust in God ........... 164
37. More Than a Formula: Faith is a Relationship .......................... 167
38. Tapping into the Source: The Wedding at Cana ....................... 173
39. "The Faith Killer: Overthinking Everything" ............................. 178

40. Holiness Isn't About Trying Harder—It's About Trusting More .... 185
41. Rest: The Fuel for Your Soul ................................................. 192
42. Led by the Spirit: Living a Supernatural Life ........................... 197
43. Everyday Faith: Taking God Home ........................................ 202
44. Silence the Negative Voices .................................................. 208
45. Wisdom 101: Start with Common Sense ................................ 214
46. Pray Boldly: Asking God Without Hesitation ......................... 221
47. Heart Surgery: Let God Transform You From the Inside Out . 227
48. Jesus the Disrupter: Get Ready for Change ........................... 233
49. Jesus: The Author and Finisher of Your Faith ....................... 239
50. "Grace That Changes Everything" ....................................... 244
51. Faith in the Real World How to Be Social ............................. 251
52. Obedience is the Most Spiritual Thing You Can Do .............. 258
53. God's Word Works—Let It Do Its Job .................................. 264

**SECTION FOUR: Bible Study Learning The Mechanics ......... 273**
54. A Bible Study: "It Will Not Be Forgiven" .............................. 275
55. Bible Study: Understanding John 3:1–15 .............................. 285
56. Bible Study: Reading Matthew 24 with Care ........................ 294
57. Bible Study: The Parable of the Ten Minas (Luke 19) ........... 301
58. "Take Up Your Cross"—Embracing His Cross, Not Ours ..... 309
59. Cross-Examining Jesus' Words ............................................. 316
60. When the Bible Interprets Its Own Story .............................. 324
61. "Faith Without Works Is Dead" ............................................ 330
62. When We Stretch the Text Too Far ...................................... 338

**SECTION FIVE: Seeing the Big Picture ..................347**

63. How to Read the Gospels ........................................349
64. The Forest for the Trees on the Binary Outcome......................366
65. The Forest for the Trees – Progression ...........................372
66. The Forest for the Trees—Divine Concessions and Adaptability.....378
67. The Forest for the Trees – The Kingdom................................386
68. The Forest for the Trees on Sin ....................................392
69. The Forest for the Trees on Intimacy...............................397
70. The Forest for the Trees — Divine Communication Within Human Limitations................................................................403
71. Forest for the Trees – All Things Fulfilled in Christ ................412
72. The Menu Was Only the Beginning .............................................417

Works Cited................................................................422

# For the Skimmers

*(Or why just ordering an appetizer might change everything)*

Listen, I get it. You're busy. There's an excellent chance you'll never read this book cover to cover—and that's fine. This book was designed as a menu you can dip in and out of according to your spiritual appetite.

But if I could slide four "must-try" dishes across the table, these would be the ones that capture the heart of what makes this perspective different. Consider them the signature dishes that might just change how you taste everything else:

***We've Been Reading the Gospels Too Small*** **(Section 5)** This isn't just another chapter—it's the heartbeat of the entire book. What if we've been approaching the Gospels primarily as moral lessons when they're showing us the explosive drama of God Himself walking among His covenant people? This chapter reframes the entire Gospel narrative away from "what should I do?" to "who is showing up here, and how are people responding?" Trust me on this one.

***The Forest for the Trees - Divine Communication Within Human Limitations*** **(Section 5)** How does an infinite God speak through finite human language? This chapter explores how God's truth passes through the medium of human understanding—like sunlight through stained glass—without diminishing the divine message. Not a bug, but a feature.

***"Eyes on Jesus, Not Yourself"*** **(Section 3)** The most common error in modern Bible reading isn't skepticism—it's self-focus. We turn every passage into a story about our spiritual performance rather than fixing our gaze on Jesus Himself. This chapter might shake up how you approach Scripture tomorrow morning.

***"Stop Treating the Bible Like a Self-Help Book"*** **(Section 2)** In our productivity-obsessed culture, we've reduced Scripture to a tool for self-improvement. This chapter challenges the assumption that everything in the Bible needs to "do something" for us, inviting us instead to simply bask in the beauty of divine revelation.

If these resonate with you, you'll find the rest of the book builds on these core insights. But even if you read nothing else, these four perspectives might transform how you approach Scripture—and that's what this whole menu is about.

*Bon appétit.*

31 Then their eyes were opened, & they knew him, and he vanished out of their sight.

32 And they said betweene themselues, Did not our hearts burne within vs, while hee talked with vs by the way, and when hee opened to vs the Scriptures?

33 And they rose vp the same houre, and returned to Ierusalem, and found the eleuen gathered together, and them that were with them,

34 Saying, The Lord is risen in deede, and hath appeared to Simon.

35 Then they told what things were done in the way, and how hee was knowen of them in breaking of bread.

36 ¶ And as they spake thus, Iesus himselfe stood in the mids of them, and said vnto them, Peace be to you.

37 But they were abashed and afraid, supposing that they had seene a spirit.

38 Then he said vnto them, Why are ye troubled? and wherefore doe such doubts arise in your hearts?

39 Behold mine hands, and my feete: for it is I my selfe: handle me, and see: for a spirit hath not flesh and bones, as ye see me haue.

40 And when he had thus spoken, he shewed them his hands and feete.

41 And while they yet beleeued not for ioy, and wondered, he said vnto them, Haue ye here any meate?

42 And they gaue him a piece of a broyled fish, and of an hony combe.

43 And hee tooke it, and did eate before them.

44 ¶ And hee saide vnto them, These are the wordes, which I spake vnto you while I was yet with you, that all must bee fulfilled, which are written of mee in the Law of Moses, and in the Prophets, and in the Psalmes.

45 Then opened hee their vnderstanding, that they might vnderstand the Scriptures,

46 And said vnto them, Thus it is written, and thus it behoued Christ to suffer, & to rise againe from the dead the third day,

47 And that repentance, & remission of sinnes should be preached in his Name among all nations, beginning at Hierusalem.

48 Now ye are witnesses of these things.

49 And behold, I doe send the promise of my Father vpon you: but tarie ye in the citie of Hierusalem, vntill yee bee endued with power from on high.

50 ¶ Afterward he led them out into Bethania, and lift vp his hands, and blessed them.

51 And it came to passe, that as he blessed them, hee departed from them, and was caried vp into heauen.

52 And they worshipped him, and returned to Hierusalem with great ioy,

53 And were continually in the Temple, praysing, and lauding God. Amen.

# THE HOLY GOSPEL OF IESVS CHRIST ACCORDING TO IOHN.

## CHAP. I.

IN the beginning was that Word, and that Word was with God, and that Word was God.

2 This same was in the beginning with God.

3 All things were made by it, and without it was made nothing that was made.

4 In it was life, and that life was the light of men.

5 And that light shineth in the darkenesse, and the darkenesse comprehended it not.

6 ¶ There was a man sent from God, whose name was Iohn.

7 This same came for a witnesse, to beare witnesse of that light, that all men through him might beleeue.

8 Hee was not that light, but was sent to beare witnesse of that light.

9 This was that true light, which lighteth euery man that commeth into the world.

10 He was in the world, and the world was made by him: and the world knew him not.

11 He came vnto his owne, and his owne receiued him not.

12 But as many as receiued him, to them he gaue prerogatiue to be the sonnes of God, euen to them that beleeue in his Name,

13 Which are borne not of blood, nor of the will of the flesh, nor of the will of man, but of God.

SECTION ONE

# Clearing Up Misconceptions

# 1

# Why Christians Can Be the Worst Bible Readers

*And Why Skeptics Sometimes Read It Better*

It's a startling thought—those who profess to love Scripture the most might be the ones most likely to misread it. While I'd never suggest abandoning faith to become better Bible readers, there's something counterintuitive at work: the very devotion that draws Christians to Scripture can sometimes prevent them from truly seeing what's on the page. Meanwhile, the detachment skeptics bring to the text occasionally allows them to spot what believers miss.

This isn't about who loves the Bible more. It's about recognizing how familiarity, agenda, and religious identity can create blind spots—and how we might all become better readers by understanding these dynamics.

## THE PROBLEM OF FAMILIARITY

Have you ever driven home so habitually that you arrived with no memory of the journey? Your brain operated on autopilot, seeing without seeing. This happens with Scripture, too.

Christians grow up hearing the same stories, the same interpretations, the same applications. "David and Goliath is about facing your giants." "The Prodigal Son teaches God's forgiveness." These pre-packaged readings become so embedded that we stop reading the text. Instead, we recite what we've always known it to mean.

As I wrote in the introduction, "We confuse familiarity with faithfulness. We treat what we've already learned as the final word." The danger isn't ignorance—it's the *illusion* of understanding.

Skeptics don't suffer from this ailment. When they open Scripture, they often truly read it for the first time. They notice details believers have glossed over for decades: Why did God harden Pharaoh's heart? Why does Jesus speak so differently in John compared to Mark? These questions aren't hostile—they're the natural response of someone encountering the text with fresh eyes.

I once discussed the story of Abraham binding Isaac with a friend who had never read the Bible. He was horrified: "This isn't the inspiring story I expected—it's disturbing!" His reaction made me realize I'd become numb to the text's raw power. My familiarity had sanitized a story that *should* be unsettling. The skeptic saw what was there; I saw what I'd been told to see.

## THE APPLICATION-FIRST MENTALITY

Perhaps the most pervasive problem in Christian Bible reading is what I call the "application-first" approach. Before the text has been understood in its historical and literary context, before the drama of God's revelation has been absorbed, we're already asking, "How does this apply to my life?"

This isn't mere impatience—it fundamentally distorts Scripture. When every passage must yield an immediate moral lesson or practical application, we flatten the Bible's rich complexity into a self-help manual.

As I explored in "We've Been Reading the Gospels Too Small," this approach especially damages our understanding of Jesus' ministry. The cosmic drama of God incarnate walking among His covenant people becomes reduced to principles for effective living. We turn the Gospels into moral instruction when they're primarily revealing God's nature and human response to divine presence.

Consider Jesus healing on the Sabbath. Christians typically extract the lesson: "Human needs matter more than religious rules." That's not wrong, but it misses the deeper revelation: God Himself is redefining what it means to honor the Sabbath He instituted. The religious leaders aren't just being inflexible—they're rejecting the Lord of the Sabbath standing before them.

Skeptics rarely approach Scripture with this application-first mindset. They don't need the Bible to teach them how to live better today. Instead, they read to understand what the text says and what it meant in its original context. Ironically, this more detached approach sometimes yields greater insight into Scripture's actual message.

## THE PROBLEM OF RELIGIOUS IDENTITY

For many Christians, the Bible isn't just a sacred text—it's bound up with their entire identity. Denominational commitments, theological frameworks, and cultural expectations all shape how believers approach Scripture. The Bible must conform to what they already "know" to be true.

In "When the Temple No Longer Makes the Gold Sacred," I discussed how religious identity can become self-reinforcing, leading us to defend God against God. We cite Scripture to resist the Author of Scripture. When the Bible challenges our theological system or moral assumptions, we find ways to reinterpret or contextualize the problematic passages.

A Baptist might read passages on baptism differently than a Presbyterian. A charismatic might emphasize different verses than a cessationist. A progressive Christian might navigate difficult Old Testament texts differently than a conservative one. These aren't necessarily dishonest readings, but they reveal how prior commitments influence our interpretation.

Skeptics bring fewer theological presuppositions to the text. They might miss important context or tradition, but they're also less likely to engage in interpretive gymnastics to protect a doctrinal position. They can acknowledge that Paul sounds different from Jesus, that Ecclesiastes presents a worldview unlike Proverbs, that James emphasizes works while Romans stresses faith—all without needing to harmonize these tensions into a seamless system.

I've witnessed profound insights from skeptical readers who simply point out what the text says rather than what it's supposed to say according to a particular tradition. Their freedom from religious identity sometimes allows for greater textual honesty.

## THE FEAR OF AMBIGUITY

Christians often approach Scripture with an expectation that everything must fit together perfectly. Every apparent contradiction must be resolved. Every morally troubling passage must be explained. Every verse must yield clear, applicable truth. This anxiety around ambiguity stems from a sincere desire to honor God's Word but can lead to forced readings and *artificial harmony*.

In "Divine Communication Within Human Limitations," I explored how God's revelation comes through human language, culture, and understanding—like sunlight through stained glass. This means Scripture contains genuine tensions, culturally embedded expressions, and passages that resist easy explanation.

Christians frequently rush to resolve these tensions. But what if—and hear me out—we just didn't?

I once had a coworker at the gas company whose mantra was "Remember, doing nothing is an option." He wasn't advocating laziness; he was acknowledging a profound truth: our instinct to immediately act, fix, or manage doesn't always improve the situation. Sometimes the wisest response is to wait, observe, and resist the impulse to control.

This wisdom applies surprisingly well to Bible reading. Look at what happened when we couldn't resist the urge to explain everything. The Talmud, intended to clarify the Torah, eventually expanded so vastly it overshadows the very Scriptures it aimed to explain. The Protestant Reformation, launched in pursuit of biblical clarity, fractured into countless denominations, each claiming the clearer biblical interpretation. We talk and explain and resolve so much that we rarely stop to simply absorb what's written. It's the theological equivalent of nervously filling conversational silence. God says something complex, and before the echo of His voice has faded, we're already explaining what He *really* meant. Perhaps faith mature enough to say, "I don't understand this fully yet, and that's okay. "The ability to sit with biblical tensions—to do nothing when encountering apparent contradictions—might be the spiritual discipline we're missing. Not every mystery needs immediate resolution.

Skeptics tend to be more comfortable with textual complexity. They're willing to acknowledge tensions without immediately resolving them. They can recognize that different biblical authors present different perspectives without feeling compelled to harmonize everything into a single viewpoint. This comfort with ambiguity sometimes allows them to engage the text more honestly than believers who need everything to align with their theological system.

## WHEN DEVOTION OBSCURES DISCOVERY

The ultimate irony is that Christians' deep reverence for Scripture can sometimes prevent them from truly hearing it. *When a text is elevated to such sacred status that questioning or wrestling with it feels blasphemous, genuine engagement becomes impossible.*

I've seen Bible studies where someone raises a legitimate question about a difficult passage, only to be quickly shut down with, "We just need to have faith" or "God's ways are higher than our ways." While these responses contain truth, they can function as conversation-stoppers that prevent deeper exploration.

The skeptic feels no such constraint. They can ask hard questions, notice problematic passages, and challenge traditional interpretations without feeling spiritually threatened. They can engage the text as it is, not as they need it to be.

Yet here's the tragedy: the skeptic's clearer vision often lacks the devotion that makes Scripture truly transformative. They might see the text more accurately in some ways, but they miss its deeper purpose—to reveal the living God who seeks relationship with His creation.

## LEARNING FROM BOTH PERSPECTIVES

The solution isn't for Christians to become skeptics or for skeptics to stop questioning. It's for believers to cultivate a faith that embraces both ***devotion and discovery***.

Imagine approaching Scripture with:

- The freshness of someone reading it for the first time, even when you've read it a hundred times before
- The patience to understand before applying, to absorb before acting

- The courage to question traditional interpretations without abandoning the tradition that sustains you
- The humility to acknowledge tensions and ambiguities without needing to resolve every one
- The wisdom to see that wrestling with the text honors it more than passive acceptance

This approach doesn't diminish Scripture's authority—it takes that authority seriously enough to engage with the actual text rather than our preconceptions about it.

## TRANSFORMATION THROUGH HUMILITY

The path forward begins with humility. Christians must acknowledge that familiarity, application-focus, religious identity, and fear of ambiguity can distort their reading. Skeptics must recognize that detachment, while providing clarity in some areas, may miss the transformative purpose of Scripture.

As I suggested in "Eyes on Jesus, Not Yourself," the key is shifting focus from self-improvement to divine encounter. When we read Scripture primarily to mine it for practical applications or to reinforce our theological positions, we remain at the center of our interpretive universe. But when we read to encounter the living God—to be challenged, comforted, disturbed, and transformed by His presence—we position ourselves rightly before the text.

The best Bible readers combine the skeptic's willingness to see what's there with the believer's openness to be changed by what they find. They approach Scripture with both critical intelligence and humble receptivity. They understand that, as I wrote earlier, "the temple makes the gold sacred"—it's not our doctrines about the Bible that give it value, but the God who reveals Himself through it.

## CONCLUSION: READING WITH BOTH EYES OPEN

If there's one lesson we might learn from the skeptic, it's to read with both eyes open—to see the text as it is, not merely as we wish it to be. This doesn't mean abandoning faith. It means allowing that faith to be robust enough to withstand honest engagement with Scripture's complexities.

The worst Bible readers, whether believers or skeptics, are those who use the text rather than being used by it—who come with agendas so firmly fixed that nothing can challenge them. The best readers, from any perspective, are those who remain open to surprise, to challenge, to having their understanding expanded rather than merely confirmed.

So let us read with the freshness of the skeptic and the devotion of the believer. Let us approach Scripture not as a mine for extracting moral lessons or proof texts, **but as a living revelation where God speaks within and sometimes beyond our expectations.** Let us be willing to be disturbed, confused, challenged, and transformed by what we find there.

For in the end, the purpose of Scripture is not merely to inform us but to transform us—not by confirming what we already believe, but by conforming us to the image of the One who speaks through its pages.

# 2

# Did the Bible Copy Other Ancient Texts?

*The Wrong Question Built on the Wrong Assumption*

You've probably heard it before—maybe from a late-night documentary or a viral comment under a YouTube sermon:

"The Bible isn't even original. The Epic of Gilgamesh came first. So did Egyptian creation myths. Your book just borrowed from older stuff."

It sounds like a mic-drop moment. But behind that claim is a sneaky assumption—one that even some well-meaning Christians accidentally reinforce.

Here it is:

**If something is truly divine, it must be completely unlike anything human.**

Sounds noble, right? But it creates an impossible standard that neither skeptics nor believers can live with.

## THE FUNDAMENTAL CONTRADICTION

We want God to speak to us, but we also demand that what He says:

- be **completely otherworldly**,
- **entirely original**, and
- somehow still **perfectly clear** to us.

That's the contradiction. We expect divine revelation to sound like it came from another universe—and then get frustrated when we can't understand it.

It's like asking someone to sing in a frequency the human ear can't hear and then blaming them when we don't hear anything.

## THE PARALLEL PLANES FALLACY

Skeptics say, "See? The Bible shares patterns with older myths. That proves it's just human."

Defenders sometimes say,

"No! Our faith is totally unique, totally unlike anything that came before. That proves it's from God."

The funny thing is—they're arguing from the same flawed assumption:

That God and humanity operate on two completely separate planes. And that real revelation must exist entirely apart from human culture, language, or literary devices to be legit.

That's not how communication works.

That's how *confusion* works.

## THE ACCESSIBILITY PROBLEM

Let's say God wanted to tell humanity something. But instead of using any familiar words or concepts, He invents a new language from scratch—no grammar, no shared references, no overlap with anything we know.

Would we call that "divine"? Or just completely incomprehensible?

---

**Real communication requires shared understanding.**

---

It's not plagiarism when someone speaks in your language. It's called being kind. It's how connection works.

God didn't avoid our frameworks—He entered them.

## JESUS: THE FINAL ANSWER TO THE WHOLE DEBATE

This is why the incarnation matters so much.

Jesus didn't show up to be *totally other*. He came to be fully **God** *and* fully **human.**

He didn't drop out of the sky wrapped in alien symbols and cosmic jargon. He was born into a specific culture, with a specific language, at a specific time—and He didn't apologize for it.

*"The Word became flesh and made his dwelling among us."*
—JOHN 1:14

God didn't bypass humanity to reveal Himself. He **embraced** it.

---

**So… Did the Bible Copy Other Ancient Texts?**

---

If what you're asking is, *"Does the Bible contain familiar literary structures or themes that appear in other ancient texts?"*—then sure. But that's not evidence *against* its divine origin.

That's evidence it was written in a real place, in real time, using real human frameworks—exactly what we'd expect if God's goal was to communicate with people, not confuse them.

And if Jesus—the full expression of God—didn't avoid being human, then why would we expect Scripture to sound like something dropped from Mars?

## FINAL THOUGHT

Sometimes we want revelation to feel so "divine" that it's basically unusable. We want it to be so untouched by human fingerprints that we forget—*we're the ones it's meant for.*

---

**The goal of Scripture was never to sound impressive. It was to be understood.**

---

So no, the Bible didn't copy ancient texts.

It entered a human conversation—on purpose.

And through that conversation, God said exactly what He wanted us to hear.

# 3

# One Verse Doesn't Topple the Whole

Imagine you're playing a game of Jenga. You gingerly pull out one wooden block, heart pounding, sure that if you so much as wiggle it, the entire tower will come crashing down. Some folks treat the Bible like that—assuming a single questionable word or passage might topple Christianity. It's a nerve-wracking perspective, and it's not how the Bible works.

This chapter is your front-row seat to a different point of view: The Bible is more like a solid house on a robust foundation, and tugging at one block won't bring down the entire structure. Even if there's a minor translation hiccup, or a passage missing from early manuscripts, the overarching message stands firm.

- If you're skeptical about the Bible's trustworthiness, you're in the right place. Throughout this book, we'll look at why the biblical text remains intact (see The Bible's Historical Reliability)

- Presents evidence (manuscript counts, time gaps, comparative analysis) to demonstrate that the Bible is remarkably well preserved compared to other ancient texts.

For how it was preserved and translated over centuries **The Bible's Incredible Journey**

- Traces the human story behind Scripture's transmission—from ancient scrolls to modern translations—and highlights the dedicated, often sacrificial, efforts that safeguarded its message.

And whether it's just a human invention for control (see **Who Decided What's in the Bible?**

- Explains how the biblical canon formed through a broad, community-based recognition of inspired writings rather than a secretive, top-down process but first, let's tackle the idea that one shaky word or verse can discredit the whole thing.

## A QUICK VISUAL

Try this mini exercise: read the sentence below, even though it's missing a couple of key words.

"One _____ translation can't overshadow the core _____ of Scripture."

Even with those blanks, you probably get the idea. A single flawed translation doesn't erase the central content. The Bible is like that, too. Across thousands of manuscripts and centuries of study, no single scribal slip or subpar translation has ever truly threatened its main narrative.

## COMMUNICATION IS TOUGHER THAN WE THINK

Here's what's fascinating: we've somehow convinced ourselves that the Bible—supposedly containing the most important communication in human history—is also the most fragile document ever created. One mistranslation and the whole thing crumbles? That's not how communication works anywhere else in life.

Consider this garbled text message you probably received at some point: "Hey can u meet me at the coffe shop on 5th street at 3pm? My phone is acting weird and i need to tlak to you about the projct."

Did you panic and think, "I have no idea what this person wants"? Of course not. Despite multiple typos and a misspelling, the meaning came through crystal clear. You knew exactly where to go, when to be there, and why you were meeting.

## THE AI REVOLUTION PROVES THE POINT

If you've used any AI assistant, you've discovered something remarkable: you can communicate with broken grammar, incomplete thoughts, and even foreign language mixed in, and it still understands you perfectly. Type "write me email boss about vacation next week need approve" and AI doesn't respond with "ERROR: GRAMMAR INSUFFICIENT. COMMUNICATION FAILED." It writes you a professional email because it grasps your intent through the mess.

AI demonstrates daily what linguists have known for decades: meaning is incredibly resilient. Communication has built-in redundancy. Context fills gaps. Intent transcends imperfection.

Now think about this: if human-created technology can parse meaning from our verbal fumbling, how much more robust is communication designed by God himself? We've created artificial intelligence that handles broken language better than many Christians handle biblical manuscripts. The irony is staggering.

## AUTOCORRECT AND THE RESILIENCE OF MEANING

Your phone's autocorrect provides endless examples of how meaning survives translation hiccups. "I'll bring desert to dinner" instead of "dessert"—yet nobody shows up expecting sand dunes. "Can you pick up some bread form the store" doesn't leave anyone confused about where to shop or what to buy.

These aren't communication failures; they're proof that understanding operates on multiple levels simultaneously. We process words, context, relationships, and intent all at once. One garbled element rarely derails the entire message.

## THE MANUFACTURED FRAGILITY

Here's the uncomfortable truth: both aggressive atheists and anxious Christians have conspired to make the Bible artificially fragile. Atheists insist that any textual variation proves it's unreliable. Nervous believers respond by insisting every single word must be perfect or their faith collapses. Both positions are ridiculous.

This fragility isn't inherent to Scripture—it's manufactured by centuries of human anxiety and argument. God didn't create a communication so delicate that one copyist's-tired hand could destroy it. That would make divine revelation weaker than a text message, less resilient than broken English, more fragile than AI can handle.

## WHAT GOD ACTUALLY MADE

Remember what Paul said in Romans: creation itself reveals God's character and power. The mountains, stars, and oceans don't speak in perfect Hebrew or Greek, yet their message about God's majesty comes through unmistakably. If God can communicate through wordless creation, surely His written revelation can survive the difference between "blessed" and "happy."

The Bible was designed for human beings—real people with real limitations who would copy it by hand, translate it across cultures, and read it in candlelight. God knew exactly what He was doing. He made His message robust enough to survive the beautiful mess of human handling while remaining clear enough to transform lives across every culture and century.

## NOT JUST BITE-SIZED NUGGETS

Part of why we get anxious about "one missing word" is that we often read the Bible in bite-sized portions. Our modern practice of dividing the text into chapters and verses is handy (we'll talk about these tools in more detail later), but it can make us hyper-focus on tiny fragments. When you focus on one verse in isolation, it's easy to wonder if a missing or changed word could derail everything.

The original writers didn't label their paragraphs with verse numbers or headings. That's a modern navigation system added for clarity. If you're curious about how these "chapter and verse" conventions arose—and how they sometimes shape our reading—we'll explore this in Chapter **14, "Modern Navigational Tools: Chapters, Verses, and Subheadings."**

## CASE STUDIES: JOHN 8 AND MARK 16

If you flip through some modern Bibles, you might see a footnote or bracketed disclaimer around two well-known passages:

- John 8 (the woman caught in adultery)
- Mark 16:9–20 (the longer ending of Mark)

Scholars note these sections don't appear in some of the earliest available manuscripts. That can sound alarming at first: *Did somebody add or remove Scripture?* But here's the key point: **none of Christianity's core teachings hinge on these specific passages**. The doctrine of Jesus' divinity, His resurrection, and His call to love one another are all established across many other portions of the Bible. If, hypothetically, these passages turned out not to be part of the original text, the central themes of the Christian faith would remain untouched.

## WHICH TRANSLATION IS BEST?

People often ask, "What's the best translation?" The simplest answer **is the one you'll actually read**. Having a scholarly masterpiece on your shelf means nothing if it never gets opened. Different translations aim at different audiences—some lean more literal, others strive for accessible language. They can all guide you to the deeper truths of Scripture.

Later, in **The Bible's Historical Reliability**, you'll discover just how many ancient manuscripts scholars compare to ensure we have a trustworthy text. And in **The Bible's Incredible Journey**, we'll see how devoted people over many generations toiled—often at great personal cost—to keep the message of the Bible accurate and available in a variety of languages.

## BOTTOM LINE: JENGA TOWER MYTHS

The big idea: **the Bible isn't a Jenga tower.** One misaligned verse or questionable word doesn't make it implode. Historically and practically, the Scriptures have proven remarkably resilient—no single "block" can topple them. If you're feeling nervous about one verse, step back and look at the entire house. You'll find it stands on a far more robust foundation than you might have guessed.

So, before you lose sleep over whether John 8 belongs in every manuscript or how Mark's Gospel really ends, remember: the heart of the Christian faith isn't balanced on a single precarious piece. Rather, it's woven throughout thousands of manuscripts, centuries of study, and the lived experience of communities worldwide. And that's a story no single slip or missing word can ever erase.

# 4

# The Bible's Historical Reliability

When someone mentions that Julius Caesar wrote *The Gallic Wars* or that Plato's dialogues really do capture his philosophy, few people bat an eyelash. But if someone says, "We can trust the New Testament just as much," eyebrows tend to rise. This chapter will explore why that reaction deserves reconsideration.

In One Verse Doesn't Topple the Whole, we saw how minor missing words or questionable verses don't crumble the biblical narrative. Now, let's widen our scope and see how, by standard historical measures, the Bible is truly in a league of its own.

If you're skeptical about claims of the Bible's reliability, you're not alone. It's healthy to question how an ancient text—copied across centuries—could remain trustworthy. Before we tackle those concerns directly, let's compare the Bible's manuscript record to other widely respected ancient documents. By the end, you might find yourself assigning the Bible at least the same historical credibility as Homer, Caesar, or Plato—or even more.

## MANUSCRIPT MATCHUPS

Historians look at how many copies of an ancient text survive, and how old those copies are relative to the original. The more copies we have, and the closer they are to the source, the less guesswork is needed to reconstruct the original.

| ANCIENT DOCUMENT | MANUSCRIPT COUNT |
|---|---|
| Homer's *Iliad* | 1,757 manuscripts |
| Caesar's *Gallic Wars* | 240 manuscripts (9–10 highly reliable) |
| Plato's Writings | 250 manuscripts |
| Marcus Aurelius' *Meditations* | 2 primary manuscripts |
| Shakespeare's Early Plays | Many originals lost |
| **NEW TESTAMENT** | **MANUSCRIPT COUNT** |
| Greek manuscripts | 5,800 |
| Caesar's *Gallic Wars* | 10,000+ |
| Plato's Writings | 9,300 |
| **TOTAL** | **25,000** |

No other work of ancient literature comes close[1]. In The Bible's Incredible Journey, we'll dive deeper into how these texts were meticulously copied and distributed, but for now, simply note the extraordinary numerical and geographical advantage.

---

[1] Institut für neutestamentliche Textforschung, University of Münster; Clay Jones, "The Bibliographical Test Updated" (2012).

## TIME GAPS: SOONER IS BETTER

The second key factor is how much time passed between when the text was written and our earliest surviving copy. The smaller the gap, the less opportunity for textual corruption or legendary embellishments.

| ANCIENT DOCUMENT | WRITTEN | EARLIEST SURVIVING COPY | TIME GAP |
| --- | --- | --- | --- |
| Homer's *Iliad* | 800 BC | c. 400 BC | 400 years |
| Caesar's *Gallic Wars* | 50 BC | c. AD 900 | 950 years |
| Plato's Dialogues | 350 BC | c. AD 900 | 1,250 years |
| Marcus Aurelius' *Meditations* | AD 170 | c. AD 900 | 730 years |
| **New Testament** | AD 50-100 | c. AD 125-150 | 25-100 years |

Compared to the substantial gaps for other ancient texts, the New Testament's textual proximity is exceptionally short.

## SAME STANDARD, SURPRISING OUTCOME

Applying consistent historical standards, if we consider Homer, Caesar, or Plato authentic based on their manuscript evidence, we must acknowledge the New Testament holds a far stronger case. As we saw earlier, minor textual variants don't threaten the Bible's core message[2]. Here, we're simply doubling down: the textual evidence for

---

[2] Bart Ehrman, *Misquoting Jesus: The Story Behind Who Changed the Bible and Why* (2005).

what was originally written in the New Testament surpasses nearly every ancient text accepted without hesitation.

This doesn't compel anyone to accept every biblical claim—that's a different discussion. But strictly on the question, "Has this document been reliably preserved?" the evidence strongly supports a "yes."

## NO NEED FOR A DOUBLE STANDARD

Some might say, "But the Bible is religious, so we should be more skeptical." Higher scrutiny is reasonable when a document claims divine inspiration. Yet if that scrutiny reveals even more historical reliability, it should encourage us to acknowledge its authenticity—even if we're not ready to embrace its spiritual claims.

If you're concerned about centralized manipulation, **Who Decided What's in the Bible?** addresses these conspiracy theories. For now, simply recognize that widespread manuscripts across diverse communities reduce the likelihood of centralized tampering.

## WHAT IT MEANS FOR YOU

**In Chapter 5**, we'll explore the human story behind Scripture's spread across cultures. The main takeaway here is that the Bible's textual reliability is stronger than people typically realize. Whether you're new to all this or have been around church for years, it's helpful to understand the foundation is strong.

So, if someone tells you, "You can't trust the Bible—who knows what got changed?" remind yourself that these same people probably don't hesitate to trust Julius Caesar or Plato. The manuscript evidence for those texts pales compared to the Bible's. It's a simple observation, but a vital one.

And remember, **solid historical preservation** doesn't automatically mean you'll agree with the *content* of the Bible. But if you discard it based on the idea "it's been changed too much," you'd logically have to discard most other ancient writings as well.

If the textual reliability of the New Testament is illegitimate, then virtually all written history must also be questioned, because the Scriptures stand as the most textually attested documents in human history.

## BOTTOM LINE

The Bible isn't some flimsy text teetering on the brink of collapse. In short, if you're someone who trusts the general reliability of ancient history, then you already trust a standard the Bible meets— and then exceeds. From here, we'll look at how thousands of manuscripts cross time and geography, and how translators throughout history risked life and reputation to put scripture into everyday languages. That's where Chapter 5 steps in, showing us the remarkable journey from ancient scrolls to the Bible apps on our phones.

# 5

# The Bible's Incredible Journey

By now, you've seen that the Bible's message doesn't crumble from a single shaky verse (**"One Verse Doesn't Topple the Whole"**) and that its manuscript record surpasses most ancient texts (**"The Bible's Historical Reliability"**). But those facts might leave you wondering *how* an ancient collection of Hebrew, Aramaic, and Greek writings ever got from dusty scrolls into your modern hands—especially if you're reading it in English, Spanish, or any other language.

This chapter focuses on the **human story** behind that process. It's not just about big numbers of manuscripts—it's about real people who believed so strongly in making Scripture accessible that they risked persecution, poverty, and even death.

If you're skeptical, maybe you've heard rumors that powerful groups manipulated or suppressed parts of the Bible to maintain control. In (**"Who Decided What's in the Bible?"**, we'll tackle those theories head-on. For now, let's explore the remarkable journey of how the Bible traveled across languages, cultures, and time—usually in a very public, collaborative manner.

## IT STARTED IN THREE LANGUAGES

1. **Hebrew** – Most of the Old Testament was written in the language of ancient Israel.

2. **Aramaic** – Portions of Daniel and Ezra emerged from the era of Babylonian exile.

3. **Greek** – The New Testament was recorded in Koine Greek, the everyday speech of the Roman Empire.

Each of these languages has its own rules, idioms, and historical context, and the earliest believers painstakingly guarded these original texts. Because before anyone could translate them, they had to be preserved accurately (as we discussed in **Chapter 4**). Scribes often worked in communal settings, double-checking each other's copies to guard against errors.

## THE FIRST GIANT LEAP: THE SEPTUAGINT

Around 250 BC, many Jewish communities were living in Greek-speaking regions. They needed a version of their sacred writings in their new common tongue. The result: **the Septuagint**—a Greek translation of the Hebrew Bible.

- It paved the way for non-Hebrew speakers to read the Old Testament.

- It became so well-loved that many early Christians, including the writers of the New Testament, quoted from it.

This moment wasn't just a linguistic convenience; it set a precedent that *God's Word didn't have to stay locked in one language.*

## JEROME'S LATIN VULGATE: SCRIPTURE IN THE ROMAN EMPIRE

Fast-forward to the 4th century AD. Latin was the universal language in large parts of the Roman world. A scholar named **Jerome** undertook a massive project: translating both Old and New Testaments into Latin. Known as the **Vulgate**, it unified the Western church for over a millennium.

- Suddenly, Latin-speaking Christians across Europe had a consistent Bible to study and recite.
- Over time, as Latin usage faded, fewer everyday people could understand it—setting the stage for later reformers to argue that Scripture should be accessible in local languages.

## THE COST OF ACCESSIBILITY

During the Middle Ages, only clergy and scholars generally read Scripture, leaving ordinary people to hear it secondhand. Enter bold translators who believed everyone should read the Bible for themselves. Two standouts were:

### JOHN WYCLIFFE (14TH CENTURY)

- Led a translation from Latin into Middle English.
- So enraged religious authorities that, years after his death, they **exhumed** and burned his remains to make a statement.

### WILLIAM TYNDALE (16TH CENTURY)

- First to translate directly from Hebrew and Greek into English.
- His dream was that even common laborers could grasp Scripture. For this, he was **executed**.

Their stories remind us that the Bible didn't spread through backroom deals—but rather through courageous individuals willing to suffer for the belief that *no one* should be barred from reading these texts.

## THE KING JAMES ERA AND MODERN TRANSLATIONS

In 1611, **King James I** of England authorized a new English Bible translation. The resulting **King James Version (KJV)** shaped the English-speaking world for centuries. Its elegant language influenced literature, worship, and devotion so thoroughly that many still favor it today.

However, language never stops evolving. Enter modern translations like the **NIV, ESV, and NLT**—offering fresh, accurate language for new generations. These aren't "competing" with the KJV so much as updating it to ensure clarity, using the ever-growing wealth of ancient manuscripts we discussed in **Chapter 4**.

## SPREADING ACROSS THE GLOBE

Today, organizations like **Wycliffe Bible Translators** and various Bible societies continue the same tradition—striving to bring Scripture to every known language on Earth. Whether that's a printed book, a smartphone app, or an audio recording for oral cultures, the heart behind it is unchanged: *everyone deserves access to Scripture.*

Given that the Bible is translated into more languages than any other book, it's hard to imagine a secret group successfully controlling or rewriting it. Thousands of different translators, scholars, and church communities around the world have been involved in the process, **providing a public, collective safeguard against major alterations**.

## WHY IT MATTERS

1. **Humanity, Not Conspiracy**

The chain of translation is a tapestry of real people—scribes, monks, scholars, reformers—often working with the best resources they had in their day. A grand conspiracy theory doesn't align with how widely dispersed these efforts have been.

### 2. A Legacy of Sacrifice

Wycliffe and Tyndale are just two names in a long list of individuals who paid dearly so others could read the Bible. That kind of sacrifice suggests the text wasn't a casual, politically driven project, but something believed to be vital for all people.

### 3. Consistency with the Manuscript Record

Having so many early manuscripts (Chapter 4) mean any serious deviation or tampering would be exposed by the historical record. This makes the Bible *less* likely to have been stealthily manipulated.

### 4. It's for Everyone

This resonates with the idea we explored in **Chapter 3**—no single misplaced word topples the Bible. Because the text's core message has been intentionally preserved and spread far beyond one language or region.

## LOOKING TO THE NEXT CHAPTER

Still, some folks suspect the Bible might be a product of power-hungry church leaders. **Chapter 6** tackles that idea directly Who Decided What's in the Bible? If you've heard that claim or wrestled with it yourself, you won't want to miss what's coming next.

For now, take a moment to appreciate the vast, multi-lingual, centuries-long chain that brought Scripture from scrolls to smartphones. It's a living transmission rooted not in secrecy, but in open, determined commitment—often at a huge personal cost—to give everyone a chance to read these ancient words for themselves.

# 6

# Who Decided What's in the Bible?

For some people, the most unsettling question isn't whether a single verse can topple Scripture (**Chapter 3, "One Verse Doesn't Topple the Whole"**) or if it's historically reliable (**Chapter 4, "The Bible's Historical Reliability"**), or even how it moved from ancient scrolls to modern translations (**Chapter 5, "The Bible's Incredible Journey"**). The real sticking point is this: *Was the Bible stitched together by power-hungry leaders to manipulate the masses?*

On the surface, that sounds like a plot worthy of a spy thriller—secret councils in smoke-filled rooms, forging a text to keep people in line. But the historical reality is far less dramatic and far more compelling. It involves a careful, community-based recognition of which books bore the genuine stamp of authenticity.

If you've ever heard accusations that the Bible was cobbled together by church councils with political motives, it's natural to raise an eyebrow. People have used Scripture to justify all sorts of agendas—no question there. But that doesn't necessarily reflect *how* the text itself came to be. This chapter will show how the canon (the "official" collection of biblical books) formed over time, and why it's less about a top-down conspiracy and more about a widespread recognition of what was already seen as genuine.

## WHAT "CANON" REALLY MEANS

The term **canon** comes from the Greek *kanon*, meaning "rule" or "measuring stick." It refers to the authoritative collection of books recognized as inspired by God. The Bible didn't appear as a single bound volume overnight. Rather, believers progressively acknowledged certain texts as carrying a distinct weight—like seeing the signature of God's fingerprint on them.

### The Old Testament Canon

- By the time of Jesus, the Jewish community already had a well-established set of Scriptures: The **Torah** (Law), **Nevi'im** (Prophets), and **Ketuvim** (Writings)—collectively what Christians call the Old Testament.
- When Jesus and the apostles referenced "the Scriptures," they meant these books. (See Luke 24:44, for instance.)
- Manuscripts like the Dead Sea Scrolls (circa 2nd century BC) confirm these texts were circulating and revered long before the church councils ever convened.

### The New Testament Canon

- The Gospels and letters from the apostles or their close associates began circulating among early Christians.
- Over time, criteria emerged for recognizing an authentic, authoritative text:

1. **Apostolic Origin**: Was it connected to an apostle or their immediate circle?
2. **Widespread Use**: Did Christian communities across diverse regions use this text in worship and teaching?
3. **Doctrinal Consistency**: Did it align with the known teachings of Jesus and the apostles?

   By the time councils such as **Carthage (AD 397)** officially recognized the 27 books of the New Testament, these writings were already widely accepted in practice. The councils didn't *create* the canon; they *confirmed* a reality the church had already embraced.

## WHAT ABOUT "LOST" GOSPELS?

You might hear about texts like the **Gospel of Thomas** or the **Gospel of Judas**, claiming they were snubbed for political reasons. But these so-called "lost gospels" often emerged much later (2nd-4th century AD) and reflected teachings inconsistent with what the early Christian communities recognized as the authentic message of Jesus.

- **Timing**: Many were penned long after the apostles had passed away, making them unlikely to be eyewitness accounts.
- **Content**: They introduced Gnostic or secret-knowledge elements that contradicted **the inclusive, public ministry of Jesus** we see in the canonical Gospels.

The early church didn't reject these writings out of paranoia or a desire for control, but because they simply didn't measure up to the established criteria of apostolic teaching and consistent doctrine.

## ACKNOWLEDGING MISUSE AND HARM

Let's be honest: the Bible has sometimes been wielded as a tool for control. History bears that out—whether it's the justification of oppressive systems or manipulative sect leaders cherry-picking verses to suit their agenda. But it's crucial to differentiate between *the misuse of a text* and *the text's inherent message*.

- **Evil people use good tools in evil ways**. A hammer can build a home or be a weapon of destruction. That doesn't make the hammer itself nefarious.
- Scripture itself often **confronts** misuse of power. The Old Testament prophets regularly called out corrupt leaders, and Jesus challenged religious authorities who burdened people unnecessarily.

Just because some have twisted the Bible for harm doesn't mean the text was designed for that purpose.

## A PUBLIC, NOT SECRET, PROCESS

To say the Bible was formed by a small clique in a dark backroom is to ignore the very public and widespread nature of its preservation:

1. **Multiplicity of Manuscripts**: As seen in **Chapter 4**, tens of thousands of manuscripts exist, held by various communities and in different languages.
2. **Open Discussion and Debate**: Early Christians read these documents communally, citing them in letters and sermons. If any group had tried to sneak in a "control manual," it would've clashed with established consensus across diverse regions.

3. **Historical Councils**: Church gatherings like Nicea or Carthage were hardly hush-hush conspiracies. They were large, formal assemblies that hammered out doctrines and recognized commonly used writings.

This widespread engagement makes it extremely unlikely that a single entity could manipulate the text without leaving a massive trace—something we just don't see in the historical record.

## CANON FORMATION AS "DISCOVERY," NOT "INVENTION"

Think of the canon less like an edict handed down and more like geologists identifying genuine gemstones amid riverbed gravel. The church didn't *make* these books authoritative any more than geologists *create* diamonds—they simply recognized the authenticity of what was already there. In this sense, the process was more about *discovering* which writings bore the marks of God's inspiration, rather than *deciding* it by political vote.

## WHY THIS MATTERS

### 1. Trust in the Bible's Integrity

Understanding the transparent, community-based method by which Scripture came together can ease the suspicion of backroom power plays.

### 2. A Foundation for Faith or Further Study

Even if you're still exploring its spiritual claims, you can rest assured the Bible wasn't a last-minute marketing scheme.

### 3. Context for Conversation

When friends suggest the Bible was invented by oppressive leaders, you now have some historical footing. You can explain how widely dispersed and organic the canon's formation truly was.

## LOOKING AHEAD

In **Chapter 2**, we saw how one shaky passage won't topple the biblical message. In **Chapter 4**, we learned the Bible is better attested than many ancient texts we take for granted. In **Chapter 5**, we traced how Scripture got from ancient scrolls to modern translations, often through acts of profound dedication. And here in **Chapter 6**, we've tackled the question of whether it was all a power grab.

The short answer: The biblical canon wasn't formed in smoke-filled rooms by maniacal schemers. It emerged through centuries of open use, meticulous care, and shared recognition. While people *have* used the Bible for control, that's a story about human failings, not about an inherently manipulative text.

With that in mind, you can engage with Scripture—whether from a place of faith or simple curiosity—knowing it wasn't conjured up in some clandestine plot but lovingly recognized by generations who believed they were holding something far greater than their own ideas.

# 7

# Why Does God Seem Different in the Old and New Testaments?

*"Two Different Gods"?*

It's one of the most common questions: *"Why does God in the Old Testament and the New Testament seem like two different characters?"* For some, the Old Testament God appears harsh, distant, and authoritarian, while the New Testament God comes across loving, tender, and forgiving. This idea feeds the perception that Scripture might be inconsistent or man-made. But here's the truth: it's *not* two different characters—it's two **different emphases**.

## GOD'S REVELATION IN THE OLD TESTAMENT: SIN AT CENTER STAGE

It might sound strange, but God **isn't** the main character of much of the Old Testament—**humanity's sinfulness** is. Israel's rebellion, idolatry, and God's resulting judgment often take front-and-center focus. Meanwhile, God's **grace and love**, though present, can be overshadowed by the urgent consequences of sin.

**Why** this emphasis? The Old Testament demonstrates humanity's desperate need for a Savior, **highlighting** how deep our brokenness runs. At the same time, it foreshadows God's faithfulness and redemptive plan—He's not absent or unloving, but the immediate narrative often revolves around sin's havoc and God's response to it.

Think of it like an **industrial-era backdrop**: the Old Testament is the pre-modern build-up, setting the stage for a seismic shift. Jesus is that **historical catalyst**, turning promise into fulfillment. The Old Testament supplies the foundation; the New Testament gives the realization—two parts of the same story, **connected** by Jesus.

## BACKGROUND: ELIJAH AND ELISHA

**Context:** In the time of the prophets Elijah and Elisha, Israel was plunged into deep apostasy—**worshiping Baal**. This spiritual adultery (turning from Yahweh to another god) is what truly **drives** the narrative; God's love is still there, but it's not the main storyline. Instead, the focus is on Israel's sin and God's determination to preserve them **spiritually**.

### 1. Elijah

His ministry largely centers on **confronting Baal-worship**. He calls down fire from heaven, enacts drought, and pronounces judgment. The name "Elijah" means "My God is Yahweh," reflecting an emphasis on **God's holiness** and the urgent crisis of idolatry.

God's love exists in this period (He cares for Elijah during the famine, raises the widow's son, etc.), but the **foreground** is the darkness of Israel's rebellion and the unstoppable judgment that must come if they refuse to repent.

## 2. Elisha

Following Elijah, Elisha inherits his mantle in a time still riddled with spiritual turmoil. Yet Elisha's narrative is overshadowed by more **miracles of grace**—healing waters, multiplying oil, raising the Shunammite's son. His name means "My God is Salvation."

**Note**: Judgment doesn't vanish here: Elisha anoints Jehu, who ultimately destroys Jezebel and Ahab's house (the climax of God's judgment). But the main spotlight in Elisha's story is on **God's abundant compassion**, a more gracious thread compared to Elijah's fire-and-brimstone tone.

This **Elijah-to-Elisha** transition parallels the broader biblical shift from *Law* to *Grace*, without discarding either. Judgment remains, but a **fuller revelation** of God's salvific heart emerges.

## THE PROBLEM OF LIMITED REVELATION

In the Old Testament, God often relates to Israel as **Master**—a figure of authority and holiness. This "limited revelation" fosters a sense of **distance**. Hosea 2:16 captures the transformation God desires:

"In that day," declares the LORD, "you will call me 'my husband'; you will no longer call me 'my master.'" God envisions a relationship built on love, not fear. Under the Old Testament vantage, people see glimpses of that intimacy but still struggle with the lens of **authority**. They may know God is good in principle, yet the larger crisis (idolatry, judgment) often dominates the narrative.

## THE TRANSITION FROM ELIJAH TO ELISHA

Elijah's ministry—like the Law—**spotlights sin and judgment**. He challenges false gods, calls down fire, and **exposes** apostasy. That's crucial but not the final word. When Elijah departs in a whirlwind (2 Kings 2:11), it signifies the Law's role being **fulfilled**, not nullified.

**Elisha** picks up the mantle, performing wonders that depict **grace**, restoration, and provision. While Elijah's name ("My God is Yahweh") resonates with the call back to holiness, Elisha's name ("My God is Salvation") resonates with a wave of **healing** and **miracles**. Again, it's the same God—**both** justice and compassion—but we now see more of the latter come to the fore.

## GOD'S REVELATION IN THE NEW TESTAMENT: GRACE AT CENTER STAGE

Entering the New Testament, **sin** still exists, but it's no longer front and center. Instead, **Jesus** embodies the fullness of God's love and redemptive plan. Jeremiah prophesied a day when everyone would "know the Lord" from the heart (Jeremiah 31:34). In Christ, we see that realized: God **overcomes** sin, unveiling a dimension of **intimacy** that outshines the former focus on punishment.

**At the cross**, grace becomes the main character. Of course, sin hasn't disappeared from human behavior, and God still deals with sin. But in a **dominion** sense—**the realm of sin and death** (Romans 5)—**that** power is decisively broken by Jesus' crucifixion and resurrection. Sin is no longer the unstoppable overshadowing force; Christ dethrones it. Humans still commit sins, but the dominion and penalty that once reigned is undone for those in Christ.

## THINK OF THE CROSS AS A GAME-CHANGER

To borrow a historical analogy: *Electricity* didn't negate the pre-electric era but drastically changed how society functioned. The Old Testament isn't "wrong" or replaced—it's **foundational**. But the arrival of Jesus—like electricity—ushers in a **new era**. The story continues, culminating in Christ's redemptive work, so sin no longer dominates the narrative. Grace does.

## WHY IT MATTERS FOR YOU TODAY

### 1. Shift Your Focus

In the Old Testament's vantage, sin dominates; in the New, grace does. We live post-cross, so sin isn't your main storyline—God's **grace** is.

### 2. Peace and Assurance

If you keep seeing yourself under condemnation, you're stuck in an Old Testament lens. Christ overcame the realm of sin. Yes, we still err, but we aren't slaves to sin's dominion.

### 3. Harmony in God's Character

God hasn't changed. He's consistent from Elijah's fire to Elisha's healing, from the Law to Grace. The difference is how He's revealing Himself—once focusing on humanity's brokenness, now unveiling the victory of His love in Christ.

## FINAL THOUGHT

God is the same—**yesterday, today, and forever**—but the **focus** of Scripture shifts. In the Old Testament, spiritual adultery and judgment overshadow glimpses of mercy. In the New, **mercy** and salvation overshadow sin. Both arcs belong to one grand narrative: a just and loving God working through time to save and restore.

So, if the Old Testament feels full of fire and distance, remember it was written in a context of profound rebellion—**God** was not absent of love, but that love was overshadowed by dire crises. When Jesus arrives, grace steps to the forefront, dethroning sin's dominion. The conclusion? We see a **complete** picture: God is holy, yes, but also relentlessly gracious. That's not two gods—it's one God revealing Himself through different vantage points of the same redemptive story.

# 8

# Why Doesn't God Just Show Up on TikTok?

**"If God Wants Us to Know He's Real, Why Not a Cosmic Billboard?"** We've all heard it: *"If God's real, He should do something jaw-dropping on social media—or maybe Times Square. That'd settle all debate!"* The assumption is that spectacle **guarantees** faith and closeness to God. But biblical history—and even Jesus' life—suggest otherwise.

## WHEN GOD DID GO BIG

**Exodus 20**: God reveals Himself on **Mount Sinai** with thunder, lightning, and earthquakes. Did that lead to intimacy? No—people recoil, pleading, *"Don't let God speak to us directly or we will die."* (Exodus 20:19). Overwhelming divine power can breed **fear** rather than relationship.

**1 Kings 18**: The prophet Elijah publicly defeats the prophets of Baal on **Mount Carmel** with an undeniable display of God's fire. The crowd proclaims, "Yahweh is God!" For a moment, it seems like a national revival. Yet soon enough, the people drift back into idol worship. The **spectacle** produced a fleeting confession, not lasting devotion.

**Jesus' Public Ministry**: Healing the blind, casting out demons, feeding thousands—miracles that were undeniable. Yet in the end, many who witnessed these signs cried "Crucify him!" Undeniable acts didn't secure their faith; it only highlighted that seeing truth doesn't guarantee *embracing* it.

## THE OTHERNESS PROBLEM

God is **infinite** and **holy**; we are **finite** and **fallen**. A massive, unfiltered display of His majesty might magnify that gulf rather than close it. It can **overwhelm** rather than **invite**. True closeness requires a gentler approach—one where God meets us in ways we can handle: through prophets, **Scripture**, and ultimately **Christ** in human form.

## ENTER THE HUMAN ROUTE

Rather than dazzle the masses with unstoppable force or flashy wonders every day, God typically **reveals Himself** through human means:

- **Prophets & Scripture**: He spoke via real people in real cultural contexts. That's not a compromise; it's a relational way to engage us without raw intimidation.
- **Jesus' Incarnation**: The ultimate self-disclosure—personal, approachable. Yes, Jesus did miracles, but they were never just "ta-da" moments; they pointed to God's **compassionate kingdom**. Still, many who saw them remained unpersuaded or later betrayed Him.

**Point**: "Undeniable" signs often fail to produce enduring faith. The biblical record shows repeated examples—*Sinai, Mt. Carmel, Jesus' own ministry*—where grand displays yield, at best, a superficial or short-lived compliance.

## WHY THE BIBLE IS MORE RELIABLE THAN A VIRAL SENSATION

Sure, God **could** dominate TikTok with daily miracles. But would that foster real **trust** and **love**? History suggests it would cause **temporary** awe, sensationalism, or controversies—like tabloids chasing the next big thing.

By contrast, **Scripture** provides a stable, enduring revelation:

- **Written Preservation**: It stands above fleeting trends, preventing emotional or cultural distortions.

- **Depth and Reflection**: The Bible invites slow engagement, not just a 10-second scroll that might vanish in digital noise.

- **Accessible in All Ages**: It transcends any single platform or media craze.

If God chose constant cosmic announcements, the risk of trivialization would be immense. Instead, the Bible ensures the message endures objectively, studied across generations—not sidelined as entertainment or ephemeral hype.

## POWER VS. RELATIONSHIP

Yes, spectacle **grabs attention** for a moment, but it rarely kindles **authentic closeness**. Throughout Scripture, God reveals Himself relationally—through personal stories, encounters, and ultimately **Jesus** stepping into our world as one of us. That's far more transformative for **the heart** than cosmic theatrics or daily fireworks.

**Even in daily life**: Consider an argument with a significant other. Sometimes, even when you see they're right, you **double down**. A "won" argument doesn't guarantee changed hearts or real reconciliation. Likewise, witnessing some God-sized phenomenon doesn't automatically yield surrender. Belief is a **heart** matter, not just mental assent.

## FINAL THOUGHT

Grand displays might **grab attention** but seldom produce lasting faith. The **Bible** and its relational approach—a God who slowly but surely engages us in **human** form—speaks more powerfully to **heart transformation**. God didn't choose Scripture or the Incarnation because He lacked other flashy options. He chose them because they foster real **encounter**, real **choice**, and authentic **love**.

**So, no**, a cosmic viral event wouldn't necessarily convert the masses. We have Sinai, Carmel, and even Jesus' public miracles as proof that "undeniable" acts can be acknowledged yet ultimately ignored. God's Word offers a **different** path—one that, in the long run, has demonstrated a deeper, longer-lasting impact on hearts.

# 9

# Wait... Can We Curse Our Enemies or Not?

**Q: My fiancé asked me to answer this question that someone posted to her women's Bible study group:**
*"If we're supposed to love our enemy, why in the Psalms are they always cursing their enemies and wishing them the worst?"*

That question stops people in their tracks. The Psalms read like an Old Testament diss track—prayers for disaster, ruin, and divine payback on enemies.

And it's not just David venting in his prayer journal. Paul pulls these same Psalms into the New Testament. Case in point: *Romans 11:9–10*, where he quotes *Psalm 69*:

*"Let their table become a snare and a trap,*
*a stumbling block and a retribution for them;*
*let their eyes be darkened so that they cannot see,*
*and bend their backs forever."*

Wait... *didn't Jesus tell us to love our enemies*? So why does Scripture seem to send mixed signals?

## IS EVERY VERSE A DIRECTIVE?

The tension here comes from a **common Bible-reading misconception**: *"If it's in the Bible, God must want me to do it."*

Not quite. The Bible is **not** a collection of flat, one-size-fits-all rules. It contains God's commands, yes, but it also records:

- Raw human experiences—some faithful, some flawed.
- Honest prayers—some wise, some emotional.
- Prophetic declarations—some immediate, some unfolding over time.

Not every verse is a *"Go and do likewise."* Sometimes, it's a *"Watch, listen, and learn."*

Take the Psalms, for example. They give us everything—worship, lament, thanksgiving, and, yes, some of the most unfiltered, emotionally charged prayers for revenge you'll ever read.

But that doesn't mean the Psalms are a free pass for us to start praying for fire and brimstone on our office rivals.

## WHAT ARE THE PSALMS DOING?

The Psalms aren't just about venting. They do three key things that shift how we should read them:

### 1. They Show Honest Human Emotion

David and the psalmists weren't sanitizing their prayers. They laid everything before God—their fears, their anger, their desire for justice. That's a lesson for us: **God can handle our real, unfiltered emotions.** He doesn't need polite, pre-packaged prayers. He wants us to be honest with Him.

## 2. They Contain a Prophetic Layer

Many of these seemingly aggressive prayers point forward to **God's justice—not just personal payback.** Paul's use of *Psalm 69* in *Romans 11* isn't about David's personal enemies—it's about people who have hardened their hearts against Christ. The judgment David longed for foreshadows a **greater spiritual reality.**

## 3. They Wrestle with Justice in a Broken World

The psalmists weren't asking for petty revenge; they were crying out for justice. In a world where evil often seems to win, their prayers remind us that **God is not indifferent**. He sees. He will judge. And that longing for justice? It's a longing for God to set things right.

# JESUS AND THE ULTIMATE PERSPECTIVE SHIFT

So, if these Psalms are honest cries for justice, does that mean we should start quoting them over people we don't like?

Not quite.

Jesus didn't come to erase these prayers—He came to **complete the story**. He shifts our focus from **retribution to redemption**. Instead of calling down curses, He tells us:

*"Love your enemies and pray for those who persecute you." (Matthew 5:44)*

That's not a contradiction—it's a **progression**.

The Old Testament cries out for justice. **Jesus reveals the deeper solution: justice met with mercy.**

Does that mean there's no judgment? No. Judgment is still real. But the way we engage with our enemies isn't through personal vengeance—it's through Christlike love, trusting that **God sees and will make things right**.

## So... What Do We Do with Imprecatory Psalms?

### 1. Be Honest with God

The Psalms give us permission to express our rawest emotions. Just don't stop there. Let God **refine them**.

### 2. See the Bigger Picture

When Paul uses *Psalm 69*, he's showing that **rejection of Christ has real consequences**. These Psalms are bigger than just David's personal grudges.

### 3. Follow Jesus' Lead

Jesus invites us into a higher way—not ignoring injustice, but responding to enemies with mercy, trusting that God will bring the final justice.

# THE BIBLE: MORE THAN A RULEBOOK

The Bible **isn't** a simplistic list of rules where every verse is a direct command to imitate. It's a **living narrative**—an unfolding story of how raw human cries for justice ultimately find their answer in Christ.

David's prayers for vengeance? They're not there to tell us to curse our enemies.

They're there to show us:

The depth of **human pain**.

The reality of **God's justice**.

The need for **something greater**.

And Jesus *is* that something greater.

So no, you **can't** use the Psalms as a license to pray for your enemy's downfall. But you **can** bring your frustration to God, knowing that **He hears, He sees, and He will make all things right**—just not always in the way we expect.

# 10

# Did Jesus Claim to Be God?

*Rethinking the Question That Traps Itself*

You hear it all the time—on podcasts, in YouTube comments, maybe even from your own skeptical thoughts:

"If Jesus really thought He was God, why didn't He just say so?"

It's usually said like a slam dunk: *"Show me the quote, or it didn't happen."*

But underneath that question is an unspoken rule:

"If He didn't say the exact words, 'I am God,' then He must not have been."

And that's the trap. Because the moment we make it a binary yes-or-no question, we've already missed the way Jesus revealed who He was. And we've recreated the same no-win situation He was in during His earthly life.

Let me show you what I mean.

## THE SETUP WAS ALWAYS A SETUP

When people pressed Jesus to speak plainly— *"Are you the Christ?" "Tell us who you are!"*—they weren't curious. They were setting a trap. They weren't open to understanding—they were hunting for grounds to accuse.

And He knew it.

Because here's the truth:

---

**If Jesus had explicitly said «I am God» in a hostile setting, it wouldn't have softened their hearts or cleared the air. It would've simply escalated the charge:**

---

"Look at this blasphemer. Kill Him."

So, the idea that saying it outright would have *helped* anyone? That's wishful thinking. It would have just changed the *reason* they rejected Him.

From: "He's too vague to be taken seriously"

To: "He's too bold to be tolerated."

The outcome would've been the same.

He wasn't playing hide-and-seek.

He was playing chess on a board full of traps.

And yet—despite the complexity—**those who wanted to see it, did**. The blind saw. The broken believed. The humble followed. It was never about whether Jesus was clear—it was about whether people were willing.

## NO-WIN ANSWERS IN A NO-WIN WORLD

We've all been there—when someone asks you a question, but it's not really a question. It's bait. No matter how you answer, they're not listening to understand. They're listening to accuse.

Jesus was constantly in that situation.

He wasn't afraid to speak truth—but He also wasn't foolish. He wasn't evasive—He was strategic. He knew that a *bad-faith question doesn't deserve a self-destructive answer.*

So instead of playing their game, He played **His Father's**.

## JESUS FOLLOWED A DIVINE TIMELINE

Throughout the Gospels, Jesus keeps referencing "my time" or "my hour":

*"My hour has not yet come."* (John 2:4)

*"My time is not yet here."* (John 7:6)

*"They tried to arrest him, but his hour had not yet come."* (John 7:30)

He wasn't being cryptic. He was being careful.

His mission wasn't just to tell the truth. It was to **fulfill** it. And that meant staying on **God's timeline**, not bending to human demands for clarity, spectacle, or soundbites.

Jesus didn't avoid clarity—He avoided being crucified before the right time.

Because He wasn't just trying to **reveal** who He was—He was trying to **redeem** us.

That meant protecting the timeline not just from premature execution, but also from premature *understanding*. Even His **disciples** weren't ready to grasp the full truth at once. He had to guide them gently, progressively, preparing their hearts and minds to carry His mission after the resurrection.

What looked like silence or subtlety wasn't fear. It was **faithfulness**—to a larger plan unfolding exactly as it should.

---

### When He Was Recognized, He Often Told People to Keep Quiet

---

Peter said, "You're the Christ, the Son of the Living God." Jesus didn't say, "Finally, someone got it! Broadcast that everywhere!" No—He **strictly told the disciples to tell no one.** (Matthew 16:20)

After the transfiguration?

*"Tell no one what you have seen until the Son of Man has risen from the dead." (Mark 9:9)*

Why?

Because His identity wasn't just a message to be posted—it was a reality to be **unveiled through timing, obedience, and suffering.**

## So... Did Jesus Claim to Be God?

Yes. And no.

And that's not a cop-out—it's the *only honest answer to a dishonest framework.*

He didn't say it the way we might expect.

And that wasn't a flaw in His messaging—it was **the genius of His mission.**

Because if you really pay attention, you'll see:

- He **forgave sins**, which only God can do.
- He called Himself the **Lord of the Sabbath**—which He instituted.
- He said, "Before Abraham was, *I AM*"—a reference so loaded they immediately picked up stones.
- He said, "I and the Father are one."
- He received worship.
- He spoke with divine authority.
- He acted with divine compassion.

He didn't just **say** it. He **revealed** it.

He didn't shout a label. He **embodied** it.

## THE "NO" IS PART OF THE REVELATION

Here's the part we often miss:

Even His refusal to say it outright is part of how we see **who He is.**

It shows His awareness of the stakes.

It shows His commitment to the cross.

It shows that He was never playing to the crowd—He was following the Father.

The "no" isn't a weakness—it's wisdom.

And if we understand what He was doing, we won't see it as evasiveness. We'll see it as **divine orchestration.**

## FINAL THOUGHT

We want clean answers. Simple soundbites. But Jesus gave us something better:

A revelation on *God's terms*, not ours.

A truth too holy to be reduced to slogans.

A divine identity revealed not in a press conference, but on a cross.

So, no—Jesus didn't always say it the way we might have. Because He wasn't just trying to be understood.

He was trying to **save.**

And He did.

# 11

# All or Nothing

We've all heard it: *"If God said it, I believe it. If the Bible says it, it's true."* Cute. Admirable, even. But is it just a little... over the top? Before you grab the pitchforks, hear me out.

Do you need to believe the story of Jonah and the fish to the same degree you believe in the resurrection of Jesus? *Absolutely not.* But the "all or nothing" mindset insists otherwise. It tells you that if you wrestle with one part of Scripture, you've somehow invalidated the whole thing. And that's just not true.

In fact, this mindset has been crushing people's faith for centuries. Someone asks, *"Do you believe in Jesus?"* and instead of answering, they respond with, *"Well, did Jonah really get swallowed by a whale?"* See what just happened? A single story became a stumbling block to the whole narrative. A fish tale eclipsed the main event.

## A SELF-INFLICTED TRAP

Here's the problem with "all or nothing": it's a trap we've set for ourselves. If we insist that every story in Scripture must be approached with the same level of literal, unshakable certainty, we put people in an impossible position. Their hesitation over the Tower of Babel or the sun standing still suddenly means they can't believe in the Gospel. That's absurd.

Think of the Bible as a library, not a single book. It's a collection of 66 books—history, poetry, prophecy, letters—all inspired by God but written through human hands, in different genres, for different purposes. It's not a fragile house of cards where questioning one verse topples the whole thing. It's a rich, robust narrative with its foundation in Christ.

## JONAH AND THE WHALE VS. THE EMPTY TOMB

Let's put this in perspective. The story of Jonah is powerful, whether you view it as historical fact or a vivid parable about God's mercy. But is your faith in Christ dependent on Jonah's three days in the belly of the fish? No. Your faith is dependent on Christ's three days in the tomb.

The resurrection is the cornerstone of Christianity. Paul says as much in 1 Corinthians 15:17: *"If Christ has not been raised, your faith is futile."* Notice what Paul didn't say: *"If Jonah wasn't swallowed by a fish, your faith is futile."* See the difference? One is the foundation. The other is part of the beautiful house built on that foundation.

## OVERLOADING PEOPLE WITH UNNECESSARY EXPECTATIONS

When we demand "all or nothing," we set people up for failure. A person wrestles with one story—maybe they struggle with the timeline of creation, or they're not sure what to make of the talking snake—and suddenly, they feel like they're losing their grip on all of Scripture. **The pressure becomes unbearable.**

This is why understanding the overarching narrative of the Bible is so important. It's not about perfectly reconciling every detail; it's about seeing the bigger picture: God's redemptive plan through Christ. The Gospel is the heartbeat of the Bible. Everything else—whether history, poetry, or prophecy—points to it. But the Gospel itself is the main thing.

## THE BIBLE IS NOT FRAGILE

The Bible can handle your questions. It's not a delicate tower that crumbles the moment you tug at one piece. It's more like a mosaic: some pieces might not fit perfectly in your understanding right now, but step back, and you see the bigger picture.

God doesn't demand blind acceptance of every story, every metaphor, and every cultural nuance. What He invites you into is trust. Trust in the overarching story of salvation. Trust in the God who inspired these texts. Trust in Christ, who fulfills them all.

## FOCUS ON THE MAIN THING

Faith isn't about having every answer. It's about knowing the One who is the answer. Don't let hesitation over Jonah—or Babel, or anything else—blind you to the resurrection. Don't let the details distract you from the Gospel.

So, the next time someone says, *"Do you believe in Jesus?"* resist the urge to detour into debates about fish tales or ancient towers. Instead, keep the focus where it belongs: *"Yes, I believe in Jesus, who died and rose again to save me."*

Because here's the truth: your faith doesn't have to be "all or nothing." It just must be centered on the One who is everything.

# 12

# Can the Bible Be Biased and Truthful?

We often assume truth must be a pristine, unfiltered record—free from any human vantage. But truth in **Scripture** comes through **people** with cultural backgrounds, personal experiences, and specific concerns. Does that render their testimony unreliable? Not necessarily. A partial perspective doesn't nullify truth; it can **enhance** it, providing depth a sterile, "objective" record might miss.

### TRUTH IN MULTIPLE PERSPECTIVES

Imagine two witnesses describing the same car accident from different corners: one might focus on speed, the other on the traffic light's color. Neither perspective erases what truly happened; when combined, their vantage points form a fuller picture.

**Likewise,** Scripture's authors wrote from unique contexts—yet their views converge on God's overarching work. Far from contradictions, these angles piece together a vibrant tapestry of God's redemptive story.

## A Real-Life Example: Psalm 77

In **Psalm 77**, the psalmist cries out with raw honesty:

"I remembered you, God, and I groaned... Will the Lord reject forever?"

He's wrestling with doubt, despair, and *feeling* abandoned. That emotional vantage might seem "biased," yet it **spotlights** the reality of a faith in crisis. Rather than skewing truth, it immerses us in a genuine struggle—making the psalm's eventual turn to trust in God's past faithfulness even more powerful. This personal angle isn't mere bias; it's **authenticity** that helps us relate to and grasp the psalmist's deeper truth: God remains steadfast despite our swirling fears.

## THE BIBLE'S "BIAS": A DIVINE-HUMAN STORY

Scripture doesn't read like a neutral encyclopedia. It's a **human** book telling a **divine** story:

- **Prophets, Poets, Disciples** wrote amid Israel's unfolding narrative, highlighting lessons vital to their time.
- **Gospels** each spotlight different facets of Jesus' ministry (Matthew's Jewish emphasis vs. Luke's compassion for outsiders, etc.).
- **Psalmists** like David or Asaph pour out emotional prayers rooted in personal situations—pointing us toward a relational God, not a distant deity.

Such "personal lenses" ground the text in **real** life. They don't manufacture falsehood; they convey truth shaped by living experiences.

## DOES PARTIAL PERSPECTIVE UNDERMINE TRUTH?

A partial viewpoint harms truth only if it **masks** or **misrepresents** crucial facts. In Scripture, no author contradicts the core storyline of who God is or what He's doing. They simply **accent** different attributes or contexts. That's why the Bible's variety of voices—lamenting psalmists, fiery prophets, thoughtful evangelists—deepens, not weakens, our comprehension.

**Apologetically**, when people complain, "It's biased from Israel's viewpoint," we can respond that vantage doesn't equal fabrication. Personal perspective often highlights nuances we'd miss in a purely "clinical" report. God harnesses real people, with real emotions and cultural frameworks, to convey timeless truth.

## EMBRACING HUMANITY IN SCRIPTURE

Biblical truth emerges *through* the human vantage, not despite it. Like multiple witnesses forming a fuller testimony, the distinct "biases" of each author give us a multi-layered revelation of God's nature and work.

- **Psalm 77** invites us into raw anguish, then pivots to hope, showing how genuine faith struggles can lead to deeper trust.
- **Four Gospels** unify around Jesus' divinity yet highlight unique angles—fulfilling OT prophecy, showcasing miracles, or emphasizing compassion.
- **Prophets and Apostles** address real crises in real places, their "bias" keeping God's message intimately tied to lived reality.

Viewing the Bible as both human and divinely inspired moves us beyond the idea that "bias = error." Instead, it shows God using authentic human voices—each with its own tilt—to deliver eternal truths. Far from discrediting Scripture, such vantage-laden writing assures us God meets us in real contexts, revealing Himself in a way that resonates across cultures and ages.

## CONCLUSION

A "bias" rooted in personal experience doesn't distort biblical truth; it amplifies it. Like the psalmist in Psalm 77, or the varied Gospel writers, each perspective offers a genuine glimpse of God's interaction with humanity. The result is a **multifaceted, authentic** portrayal of His unwavering purpose—proving that the Bible can be both **deeply human** and **truly divine** in its revelation.

# 13

# Do Christians Still Need the Ten Commandments?

The Ten Commandments: they're a cornerstone of Scripture, engraved in stone by God Himself. But do Christians still need them? The answer might surprise you: **no**, not because they've been **abolished** or are irrelevant, but because they've already been **fulfilled** in the believer.

That's right. What the law once demanded **externally** is now accomplished **internally**—by grace, through the Holy Spirit.

## THE LAW FULFILLED IN US

Let's start with the greatest commandment: "Love the Lord your God with all your heart, all your soul, all your mind, and all your strength" (Mark 12:30). Even this, the highest call of the law, is fulfilled in the believer. Romans 8:2–4 explains that the "righteous requirement of the law" is fully met in those who walk according to the Spirit. Essentially, **we love God because the Spirit empowers us to do so**—it's literally who we are as new creations in Christ.

Jesus hints at this in Mark 9:39, where He acknowledges the affection believers already have for Him. What the law once required—perfect love for God—has become a reality in the hearts of believers through grace. The Spirit has done in us what the law could only demand from us.

## WHY DON'T WE ALWAYS FEEL IT?

If this is true, you might wonder, *why don't I always feel like I love God with all my heart?* Or *why don't other believers seem to live like they do?*

Here's the thing: love often goes unnoticed when we **fixate** on it. Imagine trying to become hyperaware of your love for your parents. You'd likely notice your failures and shortcomings more than your genuine affection. But that doesn't mean you don't love them. The evidence of love is in your everyday actions—texts you send without thinking, the comfort you feel in their presence, the sacrifices you make naturally.

Similarly, your love for God might not always be a conscious burst of emotion. It's an **internal reality** the Spirit has created within you. Focusing solely on whether you "feel" it can obscure the fact that you do, in fact, love God—just as you sometimes fail to show love perfectly for your parents.

## THE SPIRIT, NOT COMMANDS

The Bible is clear: your love for God isn't your own doing. God sent the Spirit of His Son into our hearts, crying "Abba, Father" (Galatians 4:6). The Spirit awakens in us a love that flows naturally—like a child's affection for their parent.

Now imagine **commanding** a child to love their parents. That external demand could create confusion or even resistance. Why? Because love for their parents is already part of their nature. The same is true for believers. Commanding what the Spirit has made natural can short-circuit the relationship, turning it into anxious rule-keeping instead of free, joyful affection.

## LETTING GO, LETTING IT FLOW

So, do Christians "need" the Ten Commandments? **Not** as an external rulebook to enforce what's already been fulfilled inside. The Spirit has written God's law on our hearts (Jeremiah 31:33). Our love for God doesn't require external enhancement; it needs **freedom** to flourish.

**This doesn't mean** the moral content of the Ten Commandments disappears or that sin no longer matters. We still fall short, and we still trust the Spirit's guidance for holy living. But we **no longer** rely on the old covenant's stone-etched demands. We rely on the Spirit who naturally inclines us to love God and others, fulfilling the heart of the law from within.

So, let go of striving as if you need external commands to manufacture love. Stop scrutinizing every thought and action for proof that you measure up. Instead, trust the Spirit who has set this love in motion. **What the law demanded, grace has fulfilled.** Let go and let God.

## WHAT ABOUT SIN?

If we truly love God from within, why do we still sin? Because we're **still human**—the flesh and the world exert pressure on our outward behavior. But our **core orientation** has changed. The believer's deepest desire is no longer rebellion but to honor God, even if we sometimes fail. As we walk by the Spirit, we experience incremental transformation, growing in practical holiness over time.

**The bottom line**: our love for God isn't sustained by external mandates; it's **energized by the Holy Spirit**. The Ten Commandments aren't abolished—they're fulfilled and embedded in us. We may stumble, but our relationship with God is no longer one of external demands. It's a family bond, where love drives obedience rather than fear of breaking a rule carved in stone.

# 14

# Modern Navigational Tools: Chapters, Verses, and Subheadings

Open a typical Bible, and you'll see headings, verse numbers, and chapter divisions neatly breaking up the text. Many readers assume these were always there—like official markers that show exactly where one thought ends and another begins. **They're later aids**, not part of the inspired message. They help us find our place, but they can also lead us to treat each verse as if it's meant to stand alone—like an isolated "soundbite."

## HOW SOUNDBITES DISTORT OUR READING

Because modern Bibles insert clear breaks and headings, it's easy to believe we *should* read Scripture in small snippets. Over time, this can:

### 1. Encourage Out-of-Context Quoting

A single verse or phrase might be lifted, pinned to a bumper sticker, or posted on social media. Used well, that can be edifying. But used poorly, it may divorce the text from its larger meaning.

## 2. Make Us Miss the Train of Thought

Biblical authors wrote in a flowing sequence—whether poetry, prophecy, or epistle. Chapter breaks can artificially segment their logic, causing us to stop reading mid-thought, unaware of the full argument.

## 3. Foster Anxiety About Translation Errors

If we think every isolated word must be exactly perfect, we might fear that a tiny variation from one translation to another could unravel the entire Bible. Scripture is robust and repetitive—it often communicates the same truths in multiple contexts, ensuring no single verse holds the entire message alone.

# SCRIPTURE IS A REPETITIVE, REINFORCED MESSAGE

Think about **this book** you're reading. If someone removed one whole chapter, you might lose some detail, but the overarching argument wouldn't collapse. Why? Because key points appear throughout. **Scripture works similarly**: doctrines like salvation by grace or God's faithfulness emerge again and again across different authors and literary genres.

> **Martin Luther and Romans 1:17** Luther famously cited this verse— "The righteous shall live by faith"—as a catalyst for his understanding of justification by faith. But that didn't mean *only* this verse supported the doctrine. Throughout Scripture, from Genesis to Revelation, God's grace and our faith response appear repeatedly. Romans 1:17 was simply an inflection point where the truth jumped out vividly for Luther, not its lone basis.

## REMINDERS FROM ANCIENT MANUSCRIPTS

If you saw a **Dead Sea Scroll**, you'd note:

- **Continuous Text**: No verse numbers, no bold headings. Prophets like Isaiah didn't label "Chapter 66." They wrote an unbroken message, trusting readers (or hearers) to follow the train of thought.

- **Reading as a Whole**: Early audiences often heard large sections read aloud in one gathering—gaining the big picture rather than dissecting it line by line.

## WHY NAVIGATIONAL TOOLS STILL HELP

- **Easy Reference**: Telling someone "Check Romans 1:17" is much simpler than "Flip through Romans until you find the line about living by faith."

- **Study & Teaching**: Pastors, theologians, and everyday believers can quickly cross-reference themes across different parts of the Bible.

## AVOIDING THE PITFALLS

### 1. Zoom In, Then Zoom Out

Yes, focus on a single verse to glean insights. But *always* step back and read preceding and following verses (even entire chapters) to grasp context.

### 2. Don't Let a Heading Finalize Meaning

Subheadings are editorial choices—sometimes helpful, sometimes misleading. Let the text shape your understanding more than the label above it.

3.  **Find the Overarching Message**

When a single word or verse seems ambiguous, remember: Scripture repeats and reaffirms core truths in multiple places. You're not reliant on *just one* turn of phrase.

## CONCLUSION: BEYOND THE MILE MARKERS

Chapters, verses, and subheadings are like **mile markers on a highway**—super helpful for navigation but never meant to replace the journey itself. Similarly, a single verse can serve as a powerful spotlight on truth (as in Luther's case) without being its only foundation.

**The entire tapestry of Scripture**—sometimes repetitive, always interconnected—ensures that no single translation nuance or missing verse can uproot a vital doctrine. When we step back and read larger sections, we see a robust, harmonious message shining through. The next time you notice a bold heading or a neat verse number, be grateful for the convenience—but remember that the biblical writers intended their words to be heard or read *as a flow*, reinforcing truth upon truth. That flow is where the depth of God's story truly emerges.

# 15

# "Paul Preached a Different Message Than Jesus"

**"If Jesus is all about the new covenant, why do we see Him telling lepers to follow Moses' laws or urging commandment-keeping—while Paul says we're saved by faith, not works?"** It's a common confusion that can appear to pit Jesus and Paul against each other. The reality? They're both part of **one unfolding story**—Jesus brings the old covenant to completion, and Paul explains how the new covenant, established at the cross, transforms everything.

## JESUS UNDER THE LAW

**Before the Cross, the old covenant still reigned.** According to Hebrews 9:16–17, a covenant only takes effect after the death of the one who made it. So, until Jesus died, the Mosaic system was still operational.

### 1. He Was "Born Under the Law"

Galatians 4:4–5 says Jesus came under the Law so He could redeem us.

When He instructs a healed leper to offer sacrifices "as Moses commanded" (Luke 5:14) or tells a young man to keep the commandments (Matthew 19:17), He's not denying the coming grace—He's **fulfilling** the still-active old covenant.

### 2. Not a Contradiction, But a Completion

Jesus' death **finalized** that old system, unleashing a new era of grace.

Think of it like using the old textbooks until the new ones officially arrive: Jesus honors the Mosaic framework until the moment He ratifies the new covenant with His own blood.

## PAUL'S MESSAGE OF GRACE: SAME STORY, NEXT PHASE

After the cross, the new covenant is in full force. Paul's teaching flows naturally from this **completed foundation**:

### 1. New Covenant Ratified by Death

Hebrews 9:16–17 underscores that a covenant begins only after the testator dies. Jesus' own death triggered this monumental shift.

### 2. Unveiling Grace

Paul highlights how believers are now justified by faith, **not** by Mosaic works. The old covenant's purpose was pointing to Christ. Once Jesus fulfilled it, the veil lifted (2 Corinthians 3:14–16).

## WHY JESUS AND PAUL AREN'T AT ODDS

### 1. Old Covenant Was Necessary

Jesus upholds Moses' law because it was still in effect—He's "the end of the beginning," completing every requirement so the new can be launched.

### 2. Paul Explains the Fulfillment

Post-resurrection, Paul clarifies that we're no longer bound by rituals Jesus satisfied. That's not undermining Jesus; it's revealing the transformation brought by the cross.

## A CLASSROOM ANALOGY

**Teacher** → Jesus, using the old curriculum until the cross.
**Post-New Curriculum** → Paul, showing how the new content (grace) surpasses the old.

They're not two rival educators—just consecutive stages of the same lesson plan.

## CONCLUSION: ONE CONTINUOUS PLAN

When we see Jesus telling people to keep the Law, that's **before** His death enacts the new covenant. When Paul preaches grace, he's **after** the cross, explaining the result of Christ's work. They're not contradictory; they're sequential. Jesus closes out the old covenant by **fulfilling** it, and Paul celebrates the **aftermath**: grace made fully available. The labels in our printed Bibles— "New Testament" before Matthew—can mislead us into thinking the new covenant began at Jesus' birth. In truth, it began at His **death and resurrection**, the hinge point between Law and Grace.

# 16

# Dividing the Word: The Sermon on the Mount and the Old Covenant

Understanding how to rightly divide the word isn't just an exercise in scholarship; it's foundational to our faith. One powerful example of this is Jesus' Sermon on the Mount. While it's often viewed as the pinnacle of Christian teaching, we need to recognize its primary context—the old covenant—and how it hints at, but does not fully reveal, the new.

## THE OLD COVENANT CONTEXT OF THE SERMON

The Sermon on the Mount (Matthew 5-7) is a masterpiece of wisdom, yet every word reflects the covenant in which Jesus taught: the old covenant. Jesus' role, as He stated, was not to abolish but to fulfill the law (Matthew 5:17). At this point, the new covenant had not been established because it could only come through His death and resurrection. As a result, His teachings reflect old covenant principles, with glimpses of a greater kingdom to come.

## WHAT JESUS DOESN'T SAY

To understand this, consider what Jesus doesn't mention in the Sermon on the Mount:

- **Praying in His Name**: Jesus taught on prayer, but He never instructs His followers to pray in His name. This practice becomes part of the new covenant because of our direct access to God through Christ (John 14:13-14).

- **The Cross and Justification**: Nowhere in the Sermon does Jesus mention the cross or the justification it brings. These central elements of the Christian faith could not yet be introduced because the means of justification had not yet been accomplished.

- **The Holy Spirit**: Jesus does not mention the coming of the Holy Spirit, who would later be described as the believer's counselor, guide, and seal of the new covenant (John 14:26, Ephesians 1:13).

- **The Church**: The Sermon on the Mount does not mention the church, which would be born from Jesus' resurrection and the outpouring of the Holy Spirit (Acts 2).

- **Believing in Him**: There is no mention of salvation by believing in Christ, a core teaching of the new covenant (John 3:16).

## COULD WE HAVE CHRISTIANITY WITHOUT THESE TEACHINGS?

Imagine if none of these doctrines existed—prayer in Jesus' name, the cross, justification, the Holy Spirit, the church, and faith in Christ. Without these, Christianity as we know it would not exist. Each of these teachings is foundational to the new covenant, meaning that while the Sermon on the Mount holds timeless principles, it is rooted in an old covenant context.

## THE IMPORTANCE OF CONTEXTUAL UNDERSTANDING

Understanding the Sermon on the Mount within its covenantal context does not diminish its value; it enhances it. Jesus presented the law's fullest demands and hinted at the kingdom to come, but He had to operate within the bounds of the old covenant until it was fulfilled. This awareness prevents us from misapplying teachings intended for the old covenant and helps us appreciate the complete revelation that came through His death, resurrection, and the establishment of the new covenant.

# 17

# Even Jesus Interpreted

The Pharisees were notorious for their word-for-word understanding of Scripture. They memorized the Law, quoted it on demand, and upheld it with an intensity that would make your Bible app streak look pitiful.

And yet... they didn't understand a thing.

Jesus called them out repeatedly—not because they didn't know the words, but because they missed *the point*.

## JESUS TRANSLATED THE POINT

Jesus wasn't afraid to interpret Scripture. In fact, He often revealed the deeper meaning behind the text:

- **On the Sabbath**: The Pharisees were livid when Jesus healed on the Sabbath. But He reminded them, *"The Sabbath was made for man, not man for the Sabbath"* (Mark 2:27). He translated the point: it's about restoration, not rigid rules.

- **On David Eating the Holy Bread**: When the Pharisees accused Him of breaking tradition, Jesus referenced David eating the consecrated bread (Matthew 12:3-4). Why? To show that righteousness isn't about legalistic lines—it's about doing good.

Jesus didn't twist Scripture; He clarified it. He showed that understanding the words doesn't always mean you understand *what they mean*.

## THE PROBLEM WITH MISSING THE POINT

Occasionally, someone comes along who ridicules *the point*. They uphold a single word as sacred, claiming it's the only way to preserve truth. They ridicule interpretation as reckless and paint themselves as the ultimate authority—or worse, the lone hero fighting off some imagined conspiracy.

Here's the problem: focusing on the words without understanding the heart doesn't make you faithful—it makes you a Pharisee.

## WHAT JESUS DID

Jesus followed the words with integrity, but He never stopped at the words. He always revealed *the point*. That's why He could say, *"You have heard it said... but I say to you"* (Matthew 5:21-22). He wasn't rewriting Scripture—He was showing us its fullness.

To follow Jesus, we don't just need to know the words. We need to know the point.

## WHY THIS MATTERS

Knowing the Bible word for word doesn't automatically mean you understand it. The Pharisees had the words, but they didn't recognize the Word standing in front of them.

If we're going to engage Scripture faithfully, we need both: the integrity of the words and the clarity of the point. That's not reckless—that's what Jesus would do.

## FINAL THOUGHT

Even Jesus interpreted. Not to change the words, but to show what they meant. Don't stop at the letters—follow the Word to the truth He's pointing to.

# Bridging Barriers and Building Habits

*Transition from section 1 to section 2*

Now that we've cleared away some of the most common misconceptions about Scripture, you might be thinking, "Okay, I'm more confident the Bible is reliable—but how do I actually engage with it regularly?" That's a fair question. Understanding that the Bible is trustworthy is one thing; making it part of your daily life is another challenge entirely.

Many of us have experienced the cycle: We get inspired on Sunday, commit to reading Scripture daily, start strong on Monday... but by Wednesday, we're overwhelmed, confused, or simply distracted. The Bible sits on our nightstand, collecting dust until the next burst of motivation.

If that sounds familiar, you're not alone. And it's not your fault.

The truth is no one teaches us how to read the Bible effectively. We're told it's important but rarely shown how to make it sustainable or enjoyable. It's like being handed a complex instrument without any lessons, then wondering why we can't play beautiful music right away.

In this next section, we'll move from understanding what the Bible is to discovering how to engage with it in ways that work for real people with busy lives. These aren't generic "read more Bible" guilt trips. They're practical strategies, mindset shifts, and approaches that have helped countless readers move from sporadic, frustrating attempts to consistent, life-giving engagement with God's Word.

31 Then their eyes were opened, & they knew him, and he vanished out of their sight.

32 And they said between themselves, Did not our hearts burne within vs, while hee talked with vs by the way, and when hee opened to vs the Scriptures?

33 And they rose vp the same houre, and returned to Ierusalem, and found the eleuen gathered together, and them that were with them,

34 Which said, The Lord is risen in deede, and hath appeared to Simon.

35 Then they told what things were done in the way, and how hee was knowen of them in breaking of bread.

36 ¶ And as they spake these things, Iesus himselfe stood in the mids of them, and said vnto them, Peace be vnto you.

37 But they were affrighted and afraid, supposing that they had seene a spirit.

38 Then he said vnto them, Why are ye troubled? and wherefore doe thoughts arise in your hearts?

39 Behold my hands and my feete, for it is I my selfe: handle me, and see, for a spirit hath not flesh and bones, as ye see me haue.

40 And when he had thus spoken, he shewed them his hands and feete.

41 And while they yet beleeued not for ioy, and wondered, he said vnto them, Haue ye here any meate?

42 And they gaue him a piece of a broyled fish, and of an hony combe.

43 And hee tooke it, and did eate before them.

44 ¶ And hee saide vnto them, These are the wordes, which I spake vnto you while I was yet with you, that all must bee fulfilled, which are written of mee in the Law of Moses, and in the Prophets, and in the Psalmes.

45 Then opened hee their vnderstanding, that they might vnderstand the Scriptures,

46 And said vnto them, Thus it is written, and thus it behoued Christ to suffer, & to rise againe from the dead the third day,

47 And that repentance & remission of sinnes should be preached in his Name among all nations, beginning at Hierusalem.

48 Now ye are witnesses of these things.

49 And behold, I doe send the promise of my Father vpon you: but tarie ye in the citie of Hierusalem, vntill yee bee endued with power from on high.

50 ¶ And he led them out into Bethania, and lift vp his hands, and blessed them.

51 And it came to passe, that as he blessed them, hee departed from them, and was caried vp into heauen.

52 And they worshipped him, and returned to Hierusalem with great ioy.

53 And were continually in the Temple, praysing and lauding God. Amen.

# THE HOLY GOSPEL OF IESVS CHRIST ACCORDING TO IOHN.

### CHAP. I.

1 IN the beginning was the Word, and the Word was with God, and that Word was God.

2 The same was in the beginning with God.

3 All things were made by it, and without it was made nothing that was made.

4 In it was life, and that life was the light of men.

5 And that light shineth in the darkenesse, and the darkenesse comprehended it not.

6 ¶ There was a man sent from God, whose name was Iohn.

7 The same came for a witnesse, to beare witnesse of that light, that all men through him might beleeue.

8 Hee was not that light, but was sent to beare witnesse of that light.

9 This was that true light, which lighteth euery man that commeth into the world.

10 He was in the world, and the world was made by him, and the world knew him not.

11 He came vnto his owne, and his owne receiued him not.

12 But as many as receiued him, to them he gaue prerogatiue to be the sonnes of God, euen to them that beleeue in his Name.

13 Which are borne not of blood, nor of the will of the flesh, nor of the will of man, but of God.

SECTION TWO

# Practical Bible Engagement

# 18

# You Need to Actually Like Reading the Bible

Ever feel like **reading the Bible** is a drag? Like it's *one more* chore on the spiritual checklist, right up there with flossing? You're not alone. People say:

- "Just get up earlier."
- "Push through—God will bless your faithfulness."
- "Be more disciplined."

But here's the truth:

**No one sticks with something they hate.**

**Discipline** can help you start, but *desire* is what keeps you going.

### THE GOAL ISN'T ROBOTIC OBEDIENCE

Some folks think real spiritual maturity is about forcing yourself to do stuff you secretly despise—like waking up at 5 AM to read four chapters while half asleep.

**But look:**

- God has never been after mere external performance.
- He wants your heart (Ezekiel 36:26).
- Jesus came to change your *desires* (Matthew 5:8).
- The Holy Spirit writes God's law *on your heart* (Jeremiah 31:33).

**Yes**, discipline plays a role, but if you fundamentally dislike reading the Bible, you'll eventually give up—or do it begrudgingly, missing the joy. God wants **transformation** from the inside out, not a checklist you resent.

## IF YOU'RE BRAND-NEW: DON'T SWEAT IT

Maybe you've never cracked open a Bible. Maybe "Leviticus" sounds like a Marvel villain. That's okay. Start with **desire**, not perfection. You don't need to morph into a monk overnight.

**Think about it:** If you're new to anything—like learning guitar—you won't master it by guilt. You find small wins, you discover the *why* it matters. Same with Scripture. The key is to **like** it, even if just a little at first.

## WHY "MORE DISCIPLINE" ISN'T THE MAGIC BULLET

We're told we just need: → More willpower.
More structure.
More routine.
But the key is actually: → **More desire.**
**Discipline** is short-term. **Desire** is long-term.
When you want something, you don't need constant pep talks. You just do it.

## WHAT WOULD MAKE THIS EASIER?

You don't hate learning—you might hate archaic translations that bore you. You don't hate praying—you might just feel awkward because you think it must be "super spiritual."

You don't hate church—you may just not have found a community that feels like home.

---

**PRO TIP: Stop making it a battle every day.**

---

- If reading feels like a struggle, **try audio** Bibles while commuting.
- If morning devotionals drain you, do it **at night** or during lunch.
- If prayer feels forced, **walk and talk**—let it be natural, like chatting with a friend.

**The best kind of "spiritual discipline"** isn't about trudging through misery; it's about creating an environment where Bible reading feels life-giving.

## CHANGING THE NARRATIVE: LESS "GRIND," MORE "GROWTH"

- People who get great at something? They *learn to love* the process.
- You rarely see an elite athlete who can't stand their sport. Sure, they have tough days, but there's a core enjoyment driving them.
- Imagine if you looked forward to Scripture, if it **fed** you, **relaxed** you, and **inspired** you.

That's not a fantasy. That's the Holy Spirit's *actual plan*—to shift your heart so you crave His Word.

## RETHINK SPIRITUAL DISCIPLINE

The word "discipline" can sound militaristic, like it's all about willpower and grit. But **Jesus** said:

*"My yoke is easy and my burden is light" (Matthew 11:30).*

It doesn't mean it's never challenging; it means the central force is **love**, not gut-it-out determination.

- "If you love me, you will keep my commandments" (John 14:15).
  → Notice it doesn't say "If you're disciplined enough, you'll keep them." It says **love**.

So, it's fine to say, "Lord, help me read daily," but it's even better to say, "Lord, make me *love* your Word so I'm drawn to it—*not* just forcing it."

### Practical Suggestions for Both Newbies and Veterans

#### 1. Start Small

Don't plan a 90-day Bible marathon if you've never read more than a Psalm. Maybe just one chapter or a short passage. Let *enjoyment* grow.

#### 2. Use Modern Tools

Audio Bibles, user-friendly translations, even devotion apps can remove obstacles.

Reading the King James if it frustrates you might kill your vibe. Try an NIV or NLT for clarity.

### 3. Build a "Bible-Friendly" Routine

Place your Bible by your coffee mug or schedule a quiet 10 minutes before you head out the door.

### 4. Group Up

Sometimes reading is more fun with friends. Join a small group or do a shared reading plan.

### 5. Ask for Desire

This is **huge**. Pray specifically, "God, make me want Your Word." That's not selfish—that's inviting the Holy Spirit to shape your affections.

### A Prayer: "God, Make Me Love Your Word"

**Father,**

*I'm done with guilt-based efforts. I don't want to just force myself to read Scripture; I want to want it.*

*Please stir up a real desire for Your Word, a genuine excitement to hear from You. Transform my heart so that discipline isn't a burden, but an overflow of love for who You are.*

*For the times I feel bored or lost, show me practical ways to engage. Let me enjoy the Bible the way You intended—like a feast I can't wait to taste.*

**Amen.**

## CONCLUSION: LET DESIRE LEAD THE WAY

**You don't need to beat yourself up** for not reading the Bible enough. The solution isn't more willpower; it's a **heart shift**.

When God kindles real **desire** in you, Bible reading goes from chore to **connection**. It becomes the highlight, not the duty. Yes, you still need routine, but routine flows easily when you like what you're doing.

**So, ask** for that desire. Stop thinking you need to be some spiritual Navy SEAL. Embrace a path where you **genuinely** enjoy Scripture. That's the kind of faith—and life—God always intended you to have. Now that you're equipped with fresh motivation, let's see where to start reading..."

# 19

# Stop Overthinking It: Just Open the Book!

Here's the amateur's favorite pastime: turning molehills into mountains. A party you RSVP'd to three months ago. Suddenly feels like climbing Everest. The gym? Forget it. You're already mentally exhausted just thinking about putting on sneakers. And intimacy with your spouse? You'd rather negotiate world peace while rolling a boulder up a mountain.

Why? Because you're making it a *big deal*. That's the amateur's calling card—hyper-inflating resistance until even the smallest task feels unbearable.

## RESISTANCE LOVES DRAMA

The seasoned Bible reader knows the truth: resistance thrives on drama. It wants you to believe that opening your Bible is like launching a space mission. It whispers, *"This is going to be awful. It's going to take forever. You'll probably hate it."* And you believe it. Because, let's be honest, resistance is a pretty convincing liar.

But here's the thing—none of it is true. The task is never as bad as the build-up. How many times have you gone to the gym, opened your Bible, or followed through on that "big deal" task and thought, *"Wow, this wasn't so bad after all"*? Exactly.

## SHRINK THE TASK, DEFLATE THE RESISTANCE

The seasoned reader doesn't let resistance dictate their emotions. They know the trick is to downsize the task in their mind. Instead of thinking, *"I need to have the perfect Bible study session with deep revelations and a heavenly glow afterward,"* they think, *"I'll just open the book and read for five minutes."*

Think of it like ripping off a Band-Aid: no overthinking, no drama, just action. The moment you stop feeding resistance with your predictions, it starves and loses its power.

## BIBLE READING (AND OTHER THINGS) AREN'T THAT BAD

Bible reading is a lot like intimacy with your spouse—it's rarely as bad as resistance makes it seem. The amateur predicts doom and gloom: *"This is going to be awkward, uncomfortable, or exhausting."* The seasoned knows better: *"I might actually enjoy this once I start."*

Proverbs 16:3 says, *"Commit your work to the Lord, and your plans will be established."* Notice it doesn't say, *"Overthink your work until you're too stressed to do it."* Commit it—just start. God will handle the rest.

## DEPRIVE RESISTANCE OF DRAMA

Here's the key: stop giving resistance the satisfaction of your predictions. Don't think about how miserable the gym will be—just put on your shoes. Don't overanalyze Bible reading—just open the book.

Resistance thrives on the "what ifs" and the "maybes." Deprive it of those, and it shrinks to nothing.

The seasoned Bible reader knows this secret: it's never as bad as you think. And often, it's far better than you expected.

So, stop making it a big deal. Open the book. Start small. And remember—resistance only wins if you let it.

# 20

# Bible Reading for Beginners: Where to Start

" Once you've realized the power of loving Scripture, here's how to pick a starting point. You pick up the Bible—66 books, spanning centuries, cultures, and genres. It's not just a book; it's a **library**. Small wonder many people hesitate: "Where do I even start?" It's easy to feel paralyzed by the sheer scale.

But take heart: you don't have to read the Bible cover-to-cover immediately. Instead, **begin** where you can get a **clear** window into who Jesus is and what God's heart looks like. Then branch out, adding more depth as you go.

**START WITH A GOSPEL: Mark or Luke**

**Why a Gospel First?** The four Gospels (Matthew, Mark, Luke, John) give you a front-row seat to Jesus' life and teachings—core to understanding the rest of Scripture. But which Gospel?

### 1. Mark

**Fast-Paced**: Mark is the shortest and moves quickly, using words like "immediately" often. Jesus is constantly **on the move**, which can keep you engaged if you're new.

**Action-Oriented**: Mark spotlights miracles and Jesus' authority. If you want a quick, vivid overview of who Jesus is, Mark is a great gateway.

2. **Luke**

**Universal Themes**: Luke highlights Jesus' compassion, His prayers, and His engagement with the marginalized.

**Wider Appeal**: Because Luke wrote with a more **Gentile** audience in mind, cultural references aren't as steeped in Jewish traditions as Matthew or John can be.

**Note**: Matthew and John are wonderful—just more Jewish customs (Matthew) or intense theological focus (John). They're best tackled once you have a sense of biblical context. For now, pick up Mark or Luke to get your feet wet.

## NEXT: Psalms and Proverbs in Bite-Size

Once you've read a Gospel, consider adding **Psalms** and **Proverbs** to your routine. Why?

- **Standalone Readings**: Each psalm or proverb can be read in short chunks. You don't need tons of background knowledge to glean wisdom or encouragement.
- **Building a Consistent Habit**: A psalm a day or a chapter of Proverbs can form a healthy, sustainable pattern. These are **self-contained** enough to avoid overwhelming you.

1. **Psalms**

Poems, prayers, and honest cries of the heart. You'll see people wrestling with despair, praising God, and everything in between. **Psalm 23** is a classic ("The Lord is my shepherd..."), easy to read solo.

**2. Proverbs**

Short wisdom sayings that speak to daily life. Even if you have no deep biblical background, *"A gentle answer turns away wrath..."* (Proverbs 15:1) is straightforward and applicable.

## THEN: Genesis or Exodus

After you've tasted the Gospels, and you're enjoying Psalms/Proverbs in small doses, consider **Genesis** or **Exodus** for bigger narrative arcs.

- **Genesis**: Foundational stories—creation, Abraham, Jacob, Joseph. It sets the stage for the entire biblical story, showing God's covenant heart.
- **Exodus**: The epic liberation of Israel from Egyptian slavery. It also shows God's faithfulness, the birth of the Law, and the concept of covenant community.

With some familiarity from Mark/Luke and the wisdom gleaned from Psalms/Proverbs, you'll have a better grasp to appreciate these origin accounts.

## LET GOD GUIDE THE REST

Reading the Bible isn't a strict linear chore. You can move around, sampling stories or letters, as you feel led. And if a certain book intrigues you—like **Ruth** or **Philippians**—feel free to explore. The main thing is not to let the vastness paralyze you.

**Tips:**

- Start with shorter books if you get overwhelmed.

- Pair a narrative (like a Gospel) with something poetic (Psalms) or an epistle (like Ephesians) if you want variety.
- Look for an easy-to-read translation, like NIV or NLT, if you're totally new.

## THE POWER OF STARTING SIMPLE

**Why** do we recommend such an approach?

### 1. Immediate Connection

The Gospels let you see Jesus right away—His compassion, His teachings, His miracles. There's no better anchor for your faith.

### 2. Less Overwhelm

Psalms and Proverbs can be digested in small bites. Perfect for building a daily or weekly habit without feeling the pressure of heavy theology or lengthy chapters.

### 3. Laying a Foundation

Once you know who Jesus is and you enjoy brief, stand-alone readings, you're prepared for the **big narratives** of the Old Testament, or the more in-depth letters of Paul, etc.

## CONCLUSION: PICK UP MARK (OR LUKE), START SMALL, GROW STEADILY

In short:

1. **Begin** with Mark or Luke—a direct, clearer view of Jesus.
2. **Add** a psalm or proverb daily/weekly for wisdom and devotions.
3. **Expand** to Genesis or Exodus as you gain confidence.

4. **Keep exploring**, trusting that each book has a role in the grand biblical story.

The Bible might be vast, but you don't have to conquer it overnight. Let these entry points ease you in. As you taste bits of Scripture, your appetite for God's Word can grow naturally. And remember it's not just about knowledge, but about **encountering** the living God through His written revelation. Enjoy the journey—**one step, one chapter, one day** at a time.

## A Prayer for Beginning

**Lord,**
*I sometimes feel overwhelmed by Scripture's size and depth. Help me start in a practical way—maybe with Mark or Luke—so I can see Jesus' life clearly. Guide me as I read Psalms and Proverbs for daily wisdom. And as I move on to Genesis, Exodus, or elsewhere, let my understanding grow steadily. Make each chapter an invitation to know You better, transforming my heart as I go.*
**Amen.**

# 21

# Holy Habits: Embrace the Routine

Some people bristle at the thought of a strict routine for prayer or Bible reading—they assume it's unspiritual, that the Holy Spirit only works in spontaneous bursts. But the truth is, **habits** aren't anti-faith. They might be precisely how God grounds us in day-to-day devotion.

## JESUS MODELED HABITS

In **Luke 4:16**, it says Jesus went to the synagogue "as was His custom." He didn't wait to "feel led" every Sabbath—He showed up routinely. That's not a lack of spirituality; it's a practical discipline that He deemed important. If the Son of God embraced consistent practice, we can too.

## ROUTINE WITHOUT GOOSEBUMPS

Let's be honest: some days you **read Scripture** or pray purely from habit. No angelic choir, no tears of revelation—just routine. But that routine is far from empty. In fact, some of our **biggest** spiritual insights emerge on days we read out of sheer faithfulness. God isn't offended by our habits; He often meets us right in the mundane.

## WHY HABITS ARE HOLY

### 1. They Provide Steadiness

Much like a steady rhythm in music, habits give shape to our spiritual life, preventing us from drifting in emotional highs or lows.

### 2. They Let God Work in Ordinary Spaces

Not every encounter with God arrives in a dramatic moment. Sometimes, it's a quiet nudge during your everyday routine.

### 3. They Protect Against Overthinking

Instead of deciding each morning whether you "feel" like reading the Bible, the habit does the deciding for you, freeing your mind to focus on the Word itself.

## DON'T OVERCOMPLICATE

If you ever feel robotic or guilty for reading out of habit, pause. It's no sin to run on a schedule. Just as a balanced diet keeps your body healthy, a habitual intake of Scripture fuels spiritual growth—whether you're "feeling it" that day.

---

**PRACTICAL TIP:** If monotony sets in, experiment with a new translation or a different reading spot. Small tweaks can refresh your routine, but don't abandon the routine altogether.

---

## CONCLUSION: EMBRACE THE ORDINARY RHYTHM

Habits may not always feel "holy," but they are a powerful channel for God's grace. They're not a fallback plan when passion fails; they're often the **vessel** through which God consistently nurtures us. So, if you ever wonder, "Am I less spiritual for being routine-driven?"—the answer is no. You're simply following in Christ's footsteps, letting daily faithfulness create space for the Holy Spirit to move in subtle yet profound ways.

# 22

# DIY But Not Alone: Balancing Personal Study and Community

The Bible is **for** you, yet you're **not** supposed to handle it in isolation. Scripture calls us to learn from teachers, gather as believers, and benefit from the body of Christ. The tension is maintaining personal engagement while welcoming communal insight.

1. **Too Much Is Done for Us**

Devotionals, sermons, group studies—they can be wonderful, but they can't replace opening the Bible for yourself. If you always let others interpret, you risk secondhand faith.

2. **The Blessing of Direct Contact**

Revelation 1:3 promises blessing to those who **read** the words of prophecy. Notice it specifically mentions reading, not just hearing it secondhand. God wants you engaged firsthand.

# BALANCING PERSONAL AND COLLECTIVE STUDY

### 1. Don't Do It Alone

Community input is vital: small groups, Bible studies, commentaries—they expand your perspective and keep you grounded in truth.

### 2. But Don't Skip Personal Reading

There's a depth of discovery and intimacy that only comes from encountering Scripture **yourself**. Teachers guide, but the Holy Spirit also speaks uniquely as you read directly.

## WHY IT MATTERS

- **Prevents Collective Misinterpretations**: If nobody reads for themselves, biases or errors in a group can go unchallenged. Think of the Bereans (Acts 17:11) who tested Paul's teaching against Scripture—an ideal mix of community learning and personal verification.

- **Avoids Spiritual Apathy**: When you rely solely on others' preaching, you might grow passive. Personal reading enlivens your faith, fueling a deeper connection to God's voice.

## TOOLS TO HELP

- **Small Groups & Mentors**: Not a replacement for personal reading, but a supplement that enriches your insights.

- **Bible Software & Commentaries**: They provide background and clarify tricky passages, but you still do the reading.

- **Compare Translations**: Checking multiple versions can enhance understanding—just remember to keep reading for yourself.

## BOTH, NOT EITHER-OR

So, it's not about isolation vs. communal study. **Read the Bible for yourself**—listen to the Holy Spirit guiding your understanding—**and** bring those gleanings into the fellowship of believers. You don't want a vacuum, nor do you want spoon-feeding. Let them complement each other.

**In short**: Scripture is for you to explore personally, but also for the church to process together. By balancing these angles, you reap the blessing of firsthand experience *and* the collective wisdom of the body.

# 23

# Clear the Noise: Hearing God in a Cluttered World

Reading Scripture on your own doesn't mean **rejecting** teachers, commentaries, or sermons. Sometimes you just need a spiritual "detox"—a pause from secondhand interpretations. Think of it as recalibrating your heart to hear God's Word **directly**, without the static of other voices.

### 1. Why Detox?

Over time, we can slip into hearing Scripture primarily through our favorite preacher or YouTube teacher. Their insights might be good, but if we never listen for God's **fresh** voice, we risk confusing secondhand revelation for personal conviction.

### 2. It's Temporary, Not Permanent

This isn't about living in isolation forever—just stepping away for a bit to let God speak. When you rejoin community, you'll do so with renewed clarity.

## THE ECHO CHAMBER EFFECT

Imagine opening the Bible only to overlay it instantly with what you've heard before—like a remix overshadowing the original song. That's not all bad, but it can limit new insights. A short break from external influences **lets Scripture breathe** on its own.

- **Cluttered Kitchen Analogy**: If the counter is littered with someone else's leftover dishes, you can't cook effectively. In the same way, if your mind is crowded with past teachings, you might miss a new angle God wants to show you.

### Biblical Examples of Solitude

- **Jesus** withdrew to lonely places to pray (Luke 5:16). If the Son of God needed alone time, so do we.
- **Paul** spent time away (Galatians 1:15–17) after his conversion, letting God reshape his understanding of Scripture before diving into ministry.

### Practical Steps to "Reset"

#### 1. Scheduled Seclusion

Pick a day or weekend where it's just you, the Bible, and God. Turn off podcasts, set aside devotionals, ignore social media threads about Scripture.

#### 2. Ask Different Questions

Approach familiar passages with, "Lord, is there something I've overlooked?" Jot down new impressions in a journal.

3. **Return to Community**

After your reset, compare what God showed you with trusted mentors or small-group friends. This guards against error and deepens mutual encouragement.

## A FRESH FREQUENCY

When you temporarily purge external voices, you let Scripture resonate in a new way. You're not spurning wisdom or teachers but giving yourself space to **hear** the Word directly. Then you re-engage community with clarity. It's not about resisting outside input; it's about **resetting** so you can discern God's voice without the static.

# 24

# Remember what you read: Write it down

We walk into a room and forget why. We lose our train of thought mid-sentence. If we're that forgetful with daily life, imagine how easily profound biblical insights slip away. James 1:22-25 warns that hearing the Word but not living it is like gazing in a mirror, then immediately forgetting your reflection. The issue? **Memory**. No memory, no transformation.

## WHY WRITING MATTERS FOR RETENTION

Think of memory as the bridge from **revelation** to **application**. If you can't recall what God showed you, how will you obey it? **Writing** is your anchor:

- **Locks in Insights**: A notebook or digital journal prevents the "in one ear, out the other" syndrome.
- **Tangible Reference**: Revisiting notes cements truths, keeping them fresh in your mind.
- **Active Engagement**: Jotting verses in your own words forces you to process them deeper, driving them into your heart.

## Practical Pointers

### 1. Dedicated Journal

Give yourself a space—physical or digital—where you regularly record verses, observations, or new learnings.

### 2. Summaries & Questions

After reading, paraphrase the passage in your own words. If questions arise, write them, then search for answers.

### 3. Action Steps

Jot down how you'll apply the day's reading. Even if it's small—like "Pray for X" or "Forgive Y"—it solidifies the message in real life.

## FORGETTING LEADS TO DRIFTING

Second Peter 1:9 notes that spiritual stagnation often comes from forgetting our forgiveness in Christ. **Forgetting** kills momentum; **remembering** spurs growth. Writing is your tool to remember. When God nudges you, don't trust it solely to memory. Capture it on paper or screen, so it fuels your long-term transformation.

## CONCLUSION: HANG ON TO TRUTH

We're prone to letting vital lessons evaporate. But writing them down transforms fleeting insights into **lasting** guides. God's Word is too precious to lose in mental clutter. Make writing part of your Bible routine and watch how much more you retain—and how much deeper you live it out.

# 25

# Meditate on the Word— Hearing What God Is Saying to You

Meditation isn't about emptying your mind; it's about filling it with God's Word. It's about sitting with Scripture long enough to hear what God is saying to you. And here's the thing: sometimes that means staying with the same verse, chapter, or sermon for days— or even weeks. Repetition is not just okay; it's essential.

## THE REPETITION OF GOD

One of the first things you need to know about God is that He has no issue repeating Himself. In fact, Scripture is filled with repetition. Take the book of Proverbs, for example. Wisdom doesn't just speak once and move on. It reiterates the same truths in different ways, over and over. Why? Because God knows we need to hear it more than once for it to sink in.

Yet, how often do we resist this approach? We skim through chapters, hop between sermons, and switch from one pastor's teaching to another as if it's all interchangeable. But learning doesn't work like that. Growth doesn't work like that. And God certainly doesn't work like that.

## THE PRACTICALITY OF STAYING

Think about it practically. Imagine you're undergoing surgery, and halfway through, the surgeon walks out and a new one steps in. Or picture a courtroom where your lawyer leaves mid-cross-examination, replaced by someone else. Would that inspire confidence? Of course not. It's chaotic and impractical, and it disrupts momentum.

The same principle applies to studying God's Word. Jumping from one thing to the next without fully absorbing what God is saying can kill spiritual momentum. It's okay—necessary, even—to stay with something for a long time. When God has you revisit a verse, chapter, or sermon, it's because He's working something deep within you. Don't rush the process.

## THE COACH'S DRILL

When learning a new skill, a coach might have you repeat the same drill over and over. It might feel monotonous, but it's how you develop muscle memory and mastery. The same is true with God's Word. Meditation is like spiritual drilling. It's not about quantity—how many chapters you can read or sermons you can watch—but about quality. What is God teaching you in this moment? Are you allowing it to sink in?

## DISCERNMENT IN CONSISTENCY

There's another layer to this: discernment. Sometimes, the person or teaching you're avoiding is the very one God is using to revisit something important. Don't treat God's Word as trivial, thinking it doesn't matter who says it, when they say it, or how they say it. It does matter. God's timing and instruments are intentional.

Switching between voices, verses, or sermons too quickly can dilute what God is trying to show you. Sit down. Get comfortable. Be prepared to listen to the same thing repeatedly. There's depth in repetition. There's revelation in consistency.

## THE VALUE OF MEDITATION

Joshua 1:8 says, "Keep this Book of the Law always on your lips; meditate on it day and night, so that you may be careful to do everything written in it. Then you will be prosperous and successful." Meditation isn't just about hearing—it's about doing. And doing requires focus, repetition, and commitment.

So, the next time you're tempted to jump from one teaching to another, pause. Ask yourself: *Am I giving God's Word the time and attention it deserves?* Meditation is not a race; it's a slow, intentional journey. Allow God to speak to you repeatedly. Let Him drill the truth deep into your heart.

Because the more you meditate on His Word, the more you'll hear His voice. And the more you hear His voice, the more you'll grow into the person He's calling you to be.

# 26

# Your Soul is Hungry— Give It the Right Food

Here's the truth: the biggest myth about adulthood is that we know what we want. Spoiler alert—we don't. If you're sitting there thinking, *"No, I know exactly what I want,"* congratulations— you've just exposed yourself as an amateur.

The seasoned Bible reader? They know better. They've learned that half the time, what you *think* you want is just a poorly disguised tantrum from your soul crying out for something else.

## THE ITCH THAT WON'T SCRATCH

I can't tell you how many times I've felt off—like something was wrong, but I couldn't put my finger on it. So, like any reasonable adult, I tried all the usual fixes: Netflix, a bag of chips, scrolling through TikTok like my life depended on it. Did any of it work? Of course not.

Eventually, after exhausting every possible distraction, I reluctantly opened my Bible. And guess what? The gates of heaven opened, angels sang, and my soul sighed, *"Finally!"* Turns out, *this* was what I wanted all along.

## SOUL TANTRUMS ARE REAL

Your soul knows what it needs. When it doesn't get it, it acts out. Think of it like a toddler throwing a tantrum. It manifests as binge-watching, snacking, or doom-scrolling, but deep down, it's just screaming, *"I need the Word!"* The seasoned reader understands this. They know the more acting out, the hungrier the soul is.

## PRO TIP: SKIP THE DRAMA

The amateur waits for the soul tantrum to run its course. The seasoned? They skip the drama and go straight to the Word. No chips, no TikTok, no fake distractions. They've learned that when their soul is restless, the only thing that will truly scratch the itch is time with God.

So next time you're wandering from distraction to distraction, remember this: you don't know what you want—but your soul does. And it's waiting for you to figure it out.

# 27

# "If I Don't Feel It, Is It Even Working?"

We live in a culture that thrives on instant results. Fast food, fast shipping, fast answers. No one wants to wait. Why spend months getting in shape when you can take a shortcut? Why work for something when you can get the *feel* of it instantly?

But the problem with instant gratification? **It rarely delivers lasting results.**

A quick-fix diet might shed pounds, but at what cost? A shortcut in training might make you feel strong now, but it leaves you weak later. The same goes for the way we approach Scripture. We want it to work fast. We want to feel something right away. And when we don't, we assume nothing is happening.

But God's Word isn't a drive thru. It's a **gold mine.**

## JEREMIAH 29:11 AND THE SOUNDBITE PROBLEM

Take Jeremiah 29:11:
*"For I know the plans I have for you, declares the Lord, plans to prosper you and not to harm you, plans to give you a hope and a future."*

That verse gets passed around like a spiritual protein bar—quick energy for when you're feeling low. And sure, it's true. But **it's not the whole story.**

What most people skip over is that this promise was given to people in exile, with a **70-year wait time** attached to it (Jeremiah 29:10). God wasn't saying, "Here's your breakthrough tomorrow." He was saying, "Trust me over the long haul."

Scripture isn't meant to be plucked like a quick snack. It's meant to be *mined*—dug into, wrestled with, refined, and ultimately, transformed into something of value.

## MINING THE WORD VS. SKIMMING THE SURFACE

Think about gold mining. When you first pull something out of the ground, it doesn't look valuable. It's dirty, unrefined, and covered in rock. If you judged its worth by its *initial* appearance, you might toss it aside.

But if you refine it? If you put in the time, remove the impurities, and let the process do its work? **Now you have gold.**

That's exactly how the Word works.

- **Mining the Word** = Sticking with a passage even when it doesn't "click" right away.
- **Refining the Word** = Meditating on it, praying over it, and letting the Holy Spirit illuminate deeper meaning.
- **Gold** = The revelation, transformation, and wisdom that lasts for life—not just for a moment.

## WHY QUICK HITS OF SCRIPTURE AREN'T ENOUGH

A single verse can give you a **temporary boost**, but that's not the goal. If you only ever take in scripture through soundbites, it's like eating a sugar rush diet—quick energy, but no sustenance.

Think about Jesus. When He was tempted in the wilderness (Matthew 4:1-11), He didn't just fire off random verses for motivation. He pulled from **what was deeply ingrained** in Him.

- He didn't just *know* the Word—He *lived* it.
- He didn't just *quote* Scripture—He *embodied* it.
- He didn't just *skim* it—He had *mined* it.

## WHEN THE HOLY SPIRIT TELLS YOU TO STAY, STAY

Have you ever felt drawn to a passage, but you didn't know why? A verse or chapter that won't leave you alone? That's not random. That's the Holy Spirit leading you to **mine deeper**.

Too often, we treat these nudges like background noise. We read something, don't immediately "get it," and move on. But what if that passage is waiting to **reveal something huge—if you'd just stay long enough to see it?**

- What if *sticking with it* is the difference between a passing thought and a life-changing revelation?
- What if *meditating on it* unlocks something about God you've never seen before?
- What if *wrestling with it* is where the breakthrough happens?

## THE INVESTMENT MINDSET: PATIENCE AND DILIGENCE PAY OFF

Mining for gold takes time, effort, and patience. But no one who strikes gold complains about the work it took to get there.

The same is true with Scripture. The more you **invest**, the **greater the return.**

- The amateur skims a verse and moves on.
- The seasoned reader **digs, stays, refines, and transforms.**

Proverbs 2:4-5 says:

*"If you seek [wisdom] like silver and search for it as for hidden treasures, then you will understand the fear of the Lord and find the knowledge of God."*

This isn't about picking up quick encouragement. This is treasure hunting.

## WHAT'S YOUR APPROACH?

Next time you sit down with the Word, ask yourself:

- Am I skimming or mining?
- Am I chasing a quick pick-me-up or building something that lasts?
- When the Holy Spirit nudges me to stay, am I staying?

Because **instant gratification won't change your life—but gold will.**

So, dig deep. Refine what you find. And watch as the Word turns into something far more valuable than you ever imagined.

# 28

# When You're Too Sad to Read the Bible

"I'm far too sad to read the Word today." Sound familiar? There's probably nothing that holds us back from doing the right thing more than the insidious thought: *I'm not happy enough to do it.*

But let's be real—that thought is a trap. Jesus Himself warned us about it. In the parable of the Sower, He said, **"The cares of the world choke out the seed"** (Mark 4:19). Translation: life's heaviness—the sadness, the stress, the never-ending worries—has a way of squeezing out the little bit of Word we might have had to begin with. And once that cycle starts, it feeds on itself: unhappy leads to unproductive, unproductive leads to more unhappy.

## THE ENEMY EXPLOITS SADNESS

The enemy thrives in this cycle. **"He prowls around like a roaring lion, seeking whom he may devour"** (1 Peter 5:8). And who do you think is at the top of his list? The unhappy. The downcast. The overwhelmed. Because, let's face it, when we're miserable, the last thing we feel like doing is opening the Bible.

But that's exactly what makes us vulnerable. We let sadness become the reason we stay disconnected from the very thing that could save us from it.

## THE WAY OUT

Here's the truth: everything will fight to convince you that happiness can be found somewhere else—Netflix, food, a quick fix, or scrolling aimlessly through your phone. But happiness isn't what you need. The Word is.

The Bible isn't just for the good days when everything feels right. It's for the days when everything feels wrong. It's for the moments when you're too sad to function, too stressed to think, and too overwhelmed to care. It's the light in the darkness, the life preserver when you're drowning.

**"Your word is a lamp to my feet and a light to my path"** (Psalm 119:105). That doesn't mean it always fixes everything instantly, but it gives you the clarity, the strength, and the hope to keep going.

## BREAK THE CYCLE

The only way to break the vicious cycle of sadness and stagnation is to take control. Open the Word, even if it's the last thing you feel like doing. Read a verse, a chapter—anything. Because when you do, you're choosing to step out of the enemy's trap.

It's not about waiting for happiness to come. It's about realizing that joy, peace, and fulfillment are found in God's Word—and the only way to access them is by opening the Bible.

Don't let sadness keep you stuck. The enemy may use it to keep you down, but God's Word is what will pull you up. Start reading, even through the tears. That's where healing begins.

# 29

# Don't Spoil the Story– Read with Fresh Eyes

Ever watched a movie with someone who already knows the ending? They nudge you during a seemingly small moment, whispering, *"That guy? He's the villain."* Or they casually drop, *"Oh, this scene is way more important than you think."* And just like that, your fresh experience is ruined. You can't *un-know* what they just told you.

We do the same thing when reading the Bible. It's impossible to *unknow* the cross and resurrection. We already know how the story ends. And because of that, we subconsciously impose that knowledge onto passages where no one *in the moment* had that perspective. The problem isn't that we know the ending—it's that we forget the disciples *didn't*.

A person who doesn't realize how much they already *know* the story will read it like the friend who spoils the movie—filling in meaning where it doesn't belong and missing the raw, unfiltered impact of what's happening.

## HOW WE MISREAD JESUS' WORDS

Take *"Take up your cross and follow me"* (Matthew 16:24). Sounds like a solid life principle, right? A metaphor for self-denial, faith through hardship, or the cost of discipleship. We check the boxes:

- Church
- Devotion
- Moral alignment

But when Jesus said it, no one was checking off anything. They were *horrified*. Because when *they* heard "cross," they didn't think *personal struggles*—they thought *public execution*. At that point, no one was expecting a Messiah who *dies*. So much so that just the *mention* of it made Peter rebuke Jesus to His face.

This is why Jesus used such strong language. He wasn't giving them a spiritual life lesson. He was making it clear: *This is happening.* The cross wasn't a vague symbol of endurance; it was a warning of what was to come. Peter and the disciples weren't ready for that reality, so Jesus enlarged the scenario to make sure they grasped it.

But because we *already* know the cross is part of the story, we shrink Jesus' words into something safer. We domesticate them into an encouragement for tough seasons rather than what they were—a blunt wake-up call to men who still thought this road led to a throne.

## REDUCING OUR CLUMSY TAKES

The key to reading Scripture well isn't *unknowing* what we know (that's impossible). It's *factoring in* what the disciples *didn't* know. It's realizing that when we assume *our* perspective was *their* perspective, we miss the weight of the moment.

So, the next time you read the Gospels, pause. Ask yourself:

- What did Jesus' audience hear in this moment?
- Would this have made sense to them at the time?
- Am I filling in meaning because I already know how it all turns out?

You can't unknow the story, but you *can* read with awareness. And that awareness will keep you from being *that friend*—the one who, without meaning to, spoils the moment before it can hit the way it was meant to.

# 30

# "The Bible is a Mirror, Not a Microphone"

We all know that person who uses the Bible as a microphone—always quick to point out what's wrong with everyone else. But here's the thing: the Bible was meant to be a mirror before it's a microphone. In other words, its primary purpose is to reflect our own hearts, not to give us ammo for calling out the faults of others.

It's easy to read Scripture with other people in mind. *"So-and-so really needs to hear this!"* But when we do that, we miss out on the personal transformation God wants to work in us. The Bible is first and foremost a tool for our own growth. Before we try to apply it to anyone else's life, we need to let it do its work in our own.

Jesus made it clear in Matthew 7:5: *"First take the plank out of your own eye, and then you will see clearly to remove the speck from your brother's eye."* Start with yourself, and let the Bible be the mirror that reveals what needs to change in you.

# 31

# Healthy Fear: The Weapon You Didn't Know You Needed

Amateurs think fear is always a bad thing. They'll say stuff like, *"God's got me, so I don't need to worry about anything."* "That's cute, but it's not entirely true. The seasoned Bible reader? They know better. They've learned that fear—when it's the right kind—can be a weapon.

Think about it. If you completely abolished fear in a deer, how long would it last in a forest full of predators? Exactly. Fear keeps the deer alive. It doesn't freeze it in place; it keeps it sharp, alert, and mindful of danger.

## THE FEAR THAT KEEPS YOU GROUNDED

Here's the thing: not all fear is bad. Most fear is destructive, sure. Fear of failure, fear of rejection, fear of change—those will paralyze you. But there's one kind of fear that can save your life: the fear that says, *"I need the Word today, or I won't make it."*

Proverbs 9:10 says, *"The fear of the Lord is the beginning of wisdom."* This isn't terror—it's reverence. It's a healthy respect for

God and a recognition of how desperately you need Him. The seasoned reader takes nothing for granted. They know that without the Word, they're vulnerable. They understand that any given day can defeat them if they're not armed with truth.

## THE WEAPONIZED WORD

Let's be real—fear gets a bad rap. But the seasoned Bible reader knows it can be a motivator. It's the fear that says, *"I need God's Word today, because without it, my mind will unravel faster than I can scroll TikTok."* It's the same fear that an alcoholic has when they see a drink and know, *"That could be the end of me."*

The amateur says, *"God's got me; I'm good."* The seasoned says, *"Yes, God's got me, but I still need to remind myself of that over and over, or I'll forget."*

Jesus Himself demonstrated this in Matthew 4:4: *"Man shall not live by bread alone, but by every word that proceeds out of the mouth of God."* Even in the wilderness, Jesus reminded Himself—and us—that the Word is as essential as food.

## THE CONFIDENCE THAT COMES FROM FEAR

The irony is, healthy fear builds confidence. It keeps you dependent on the right things—like God's Word—and not on your own strength. It sharpens your focus. It's not the fear that paralyzes you; it's the fear that gets you to open the Bible and say, *"This is life to me. I can't afford to skip it."*

Psalm 119:11 says, *"I have hidden your word in my heart that I might not sin against you."* Why? Because the psalmist knew what could happen without it.

## STAY HUMBLE, STAY HUNGRY

Fear reminds us we're not invincible, and that's a good thing. The seasoned Bible reader understands this: life will try to sneak up on you like a predator in the forest. Healthy fear is what keeps you sharp, alert, and dependent on the Word.

So, if you feel that tug in your heart saying, *"You need this,"* don't dismiss it as paranoia or guilt. That's the kind of fear you want to keep. It's not weakness—it's wisdom.

The amateur thinks fear is unnecessary. The seasoned knows it's essential. Keep the fear that drives you to the Word—it just might save your life.

# 32

# It Really Is the Phone: Dealing with distraction

You sit down to read the Bible. You're ready. Focused. Holy. Then—just for a second—you check your phone. *Just a quick glance.*

Fifteen minutes later, you've watched a dog skateboard, learned why ancient Rome fell, and somehow ended up debating a stranger in the comment section.

And your Bible? Still closed.

I used to think my biggest problem was a lack of discipline. Turns out, **it really is the phone.**

## NOT ALL NOISE IS THE SAME

We live in a world drowning in noise—not just sound, but the kind that clutters your mind and fractures your focus.

But not all noise is bad. Some noise—the hum of conversation, the rhythm of work, the joy of family—doesn't interrupt God's voice. It often complements it.

Then there's the other kind. The scroll. The click. The endless cycle of notifications that don't add to your life—they just steal from it.

That's the noise that silences God's voice in your life.

## JESUS AND THE RHYTHM OF FOCUS

Jesus never demanded perfect silence to hear the Father. He moved through real life, calling His followers to do the same.

*"They will come in and go out, and find pasture."* (John 10:9)

Notice the rhythm—movement, not isolation. God's voice was meant to go with you into your daily life. But the constant hum of digital chaos trains us to be distracted, not present.

The problem isn't that God isn't speaking. It's that we're too overstimulated to listen.

## YOUR PHONE ISN'T JUST DISTRACTING YOU—IT'S REWIRING YOU

Ever notice how hard it is to read a full chapter of Scripture, but you can doomscroll for an hour without blinking? That's not coincidence—that's design.

Your phone is a dopamine slot machine, rewarding you every few seconds with new stimuli. It's not just stealing your focus—it's changing your brain.

And before you say, *But I use my phone for the Bible!*, be honest—how often do you open the Bible app only to get sidetracked by a text, a notification, or *one quick thing*?

Your phone isn't helping your spiritual life. It's hijacking it.

## CUTTING THROUGH THE NOISE: PRACTICAL STEPS

If you feel like you can't focus anymore, you're not crazy—you're just overstimulated. But you can undo it:

### 1. Physically Remove the Phone When Reading Scripture

If your phone is within reach, you will check it. **Don't trust yourself.** Put it in another room.

### 2. Create a Digital Sabbath

Set a daily window where you disconnect completely—no social media, no notifications. Give your brain space to reset.

### 3. Rebuild Your Attention Span

Start small. Read one chapter of the Bible without looking at your phone. Then two. Train your brain to sit with Scripture before feeding it the dopamine rush of the internet.

## THE TAKEAWAY: THE SHEPHERD IS STILL SPEAKING

God's voice isn't absent—it's just waiting in the quiet.

He doesn't need perfect silence, but He does need your attention. And in a world working overtime to steal it, **protecting your focus is one of the most spiritual disciplines you can develop.**

So, the next time you pick up your phone before you pick up your Bible, ask yourself:

*"Is this helping me hear God's voice—or is it silencing it?"*

The Shepherd is still speaking. The question is whether we're listening.

# 33

# The Enemy of the Word

Christians are notorious for saying, *"The devil did this"* or *"The enemy did that."* It's like every bad thing that happens in life is blamed on demonic activity. Got stuck behind a slow driver? Must be the enemy. Coworker rude to you? Obviously, the devil. Having a bad week? Yep, that's got to be the enemy's fault. At this point, the devil is probably sitting in a corner crying, saying, *"Why do they blame me for everything?"*

Now, I'm not diminishing the fact that there is an enemy who goes around like a roaring lion. That's real. But the Bible doesn't explicitly label every inconvenience or frustration as demonic activity. However, there is something that Jesus *did* directly address as a demonic attack—the attack on the Word.

In the parable of the Sower (Matthew 13:3-23), Jesus gives us a clear picture of the enemy's real target. He says that when someone hears the message of the kingdom but doesn't understand it, the evil one comes and snatches away what was sown in their heart. *That* is spiritual warfare, right there—the enemy specifically going after the Word.

It's like stealing candy from a baby. When the Word is carelessly heard, or when we're inattentive or negligent, the enemy swoops in and takes it away before it can take root. You ever notice how some people have been in church for years but barely know the Word? That's the enemy at work—keeping the Word from taking hold in their hearts.

Let me make it clear: if you don't guard the Word, if you don't read it, if you don't seek to understand it, the enemy will gladly take it away. Jesus himself warned us of this in the parable. The Word is precious, and there is a very real spiritual attack on it. The enemy knows that if the Word takes root in your life, it changes everything.

So, the next time you're tempted to blame the devil for the slow driver or the bad week, stop and think about what's really going on. The enemy's primary mission isn't to inconvenience your day—it's to snatch away the Word. Not reading, not understanding, not desiring Scripture? That's the real work of the enemy. And that's something we can know for sure

# 34

# "Stop Treating the Bible Like a Self-Help Book

We live in a world consumed by **productivity**. Everything must produce a tangible benefit or result. "What's the point?" we ask, as though value only exists in what we can measure. This mindset seeps into how we see Scripture, too. Is Bible reading crucial for the planet's survival? Will it guarantee your kids a perfect life or land you a promotion? Probably not. And that's okay.

## NOT EVERYTHING HAS TO "DO" SOMETHING

We've trained ourselves to view everything through utility: if it doesn't "work" for us, why bother? Even church culture often focuses on sermons about fixing life's problems—helpful, sure, but we risk missing something profound: simply **being** with God and His Word, enjoying it for what it is rather than treating it as a tool.

## SCRIPTURE AS ART, NOT MERELY INSTRUCTION

Think of standing before a **Picasso**. Does it *do* anything? No, but you're captivated. Or smelling a perfect fragrance—it doesn't solve a problem; you just savor it. Or the way white sand meets clear water—no one asks, "Why is this beach here?" You just **bask** in its beauty.

The Bible is the same. Yes, it has wisdom and guidance, but it's not a self-help manual. It's **God's revelation**—a masterpiece that draws us into wonder.

## LIFE IS NOT PRODUCTIVITY

We confuse **life** with endless productivity. We assume we're only living if we're *achieving*. But Jesus didn't come to hand us a to-do list—He came to give us **life to the full** (John 10:10). Reading Scripture isn't about turning it into a productivity hack. It's about **experiencing** God's story, letting His Word **feed** your soul, not just *fix* your problems.

## IRONY: THE BIBLE'S UTILITY IN ITS "INUTILITY"

Here's the paradox: the Bible is most **powerful** when we stop trying to make it serve us. If we approach it as a "tool," we limit its transformative power to immediate benefits. But when we let it stand as a **work of divine art**, it can shape our hearts far beyond what we can measure. That's more valuable than any tangible "use."

## A PRACTICAL WAY TO JUST ENJOY: PSALMS & REFLECTION

One simple step: **spend a few minutes each day** reading a passage "just because." Don't think, "How can I apply this?" or "What problem will this solve?" Simply read **for enjoyment**—to marvel at God's nature or dwell in His presence. The **Psalms** are perfect for this: they don't always offer a specific "task" or solution. They're filled with **worship**, emotion, lament, and admiration. By reading them as the psalmist wrote them—full of **wonder**—you taste Scripture's beauty without forcing utility.

> **Try This**: Open to a favorite psalm (e.g., Psalm 23). Read it slowly, savoring the words of comfort, **not** looking for an immediate "lesson." Let the imagery wash over you—green pastures, still waters—and simply enjoy God's care.

## EMBRACE THE BEAUTY

So, the next time you open your Bible, resist the urge to ask, "What's the point?" Don't approach it like a checklist item or a spiritual hammer for your life's nails. Instead, **admire** it. Stand in awe of its truth, its poetry, its divine-human narrative—like you'd gaze at a stunning painting or soak up a sunset. Because sometimes, the most beautiful things in life have no "point" other than to be treasured.

**And that's okay.**

## FINAL THOUGHT

Reading Scripture purely for **enjoyment** might feel unproductive—but that's precisely the **point**. The Bible's greatest impact often emerges when we stop making it about "usefulness." So let yourself be awed. Let yourself **enjoy**. In a world demanding everything "do" something, remember that some things—like a breathtaking beach or a perfect fragrance—are simply **worth savoring**. Scripture, at its core, is one of them. Let it move your heart, whether or not you can measure the outcome.

# From Reading to Becoming

*Transition from section 2 to section 3*

You've established some practical habits for engaging with Scripture—maybe you've found your rhythm, chosen a starting point, or discovered ways to stay consistent despite life's demands. These practical steps are vital, but they're just the beginning of what God's Word can do in your life.

Because here's the truth: the Bible isn't merely a book to be read—it's a living Word meant to transform you. Many believers get stuck in a pattern of faithful reading without experiencing profound change. They develop the habit but miss the heart-level encounter. They gain information without transformation. They know more about God without actually knowing God more deeply.

That's like learning all about swimming—the techniques, the science of buoyancy, the history of competitive swimming—without ever actually getting in the water. You might become knowledgeable, but you'll never experience the refreshment of the dive, the exhilaration of gliding through the water, or the confidence that comes from learning to float.

In this next section, we'll explore how Scripture does its deepest work—not just informing your mind but reshaping your identity, renewing your perspective, and deepening your relationship with Jesus. We'll move beyond techniques to transformation, beyond information to encounter. Because when God's Word truly takes root, you don't just become a better Bible reader—you become more like Christ.

31 Then their eyes were opened, & they knew him, and hee vanished out of their sight.
32 And they said betweene themselues, Did not our hearts burne within vs, while hee talked with vs by the way, and when hee opened to vs the Scriptures?
33 And they rose vp the same houre, and returned to Ierusalem, and found the eleuen gathered together, and them that were with them,
34 Which said, The Lord is risen in deede, and hath appeared to Simon.
35 Then they told what things were done in the way, and how hee was knowen of them in breaking of bread.
36 ¶ And as they spake these things, Iesus himselfe stood in the mids of them, and said vnto them, Peace be to you.
37 But they were abashed and afraid, supposing that they had seene a spirit.
38 Then he said vnto them, Why are ye troubled? and wherefore doe doubts arise in your hearts?
39 Behold mine hands, and my feete, for it is I my selfe: handle me and see: for a spirit hath not flesh and bones, as ye see me haue.
40 And when he had thus spoken, he shewed them his hands and feete.
41 And while they yet beleeued not for ioy, and wondred, he said vnto them, Haue ye here any meate?

42 And they gaue him a piece of a broyled fish, and of an hony combe.
43 And hee tooke it, and did eate before them.
44 ¶ And hee saide vnto them, These are the wordes, which I spake vnto you while I was yet with you, that all must bee fulfilled which are written of mee in the Law of Moses, and in the Prophets, and in the Psalmes.
45 Then opened he their vnderstanding, that they might vnderstand the Scriptures,
46 And said vnto them, Thus it is written, and thus it behooued Christ to suffer, & to rise againe from the dead the third day,
47 And that repentance & remission of sinnes should be preached in his Name among all nations, beginning at Hierusalem.
48 Now ye are witnesses of these things.
49 And behold, I doe send the promise of my Father vpon you: but tarie ye in the citie of Hierusalem, vntill yee bee endued with power from on high.
50 ¶ Afterward he led them out into Bethania, and lift vp his hands, and blessed them.
51 And it came to passe, that as he blessed them, hee departed from them, and was caried vp into heauen.
52 And they worshipped him, and returned to Hierusalem with great ioy,
53 And were continually in the Temple, praysing, and lauding God. Amen.

# THE HOLY GOSPEL OF IESVS CHRIST ACCORDING TO IOHN.

### CHAP. I.

1 In the beginning was the Word, and the Word was with God, and that Word was God.
2 That same was in the Beginning with God.
3 All things were made by it, and without it was made nothing that was made.
4 In it was life, and that life was the light of men.
5 And that light shineth in the darkenesse, and the darkenesse comprehended it not.
6 ¶ There was a man sent from God, whose name was Iohn.
7 This same came for a witnesse, to beare witnesse of that light, that all men through him might beleeue.
8 Hee was not that light, but was sent to beare witnesse of that light.
9 This was that true light, which lighteth euery man that commeth into the world.
10 He was in the world, and the world was made by him, and the world knew him not.
11 He came vnto his owne, and his owne receiued him not.
12 But as many as receiued him, to them he gaue prerogatiue to be the sonnes of God, euen to them that beleeue in his Name.
13 Which are borne not of blood, nor of the will of the flesh, nor of the will of man, but of God.

SECTION THREE

# From Reading to Becoming

# 35

# "Eyes on Jesus, Not Yourself"

Let's start with a stark truth: **Faith is less about what you do and more about where you look.** You can grit your teeth, stare at your own spiritual progress, and recite affirmations till you're hoarse—but if your eyes aren't on Jesus, you'll end up exhausted and frustrated.

**Psalm 16:8** captures faith's essence:

"I keep my eyes always on the LORD. With him at my right hand, I will not be shaken."

In Hebrew, it's a sense of "I have set the LORD before me always." Faith is a posture of seeing Him—recognizing His presence—so life's blows can't rattle you. That's the beating heart of true faith: **God-centered, not self-centered.**

## WHY WE STUDY THE WORD

We don't read Scripture to tick off boxes on a spiritual chore chart. We dive into it because we long to **know** Him more. And knowing Him means experiencing Him. When you're captivated by who God is—His faithfulness, His track record—faith grows almost automatically. It's like a lily blooming in the light.

## THE IRRESISTIBLE JESUS: HE WON'T CAST YOU OUT

Look at **John 6:37**:

*"All those the Father gives me will come to me, and whoever comes to me I will never drive away."*

In Greek, there's an emphatic double negative, "I will never, ever drive them away." If you can find a single place in the Gospels where Jesus fails to back this up—where He resists someone who truly hopes in Him—then we can shut the book right now. But we see the opposite:

1. **Blind Bartimaeus** was told to hush, but Jesus stopped for him.
2. **The woman with the issue of blood** was "unclean," but Jesus honored her faith.
3. **Naaman the Leper** (referenced elsewhere) wasn't even from Israel, yet God's grace reached him.

All these people had hope in Christ and found an open door. Meanwhile, those who approached with traps or debates ended up empty-handed.

## MODERN SCENARIO: STUCK ON "AM I FAITH-FILLED ENOUGH?"

Imagine Anna, who's been praying for a new job but constantly checks her "faith gauge." Every day, she wonders, *"Do I truly believe? Should I claim I already have it?"* The more she stares at her own spiritual performance, the more anxious she becomes—questioning if her faith "counts."

One evening, she reads John 6:37, seeing Jesus' promise to receive anyone who comes to Him. She realizes she's been missing the point.

Next time she prays, she says, "Jesus, you won't reject me. I come to You trusting **Your** heart, not my faith's level." A wave of peace settles in—her eyes on **Him**, not on **herself**.

This is what happens when we shift from *self - checking* to *Christ - focusing*.

## FAITH AS REACTION, NOT ACTION

We often act like faith is a skill to "activate," but in Scripture, faith is simply responding to Jesus. Look at:

- **The woman with the issue of blood**: She heard about Jesus' power and reacted: "If I touch Him, I'll be healed."
- **Bartimaeus**: He heard Jesus was near and cried out for mercy.

They didn't plan elaborate "faith sessions." They were reacting to **who** Jesus was and **what** He could do.

---

BIG WARNING: If you chase "faith" as a concept, you'll spin your wheels. If you cling to Jesus, faith naturally happens.

---

## THE DANGER OF SELF-FOCUSED FAITH

Sometimes church culture unintentionally pushes us to monitor our faith: "Own your healing! Claim your blessing!" While meant as encouragement, it can lead to anxiety: *"Am I doing it right? Do I really have it?"*

Yet the psalm says, "I keep my eyes always on the **LORD**"—not on my own level of faith. Focusing too much on our internal faith status distracts us from the One who makes faith potent.

## SOMETIMES YOU STAND, SOMETIMES YOU GO

Yes, we do have moments to **"stand firm"** on Christ's finished work. At other times, like Bartimaeus or the woman with the blood issue, we **"go to Jesus"** with our requests.

1. **When We Stand**

We rest in the victory He's already won. We're not trying to "get" it; we declare it.

2. **When We Go**

We actively petition Him for help. But either way, **He** is the star.

## LOOK MORE AT JESUS, LESS AT YOUR "FAITH"

If you half the time you spend analyzing your faith and **double** the time you spend contemplating Jesus—His love, power, compassion—you'll find faith springs up **organically**. Faith is the lens, but Jesus is the subject. Stare at the lens, and the subject stays blurry. Aim your lens at the subject, and everything clarifies.

**REFLECTION: Shifting Gaze**

1. **Where Are You Fixated on Your Own Faith?**

Is it healing, finances, relationships? Jot down a place you've been striving to "activate" faith instead of resting in Jesus' heart.

2. **Remind Yourself Who Jesus Is**

Choose a characteristic of Christ—He's the Good Shepherd, the Healer, or the One with all authority—and spend time daily **meditating** on that. Don't just list biblical attributes; reflect on how it changes your outlook.

3. **Apply a Jesus-Focused Prayer**

Next time you pray for a need, shift from *"I must have more faith!"* to *"Lord, I trust Your goodness and desire to bless me. Help me rest in that."*

## PRACTICE: Begin Each Day with Psalm 16:8

Give yourself 15 seconds each morning to whisper: *"I set You, Lord, before me always."* Visualize Jesus standing by your side throughout the day. Notice how this realignment pushes out self-consciousness and replaces it with a simple awareness of His presence.

# FINAL WORD: REST IN WHO HE IS

Ultimately, faith isn't about conjuring a mystical force. It's about looking at **Jesus**, the unstoppable, irresistible Light. Blind Bartimaeus, the woman with the issue of blood—none left disappointed when they looked to Him. The same goes for you.

So, whether you're a weary believer longing for breakthrough or someone battling a persistent fear—look to Jesus. Let His reality overshadow your introspection. As Psalm 16:8 says, "With Him at my right hand, I will not be shaken."

**Breathe and see**. That's when real faith clicks into gear—because **He** is the reason prayers get answered, not your perfect track record. Amen to that.

# 36

# Seeing is Believing: How to Deepen Your Trust in God

We often assume belief in God stems from **need**—the more desperate we are, the more we depend on Him. But look around—plenty of people need saving yet never turn to God. They're drowning in unbelief even while clinging to dire hope. **True faith** arises not from how big your need is, but from how **clearly you see** the One who can meet that need.

Consider the **centurion** in Matthew 8:

1. He had a **servant** suffering terribly.
2. He'd "heard about Jesus" (Luke 7 elaborates), and from that hearing came a *sight* of Jesus' capacity.
3. He concluded Jesus didn't even have to be physically present to heal.

**His faith** wasn't fueled by the servant's dire situation—plenty of people have dire situations and remain unbelieving. He saw Christ as both **willing** and **capable. That** was the difference.

## SHIFTING FROM YOUR NEED TO CHRIST

If your entire focus is "I really need help," you might still flounder in unbelief. Why? Because the pivot point of faith is not the magnitude of your need; it's **the magnitude of Jesus**. You can stand on your problem or stand on His Person. One leads to desperation, the other leads to **dependence**.

**When the centurion spoke** about being a man under authority, he was basically saying, "I recognize authority when I see it—and Jesus has it in full." That recognition let him believe Jesus could just **speak** a word. No house visit required.

## FAITH IS FOR GOD TO SEE, NOT YOU

We often get stuck introspecting: "Is my faith big enough? Am I believing correctly?" But **faith** is for God to detect, not you. When Jesus says, "Your faith has made you well," He's not saying you originated some magical force. He's **crediting your response** to who He is.

**Think**: If you're at a restaurant, you don't examine your taste buds every time you eat. You simply trust your sense of taste to respond. In the same way, **faith** is your heart's natural **response** when you've truly "tasted" Jesus—His goodness and power.

## STOP OVERTHINKING—LOOK AT JESUS

**Paul** warns us in Galatians 2 about nullifying the grace of God by turning inward instead of upward. Whenever we start obsessing over our own spiritual metrics— "Am I believing enough? Doing enough?"—we risk **frustrating** the grace God wants to pour out.

1. **Turn Your Gaze**

Don't stare at your faith, stare at **Jesus**.

## 2. Let That Sight Move You

The moment you see Him for who He is—loving, powerful, ready—that's where faith effortlessly takes shape.

**Faith** is the digestion of Christ, the way your spirit processes who He is. He's the meal; faith is what happens when you partake.

### A Prayer: To See Him Clearly

**Lord,**

*We confess we often obsess over our needs, thinking that alone will birth faith. Help us shift our eyes off ourselves and onto You. Let us be like the centurion—convinced of Your authority and goodness, not paralyzed by our own need. Keep us from the trap of overthinking our faith and teach us to simply see You as You are: fully able and fully willing.*
**Amen.**

## CONCLUSION: BELIEF BEYOND NEED

We all need God but **need alone** doesn't force faith. The centurion understood: **seeing** Jesus—His authority, His willingness—stirred a response that Jesus Himself marveled at. So, if you're overwhelmed by your own problems, shift your gaze. Remind yourself that it's **Christ** who carries the power.

Once you see Him rightly, **faith** naturally follows. You're no longer drowning in your deficiency; you're anchored by **His** sufficiency. And that, in the end, is what truly sets you free to believe—not because you're needy, but because you've laid eyes on the **One** who answers every need.

# 37

# More Than a Formula: Faith is a Relationship

Faith isn't a cold, mechanical transaction. It's not about mastering religious techniques or checking doctrinal boxes. At its core, faith is a personal revelation—a deep knowing rooted in the One it hopes in.

Good doctrine isn't lifeless theory—it's truth that flows from knowing God personally. When we reduce faith to formulas, we miss the Person standing before us with open arms.

### TWO WOMEN WHO GOT IT RIGHT

Two women in Scripture reveal this truth with stunning clarity. Neither approached Jesus "correctly" by religious standards. Both broke protocol. Yet both received exactly what they sought—not because their methods were perfect, but because their focus was on Him.

### THE SYROPHOENICIAN WOMAN: FINDING THE RIGHT DOOR

The scene unfolds in Mark 7:24-30. A Greek woman from Syria approaches Jesus, desperately seeking healing for her demon-possessed daughter. She addresses Him as "Son of David"—a Jewish title she had no cultural right to use. By all religious standards, she had no claim on Jesus' attention.

Jesus initially responds with what seems like rejection: "First let the children eat all they want, for it is not right to take the children's bread and toss it to the dogs."

But His resistance wasn't meant to discourage her. It was a divine invitation to clarity.

She was trying to enter through the door of the law—claiming rights she didn't have. Jesus was showing her that the door of religious merit wasn't her way in. She couldn't come through her own worthiness or cultural standing.

With remarkable insight, she shifts her approach. She acknowledges her position but appeals directly to Jesus' heart: "Lord, even the dogs under the table eat the children's crumbs."

In that moment, she found the right door—not the door of religious qualification, but the door of faith in Jesus Himself. She stopped trying to earn access and simply trusted His goodness.

Jesus' response is immediate: "For such a reply, you may go; the demon has left your daughter." She received her miracle, not because her approach was technically correct, but because her trust was in Him.

## THE WOMAN WITH THE ISSUE OF BLOOD: REACHING PAST THE RULES

The second woman's story is even more striking (Mark 5:25-34). After suffering for twelve years with constant bleeding, she approaches Jesus in a way that broke every religious rule in the book.

According to Mosaic law, she was ceremonially unclean. Being in public was forbidden. Touching a rabbi? Unthinkable. Everything about her approach was "wrong."

Yet she came anyway, pressing through the crowd, not even daring to make a request. She simply reached out and touched the hem of His garment, believing that would be enough.

Jesus, feeling power flow from Him, didn't rebuke her for breaking protocol. Instead, He turned, called her "Daughter," and declared, "Your faith has healed you. Go in peace and be freed from your suffering."

Why was she healed when her approach violated every religious standard? Because her eyes weren't on the rules—they were fixed firmly on Jesus.

## WHEN FAITH BECOMES TRANSACTIONAL

I remember years of struggling with what I called "formula faith." I'd study Scripture meticulously, looking for the exact pattern of prayer that would guarantee results. I'd analyze successful testimonies, trying to extract the precise sequence of spiritual steps that would unlock God's favor.

When prayers went unanswered, I'd mentally retrace my steps: *Did I pray with enough faith? Did I use the right biblical promises? Did I confess I am the righteousness of God in Christ?* Faith had become an exhausting transaction—a spiritual ATM where I needed the correct PIN code to access God's blessing.

The breakthrough came unexpectedly. During a particularly difficult season, I found myself too exhausted to maintain my usual "faith formula." Instead, I simply whispered, "Jesus, I don't know how to pray right anymore. But I know You're good, and I trust You with this."

That simple, relationship-focused prayer brought more peace and eventual breakthrough than all my carefully crafted formulas combined. My eyes had finally shifted from the method to the Man.

Have you been there? Clawing, striving, climbing through the wrong door? Trying to earn a blessing from God through perfect spiritual performance? That's what cold, transactional faith becomes—mere requests, lifeless and void of the substance that makes faith work.

The profound truth is this: Faith does not work because of faith. Faith works because of the One it hopes in.

## REQUESTS VS. RELATIONSHIP

Listen to Jesus' words in John 6:37: "All those the Father gives me will come to me, and whoever comes to me I will never drive away."

Notice the deeply personal tone. "Whoever" isn't a concept or a transaction. It's a person. Jesus isn't interested in perfectly formulated requests—He's interested in you.

Requests alone can be denied, but people whose requests are in Him are not. The difference is relationship.

## THE TENSION: DOCTRINE AND RELATIONSHIP

The Syrophoenician woman and the woman with the issue of blood were not, by any religious standard, doctrinally accurate. They were unclean, unqualified, and unworthy according to the law of Moses.

But they were theologically accurate in the way that truly matters. They knew Him—or at least knew enough about Him to trust Him completely.

They knew enough to come to Jesus. They knew enough to put their faith in Him, not in themselves or their ability to get everything right. And that's what made all the difference.

God is not a doctrine. He is not a thesis to be proven. He came to engage and be engaged with. John 1:17 puts it perfectly: "For the law was given through Moses; grace and truth came through Jesus Christ."

Do you see that word "came"? "Given" speaks of following rules. "Came" speaks of experiencing a Person.

Jesus came to be more than studied—He came to be known. The sun isn't just meant to be observed from a distance—it's meant to be felt, its light used, and its warmth experienced.

## THE PATHWAY FORWARD

Even though spiritual growth involves studying Scripture—engaging with it thoroughly, purposefully, and personally—you are not just a student of God. You are a child of God. There's a world of difference.

Faith that moves mountains is not cold and transactional. It's personal, rooted in a revelation of who God is and what He has done for you.

If you've fallen into the trap of lifeless transaction, take heart. Shift your focus. Let the Word remind you that God is not a formula to figure out. He is a Savior to trust in, a Shepherd to follow, and a Father to run to.

## LIVING FROM RELATIONSHIP

What might this look like practically? Here's how faith shifts when it moves from transaction to relationship:

- Instead of asking, "What's the right prayer formula?" ask, "What is Jesus saying to me right now?"
- Rather than focusing on perfect performance, focus on perfect trust in His performance

- When you fail, don't scramble to restore your "spiritual standing"—simply turn to the One who never left
- In place of measuring your faith by results, measure it by how quickly it returns your eyes to Jesus

## A FAITH THAT TRANSFORMS

Faith is not about getting every step right. It's about fixing your eyes on the One who is right. It's not about following all the rules. It's about following Him.

Jesus didn't come to create another system or transaction. He came to save, to heal, to forgive, and to be known.

So don't let faith become a cold transaction. Let it be a personal revelation—a knowing that changes everything because it's rooted in Him.

The women in our stories didn't have perfect theology or flawless approaches. What they had was far more valuable—an unshakable conviction that Jesus was good, Jesus was able, and Jesus was enough. And that, dear friend, is faith at its purest and most powerful.

# 38

# Tapping into the Source: The Wedding at Cana

When Jesus turned water into wine at the wedding in Cana, He wasn't just solving a hospitality crisis—He was revealing His identity as the Source who transforms the ordinary into the extraordinary. This miracle teaches us something profound about faith: it's not about ritualistic performance but about trusting Jesus enough to follow His lead.

### "DO WHATEVER HE TELLS YOU"

When the wine ran out, Mary didn't panic or devise an elaborate plan. She simply told Jesus, "They have no more wine," and instructed the servants: **"Do whatever He tells you."** This wasn't blind obedience—it was relational trust.

Mary's approach reveals two powerful truths:

1. **Trust flows from relationship, not ritual**—She knew Jesus personally and was confident in both His willingness and ability to help.

2. **God's instructions spring from His goodness**—Mary wasn't placing her hope in arbitrary rules but in Jesus' character. When we understand His commands come from His desire to bless us, obedience becomes joy rather than obligation.

## THE RELIEF OF SIMPLE OBEDIENCE

Jesus' instructions were refreshingly straightforward: fill jars with water, then take some to the master of the banquet. No complex rituals or tests of devotion—just simple actions that created space for a miracle.

### It's Not Our "Strong Faith" That Works Miracles

- The servants didn't grit their teeth trying to conjure a miracle. They just did what Jesus said. **That's** where the power is—our willingness to respond to His voice, not in the intensity of our self-effort.

- This is why faith often gives us something to do—it relieves the burden of conjuring. If faith is left without any form to adhere to, then all the weight falls back on your capacity to believe strongly enough—and that can be intimidating. But when you simply obey, the process becomes simpler. You're no longer trying to figure out "how" to believe; you're just doing what He says. Faith is not technique; it's submission.

- **We are vessels, not sources**—Like the jars at Cana, we are created to contain, not create. Our obedience provides the outlet through which He works. The pressure isn't on us to produce the miracle.

## A PERSONAL ENCOUNTER: THE FREEDOM OF SIMPLE OBEDIENCE

A few years ago, I found myself paralyzed by anxiety over a major life decision. I had prayed for clarity, read Scripture, sought counsel—but remained frozen with indecision, afraid of making the wrong choice.

The more I tried to "believe harder" for breakthrough, the more exhausted I became. I kept thinking, "If only my faith were stronger, I'd know what to do." This mental wrestling left me even more stuck and spiritually drained.

One morning during prayer, I felt a gentle nudge to simply take the next obvious step, even without complete certainty." Like filling water jars, it seemed ordinary and insufficient for my dilemma.

What a relief it was! Instead of the burden to manufacture enough faith, I just had to make a phone call. The pressure lifted immediately. I didn't have to generate the solution—I just had to follow a simple instruction.

And in that small step of obedience, something shifted, and peace replaced anxiety. I hadn't conjured the solution through intense belief—I had simply followed a simple prompting, and Jesus transformed my "water" into "wine."

The miracle wasn't just that everything worked out. The miracle was the profound relief I experienced when I realized faith wasn't about my spiritual muscle but about His faithful response to my simple obedience. Through this, I encountered Jesus Himself—His faithfulness, His sufficiency, His perfect timing. My eyes were drawn not to my faith-performance but to the One who actually does the work.

## WHY THIS MATTERS

When we reduce faith to a formula or technique, we miss Jesus entirely. He's not after perfect performance; He's after our hearts. And the wonderful news? His heart is already for us.

- **Jesus-centered faith endures**—In difficult seasons, it's not your "perfect technique" that will sustain you; it's your confidence in His goodness and willingness to do what He says.

- **He gets the glory, we witness it**—Just as His disciples saw His glory and believed, we too witness His transformative power when we allow Him to work through our obedience.

### TAKE AWAY: The Lightbulb Moment

"Do whatever He tells you" Isn't about legalistic compliance but an invitation to relief. It's the difference between:

"Believe harder until something happens" (exhausting self-effort)

and

"Just do the simple thing He's telling you" (restful partnership)

When you realize this truth, it's like a lightbulb moment: "Wait—I don't have to generate the miracle through the intensity of my belief? I just have to follow His lead?" Yes! What freedom this brings!

The next time you feel empty or face an impossible situation, remember Cana. The servants didn't strain to believe water could become wine—they just filled jars. Their simple obedience created the space for Jesus to do what only He can do.

This is the beautiful relief of biblical faith: the responsibility for the miracle rests on God's shoulders, not yours. Your role is simply to respond to His voice. This shifts the entire burden from you to Him—right where it belongs.

The servants at Cana didn't have to "believe harder"—they just had to do what Jesus said. And that same invitation extends to you today. Listen for His direction, no matter how simple it seems, and take that step. Your willingness to obey becomes the doorway through which His power flows—not because your obedience earns His favor, **but because it positions you to witness His glory.**

Faith isn't about mustering up enough spiritual energy to make something happen. It's about the profound relief of realizing you don't have to—you just need to trust Jesus enough to do what He says, then watch in wonder as He reveals Himself as the true Source of transformation.

# 39

# "The Faith Killer: Overthinking Everything"

People resist faith in Christ for countless reasons, but one of the sneakiest is the perpetual push for "enough understanding"—not a genuine hunger for truth, but a treadmill of **unending** analysis. John 9 is a prime example: the disciples see a man born blind and want a neat cause-and-effect explanation: "Who sinned, this man or his parents?" They want reasons. Jesus wants to bring a cure.

In the same way, we can analyze ourselves into paralysis—dissecting "why" darkness exists rather than letting Jesus expel it. Because at day's end, we don't need perfect clarity on the cause; we need an encounter with the **Healer**.

### A CLOSER LOOK AT THE STALLING TACTIC

**Why** do we stay in endless inquiry?

1. **Protecting Ourselves from Disappointment**

"Last time I believed, it failed. Let me detail all the reasons so I don't get hurt again."

We think caution protects us from heartbreak, but it also fences out healing.

## 2. Craving Cause-and-Effect Certainty

"If I can pin down exactly why this problem happened, maybe I can tame it."

It's a control mechanism, yet ironically it keeps us from accepting God's solution.

## 3. Safety in (Over)Thinking

Like reading 10 books on fitness but never going to the gym, we ruminate rather than receive. We stall behind questions, avoiding the risk of actual breakthrough.

> **KEY THOUGHT: Sometimes we'd rather rummage for reasons in the dark than let the Light in—because the Light might rearrange our familiar comfort zones.**

# JOHN 9:1-2—THE DISCIPLES' QUESTION VS. JESUS' RESPONSE

When they ask, "Who sinned?" Jesus effectively says, "You're missing the point. I'm here to do God's works." He's not ignoring their curiosity; He's exposing that it distracts from the grace available **right now**.

- **Not a Lack of Compassion**: Jesus cares, but He knows explanation alone doesn't heal.
- **A Subtle Resistance**: Their focus on blame or reason can prevent them from recognizing the miracle in front of them.

> **TAKEAWAY: Jesus rarely fuels your stalling. He redirects attention to His power to redeem.**

## REBUKING THE QUESTION: WHEN GOD SAYS, "STOP IT."

We assume if God "answers," He approves our question. But sometimes His response is a loving **rebuke**: "Stop analyzing—start letting Me fix this." Much of our theological wrestling is mere avoidance. We want a flicker of comfort from an explanation, but only Christ brings true transformation.

## THE DEEPER WAY FORWARD: ENCOUNTER OVER EXPLANATION

It's like the adage, "Do you want to be right, or be happy?" Spiritually, do we want to keep dissecting, or do we want to be **made whole**?

1. **Real Happiness vs. Being "Correct"**

You might nail down every angle of your issue but stay stuck. Jesus calls us beyond mental mastery into heart-level healing.

2. **Christ as Warmth, Not Just Facts**

Standing in the sun and feeling its warmth is different from knowing the sun's distance from Earth. One changes you; the other is just data.

## MY OWN EXPERIENCE: RUMINATING OVER THE DIAGNOSIS

I've been there obsessing over every detail of a hardship, convinced that *"If I understand it fully, I can control it."* But you can be thoroughly aware of your brokenness and remain just as broken. Understanding the disease doesn't cure it; **Jesus** does.

He says, "I'm here—will you let Me handle it, or bury yourself in one more wave of introspection?" The big question is whether we truly want the cure or prefer safe numbness.

## A REAL-LIFE SCENARIO: FROM BITTERNESS TO BREAKTHROUGH

In a small group I attended, there was a woman named *Michelle* who carried deep bitterness toward her estranged sister. Every week, she'd talk about **why** she felt wronged, analyzing the family history, pinpointing exactly when the rift happened. She'd say, "If I can just figure out every cause, maybe I won't be blindsided again."

But all this detailed dissection never touched her **anger**—it just kept it alive. Finally, our group leader gently reminded her: "Michelle, the real question isn't 'Why did this happen?' It's 'Are you willing to let Jesus heal your hurt?'" That simple shift—focusing on the Healer, not the history—unlocked tears and eventual forgiveness. She discovered she needed Christ's grace more than another explanation. Understanding the timeline of bitterness didn't break its power; **Jesus** did.

## WHY WE BLINDLY SEE THE PROBLEM BUT NOT THE SOLUTION

We see the problem with sharp clarity—money issues, heartbreak, addiction—but remain **blind** to the Healer before us. Why?

1. **Fear of Disruption**

Believing in Jesus might shake up our routines and illusions. We'd rather keep analyzing than risk deeper change.

2. **Habituated to Darkness**

Pain and frustration become predictable. Hope demands walking into the unknown of freedom.

But **John 9** shows that once you allow the Light in, your excuses fade. You can't hide behind "I need more info" once the Healer stands in front of you.

## THE SAFE HARBOR OF "NOT SURE"

Sometimes we prefer *stasis* to salvation. Because letting Jesus do something might demand forgiveness, repentance, or big life changes. Like *Michelle*, we bury ourselves in "why?" because it delays God's actual intervention. But Jesus doesn't come to harm us—He comes to heal us. The only real risk is forfeiting the wholeness He offers.

## THE SILVER LINING: WE DO BELIEVE— BUT ARE WE WILLING?

**Big Irony**: If we truly doubted God's power, we wouldn't hide from it so fiercely. Our elaborate stalling suggests we know He *can* fix it, but we're uncertain we want Him to. That's exactly the Pharisees' problem in John 9. They didn't question Jesus' power; they questioned **His** terms—terms that threatened their status quo.

- **We sabotage deliverance**: "I know God can, but I don't want the aftermath of His miraculous shift."
- **We must realize**: He's not wrecking us; He's rescuing us. This fear of change melts when we trust His goodness, not just His ability.

### REFLECTION: Stepping Beyond "Why" to "Who"

#### 1. Identify a Stalled Area

Where do you keep dissecting—money struggles, a hurtful past, a strained relationship—rather than letting Jesus heal it?

#### 2. Fear vs. Freedom

Are you afraid of how God's intervention might upend your life? Pinpoint that fear. Acknowledge He's both *able* and *loving*.

### 3. Small Step Toward Encounter

Like Michelle, maybe it's time to stop replaying the past and invite Jesus in. Write or pray a simple statement: "Lord, I lay down my analysis. Please do what only You can do."

**A Short Action Step**

Think of **one** question you've been circling forever—be it "Why did this happen?" or "How did I get here?" Write it down, then pray: *"Jesus, instead of me trying to solve this, I invite You to act."* Tear up the note or tuck it away. This is your act of letting go, moving from "analysis" to "encounter."

**A Prayer: Let Go of Endless "Why" and Embrace the "Who"**

*Lord,*
*We confess our tendency to hide behind endless questions, feeling safe in analysis. Today, we release that stalling tactic. We don't just want reasons; we want Your healing. If our hearts are blind to You standing here, open our eyes. Like the blind man in John 9, let us experience Your transforming power—beyond cause-and-effect. We trust You're good and able. And even if it disrupts our comfort, we choose You over the illusions we've built.*
*Amen.*

## CONCLUSION: THE INVITATION TO SEE

In John 9, the blind man gained sight while some observers stayed stuck in their "who sinned?" debate. Jesus isn't condemning honest inquiry; He's **inviting** us beyond inquiry into an encounter.

So, if you're spinning in circles, trying to decode every reason for your pain—pause. Could the Lord be nudging, "I'm here. Let Me handle this"? Real answers might not come from more logic, but from letting the Light break through. That's how the blind see. That's how you and I truly see. Embrace that call—because it's not your perfect understanding that heals, but **the Person** who stands ready to do it.

# 40

# Holiness Isn't About Trying Harder—It's About Trusting More

We often chase "holiness" as if it means never messing up, never making a wrong choice, never showing weakness. But **biblical** holiness is less about your ability to hold it together and more about letting **God** hold you together. That's why *dependence* on Him is the holiest posture you can take. It's the honest confession: "I can't do this on my own, and I'm not supposed to."

## MY STORY: THE HORSE, THE BOX, AND THE BRIDLE

Years ago, I found myself in rehab, wrestling with a drug addiction that had worn me thin. I was young, broken, and ready to change—but not by my own strength. The surrender that got me there wasn't even something I could muster myself. It was a gift—something God handed me when I had nothing left.

One day during treatment, our group was taken outside for something called equine therapy. The idea was to use horses as part of our healing process—apparently, they could reveal things about you that traditional therapy couldn't. I was all in. I had no intention of ever ending up in that place again, so I took everything seriously.

Out in the field, there was a large fenced-in area, and taped on the grass was a square—maybe 10 by 10 feet, give or take. Inside the fence were a couple of horses and a variety of items scattered around: buckets, toys, horse treats, random tools. Our task? Get the horse into the box and keep it there. That's it. Simple enough—or so I thought.

I got to work immediately. I tried everything—treats, toys, waving, guiding, pushing (which doesn't work on a 1,000-pound animal). Nothing worked. Not a single thing I tried could move that horse where I wanted it to go. An hour passed. Maybe two. I was sweating, frustrated, borderline embarrassed—and completely exhausted.

Eventually, I stopped. I stood still in silence, looked around, and asked one of the handlers, "What am I missing? This feels impossible."

The therapist smiled—gently, patiently—and just said, "Use what's in your environment."

So, I scanned again. And that's when I saw it. Hanging quietly on the fence—almost hidden—was the horse's bridle. Just sitting there, waiting. I looked at the therapist again. "Can I use this? "They smiled, same response: "Use what's in your environment. "So, I picked it up, walked over, and slid it gently over the horse's head. The moment it clicked into place, everything changed. I led the horse into the box effortlessly—what had felt impossible for hours was done in seconds.

And right then, God whispered something I'll never forget: *"This is surrender."* "He wasn't asking me to have the power. He was the power. He wasn't demanding I muscle my way through it. He was waiting for me to stop striving, notice Him, and trust.

That day, I learned something about holiness I had never understood: It's not about trying harder. It's about recognizing that God is the bridle. He does what I can't.

Holiness isn't in the performance—it's in the posture. It's what happens when you finally stop flailing, look up, and let Him lead.

## SELF-DEPENDENCE: THE REAL ENEMY OF HOLINESS

**Isaiah 30:1–5** paints a grim picture of self-dependence. God calls His people "obstinate children," running to Egypt instead of turning to Him. Rather than relying on their covenant God in crisis, they chase worldly solutions—leading to more confusion and eventual shame.

### 1. Religion Without Reliance

Worse than overt sin is a religious veneer that masks self-dependence. We do rituals, say the right words, but rely on our own cleverness or external fixes.

### 2. Running to the Wrong Helpers

In modern times, "Egypt" might be TikTok for advice, a friend's counsel over God's Word, or burying ourselves in social media or Netflix. Anything that replaces God as our first go-to can reveal self-reliance.

---

**KEY THOUGHT:** If our first instinct is always something other than the Lord, we're stuck in self-dependence.

---

## HOLINESS BEGINS WHERE SELF-RELIANCE ENDS

Often we assume we have a "holiness problem," but it's really a **dependence** problem. Holiness isn't "never sinning"; it's being set apart by *God's* power because we rely on Him instead of ourselves.

- **Money Troubles?** Not just "Am I bad with finances?" but "Do I trust God's wisdom in stewardship?"
- **Relationship Issues?** Not "Why do I always pick the wrong people?" but "Do I trust God to guide my heart?"
- **Struggling with Discipline?** Not "Why am I so weak?" but "Do I believe He can transform my habits?"

**Eyes up theology**: get them off yourself and onto **the One** who provides all you need.

## DEPENDENCE AS YOUR DAILY POSTURE

**Isaiah 30:15** offers the solution: "In repentance and rest is your salvation, in quietness and trust is your strength."

### 1. Repentance and Rest

Turning from self-reliance (repentance) and truly resting in His sufficiency.

### 2. Quietness and Trust

Not frantically fixing every problem yourself but believing God is actively for you. When He says, "Be still," it's an invitation into a deeper, calmer way of living.

---

> **PRACTICAL TIP:** Next time you feel panicked, *pause* and pray, "Lord, lead me." Let His presence interrupt your frantic self-effort.

---

## GOD ALREADY KNEW WE WOULD NEED HIM

Holiness was never a *DIY* project. From the start, God designed us to need Him—like our bodies need oxygen or sunlight.

- **A Loving Parent.** Doesn't birth a child and then say, "Fend for yourself." God is the same. We can't produce true righteousness alone; we need His grace daily.
- **John 15:5,** "Apart from Me you can do nothing." That's a direct invitation to dependence, not condemnation.

**Connection**: Holiness isn't a moral badge. It's the fruit of abiding so close to Jesus that **His** holiness permeates our every action.

## WHEN FRUSTRATION FORCES US UPWARD

Repeated failures can drive us to our knees. Sometimes we blame the devil or external forces. But often God allows those frustrations to highlight our need for *Him*.

- **Boredom or Emptiness.** Might be God's nudge: "Look up; let Me fill the void you're trying to self-medicate."
- **Blah Feelings.** Could be the Holy Spirit calling you to put out distractions, to create space where He can speak.

**Hebrews 12:11** reminds us no discipline is pleasant initially, but later yields righteousness. Sometimes that discipline is just seeing how futile life is without leaning on the Lord.

1. **Surrender**

Instead of a thousand DIY strategies, try this faith-step: "Lord, I'm in over my head. I need You."

### 2. Fill the Jars With Water

Like the servants at Cana (John 2), offer Jesus what you have. He'll do the miracle, but He wants your readiness.

### 3. Choose Quietness

Let your sense of restlessness or failure push you *upward* to God, not into more frantic fixes.

---

**ACTION POINT: Catch yourself reaching for a quick fix—pause and say, "Jesus, I rely on You first."**

---

## HOLINESS IS DEPENDENCE

Truly holy people aren't the ones who "appear perfect" but the ones who daily acknowledge, "I can't do this without God."

- **2 Corinthians 12:9**: "My grace is sufficient... My power is made perfect in weakness."
- They see weakness as a doorway for God's power, not an obstacle.

### Reflection Questions

---

#### 1. Pinpoint Your Self-Reliance
- Where are you frantically trying to "fix" things alone—finances, relationships, spiritual growth? How might inviting God in first change your approach?

#### 2. Where do you run to?

Identify one coping mechanism you run to when anxious (social media, comfort food, Netflix). How can you replace that habit with a simple prayer of dependence?

3. **One-Minute Surrender**

Challenge yourself daily: pause for 60 seconds, say, "Lord, I lean on You," and see how it shifts your attitude toward any problem.

## A Prayer: Surrendering Self-Dependence

*Lord,*
*I've tried. I've pushed. I've exhausted myself trying to fix what only You can carry. I confess—I've mistaken striving for strength, and self-reliance for faith. But You're not asking me to be strong. You're asking me to trust. Like that bridle resting quietly on the fence, You've always been there—ready, steady, able. So today, I stop. I surrender. I invite You to lead. Teach me that true holiness isn't in having it all together, But in letting You hold me together. In my weakness, show Your power.*
*In my stillness, speak Your wisdom. And when I forget again—because I will—gently remind me: You never asked me to do it alone. I don't want control. I want You.*
*So here I am—led, not leading. Yours, not mine.*
*Amen.*

## CONCLUSION: EYES UP, HEART AT REST

Holiness is impossible without **dependence** on the Lord. God designed you to need Him daily, like a child needing a parent's care. Don't let frustration or failure discourage you; let it drive you closer to His sustaining grace. True holiness isn't a self-help plan—it's a continual "Yes, Lord, I need You." The moment you embrace that, you step onto the path where He fills your weakness with His strength, shaping you into the person you were always meant to be.

# 41

# Rest: The Fuel for Your Soul

When you truly grasp God's character—that He delights in communicating His will, leading you, protecting you, and granting you all you need—you find yourself **fueling** on **rest** rather than frantic effort.

**John 10:27**: *"My sheep listen to my voice; I know them, and they follow me."* Jesus lays it out plainly:

1. You **hear** His voice.
2. You **learn** from Him.
3. You **obey** what He says.

He's not framing these as unattainable. He's pointing out a **present reality**: If you're coming to Him at all, it means you're capable of discerning, receiving, and responding to His voice.

**The Holy Trifecta: Hearing, Learning, Obeying**

**Hearing** is about receiving the message, **learning** suggests absorbing the truth within, and **obeying** seals it into action. Many of us doubt our ability to hear God ("What if I can't? What if I mishear?") but Jesus counters that fear head-on: *"All those that have learned from God come to me."*

**Translation**: If you found your way to Him, you've already been "tuned in" more than you realize.

## TAKE MY YOKE—AND FIND REST

*In* **Matthew 11:29**, *Jesus says: "Take my yoke upon you and learn from me... and you will find rest for your souls."*

Notice He doesn't promise rest by handing you a checklist; He promises it by **yoking** you together with Himself. This yoke isn't burdensome; it's a synergy—**His** gentle leading combined with **your** capacity to respond. The result? A restful, yet fruitful life.

1. **Movement Without Exhaustion**

When you're yoked with Him, you don't labor alone. You mirror **His** pace.

2. **Confidence in His Guidance**

He doesn't drag you into confusion. He leads you into clarity and rest.

## NO ENDLESS SELF-MANAGEMENT

This life in Christ isn't about waking up each day, scanning for a new set of rules to follow, or hyper-managing your spirituality. **He** is the Shepherd; **you** are the sheep who trust and follow. That dynamic displaces anxiety because you realize:

- **God's Voice**: You're not left guessing your next move; you're listening for His nudge.
- **God's Intention**: He's committed to bringing good into your life, so you're not fighting for blessings; you're receiving them by faith.

**Rest** blossoms from knowing the outcome doesn't hinge on your intense spiritual maintenance. Instead, you rely on **His** capability to lead.

## THE LIVING SCRIPTURE: MORE THAN SELF-HELP

Why is Scripture so transformative? Because it's not a static text of bullet points. It's **alive**, a "symbiotic" interaction where the Word **reads** you as you read it. You're encountering the **living God**—His breath, His wisdom, His personal guidance—woven into written words.

- **Self-Help**: Instructs you, but you must power the change.
- **Scripture**: Embodies **God's** power and presence, generating life **with** you and **in** you.

It's that synergy, that interplay of hearing and obeying, which fills your soul with rest rather than burden.

## AN ENVIRONMENT OF CONFIDENCE

All this talk of hearing, learning, and obeying might sound daunting, but look how bright it is:

1. **Generous Communication**: He doesn't grudgingly speak; He delights in guiding you.
2. **Inherent Capability**: You're wired to respond—Jesus said so.
3. **Gentle Pace**: By walking at His tempo, you find **rest** rather than burnout.
4. **Life-Producing Atmosphere**: You're not mustering up illusions; you're receiving from the Fountainhead of life.

In such an environment, confidence grows organically—your soul simply thrives because you see how close and committed, He is to your flourishing.

## A Prayer: Embrace the Yoke of Rest

**Lord,**
*Thank You for showing us a way of living that's fueled by rest instead of anxiety. We confess we sometimes doubt our ability to hear You, to learn from You, to obey. But Jesus says we do—so help us trust that truth.*
*Wake us to the life-giving synergy of Your Word and Your Spirit. Let our hearts absorb Your voice until obedience flows naturally, leading us into genuine rest.*
**Amen.**

## CONCLUSION: MOVE FORWARD IN REST

If you've been trying to self-manage your faith, scanning for a thousand how-to's each day, **stop**. **Hear** the One who wants to lead, **learn** from Him as He reveals His heart, and **obey** in the peace that He's carrying the heavier load.

This is no naive optimism; it's the **biblical** reality: *"My sheep hear my voice."* You're not stumbling alone. You're living in a lush, life-producing environment—one where the living Word interacts with you, God's intention for you is always good, and your confident trust is met with His unfailing provision. Let that sink in: You can **move about life** restfully, powered by the unforced rhythms of grace.

1. **Where Are You Over-Managing?**

Think of a specific area (work, relationships, personal devotions) where you're micromanaging instead of resting in Christ. How can you practice listening more than controlling this week?

2. **Hearing, Learning, Obeying**

Identify one way you can "hear" (maybe by reading Luke 10 or John 10), one way you can "learn" (journaling insights), and one way you can "obey" (a small action step) in the next few days.

3. **Embrace the Yoke**

Picture your daily routine. What's one way you can intentionally slow down, remember His presence, and do tasks with a heart of rest rather than stress?

# 42

# Led by the Spirit: Living a Supernatural Life

Living by the Spirit sounds like **the** most challenging aspect of faith, yet it's not difficult in the sense of complicated formulas. It's "hard" because it demands **surrender**. Commands and instructions are visible checklists; we can wrap our brains around them. But the Spirit? He's invisible—like **radio waves**—yet no less real. When we yield, we discover He's the One searching and revealing, not us trying to claw for clarity.

## THE SPIRIT IS THE KNOWING

Think about it: you can be in dire need and still never truly depend on God. Dependence isn't measured by how much you **lack**, but by how much you **see** the Lord at work. And the Holy Spirit is that pipeline of seeing. He doesn't just inform you; He **shapes** your perception. It's the difference between rummaging through your own logic and being carried by divine awareness.

**1 Corinthians 2:10** declares:
*"The Spirit searches all things, even the deep things of God."*

This searching isn't a rummaging like the Spirit's lost or clueless. It's a thorough, intentional dive into God's depths—His intentions, His blessings, His timing—and then He relays them **to us**.

## SURRENDER: THE KEY TO THE FOUNTAIN

Surrender precedes life in the Spirit. Without it, we stay in control mode—only applying rules or instructions we think we understand. But the Spirit's movement surpasses mere instructions; He's a **fountain** within us. Yet that fountain needs an open channel:

1. **Self-Reliance Blocks the Flow**

We're so used to tangible checklists. But rules can keep us from noticing the Spirit's gentle nudges.

2. **Surrender Opens the Spigot**

When you finally give up your illusions of control, the Spirit's living water flows freely.

## THE SEARCHER FINDS WHAT'S LOST

Life wears us down: priorities drift, hope fades, spiritual riches get buried beneath daily chaos. But the Holy Spirit's role is to "find what's lost and bring it to you." He searches, not because He's clueless, but because He's **determined** to restore your perspective:

- **Motivation**: That fire you once had for God, rekindled.
- **Joy**: Rediscovering that deep assurance you'd shoved aside.
- **Riches of God**: Recalling promises you forgot were even for you.

**David** prayed, *"Search me, God"* (Psalm 139:23). This isn't a stadium security check—this is intimate knowledge, an up-close-and-personal rummaging for every trace of good God wants to reaffirm in you.

## DEEP CALLS TO DEEP: THE PIPELINE ILLUSTRATION

Think of those fiber-optic cables lying unseen on the ocean floor, carrying signals across continents. You never see them, but they're facilitating **clear communication**. That's life by the Spirit: an **unbroken** line of fellowship with God that can't be observed physically but is entirely real.

- You might catch a sense: *"I just know the Lord wants to do me good."*
- Or a sudden reassurance: *"He's determined to fulfill a promise."*

These aren't random vibes; they're the Spirit delivering truths from the **depths of God** to the depths of **you**.

## PERSONAL TESTIMONY: A GOD-DETERMINED GOOD

I remember being 25, freshly delivered from addiction. Deep inside, I **knew**—with no tangible reason—that God had set His eyes on me for something good. It wasn't just me hoping; it felt like a firm, divine intention overshadowing me.

Soon after, I won an all-expense-paid trip to Israel through TBN with my favorite pastor, able to bring my brother along. But get this: I knew it was mine **before** it materialized. That's the Spirit's radio-wave moment—**invisible** but delivering crystal-clear certainty.

---

### "I Will Never Stop Doing Good to Them"

---

The Bible captures God's heart in **Jeremiah 32:40**: *"I will make an everlasting covenant with them: I will never stop doing good to them."*

It's that unstoppable kindness. The life of the Spirit is a daily invitation to become **aware** of it, to see that covenant at work. You're not just reading a promise in Scripture; you're feeling it resonate within your spirit.

- **Come Alive**: "Wake up" to the Spirit's presence.
- **Abide**: Let that unbroken pipeline remind you you're never alone.
- **Moments of Visitation**: Like Abraham at 100 years old, God may show up at a distinct point to confirm, "Yes, now is the time."

## SEARCHING IS NEVER QUIET

When God searches you, He wants you to **know** it. He's not sneaking around in silence; He's revealing that **you have His full attention**. This fosters joy because you sense the divine gaze on your life—He's determined to bless you, shift your season, accomplish what He promised.

### 1. Abiding and Unbrokenness

We live in constant connection with God (John 15:4). The Spirit is always present, always guiding.

### 2. Times of Visitation

Certain moments become *extra* tangible—like the Lord physically stepping into your situation, announcing, "It's time."

**Abraham** experienced it at 100: the moment he hears the final confirmation that Sarah would bear the promised child. That "visitation" changed the trajectory forever.

## A Prayer: Embrace the Searcher's Work

**Lord,**
*I invite Your Spirit to search me—not in condemnation, but in committed love. Reveal what I've lost: joy, vision, passion for Your kingdom. Let me see the good You've prepared, so I can rest in what You're determined to do. Wake me up to that unbroken line of communication, that deep calls to deep reality. May I surrender enough to let Your fountain flow, and when You visit in a special way, help me recognize it's my moment of fulfillment.*
**Amen.**

## CONCLUSION: THE SPIRIT'S UNSEEN BUT UNMISTAKABLE HAND

The life by the Spirit is more than rule-following or moral improvement. It's an **invisible** but **magnificent** communion where God's own Spirit searches out the depths of God—and shares them with you. No set of commands can replicate that.

**This** is the reality Jesus promised: that you'd know Him intimately, not by rote instructions but by **inner revelation**. So be keen to those nudges, that sense of unwavering good He has for you. Surrender paves the way; the **searcher** then reveals what's hidden in God's heart for you—and at that moment, your life transforms into a testimony of His relentless love. "Remember, living by the Spirit isn't an optional 'advanced' level of faith—it's the normal Christian life, where God's Word and Spirit continually shape your journey in real, everyday ways."

# 43

# Everyday Faith: Taking God Home

We've all been there soaked **in God's presence** during a Sunday service or Bible study, feeling invincible. Then Monday hits, and we're slapping the snooze button, grabbing a coffee, and wrestling with traffic-induced road rage. Suddenly, that **holy hush** evaporates. We think, "How can something so powerful be undercut so easily by...nothing?"

**John 10:9** might sound poetic— "They will come in and go out and find pasture." But it's more than a nice line. It's Jesus describing a **lifestyle** of spiritual **movement** and **freedom**. You can't camp out in Bible study forever. You have errands, chores, family obligations, and a world that doesn't stop spinning. **Jesus knows**; He walked that same ground, worked jobs, attended family functions, and navigated daily life. So how do we follow Him off the church pew and into the grocery store aisle?

## THE "COME IN AND GO OUT" FREEDOM

Jesus tells us we have the freedom to **come in** (commune with Him) and **go out** (live our everyday lives) while **finding pasture**—a steady source of nourishment and rest.

1. **Security in the Shepherd**

This freedom comes from **security**. We move confidently because **He** leads us. We're not stuck in frantic self-management, but living from a **place of rest**—His rest.

2. **Practical Rhythm**

Think of it like **breathing**: inhaling God's presence in times of focused devotion (prayer, worship, study), then exhaling it into daily tasks. That rhythm keeps your spirit aligned with **His voice** rather than the world's chaos.

> **KEY INSIGHT:** "Come in, go out" is Jesus' promise that both your spiritual highs and your everyday lows matter to Him. He's not just Lord of Sunday worship but also Lord of Monday's conference calls.

## LIVING FROM A PLACE OF REST

**Rest** doesn't mean inactivity; it means an internal posture of **peace**. You can be bustling around at work yet remain spiritually calm.

- **Example**: A coworker starts complaining, and you find yourself sliding into negativity. Suddenly, you sense the Shepherd's nudge: "Hey, maybe step away or redirect the convo." It's not about hearing an audible voice—it's about being **open** to His leading in small shifts.

- **Another Example**: You're having a lazy day at home, feeling restless. Then a gentle prompt: "Cook the chicken that's about to go bad." That simple act redirects your focus, breaks the restlessness, and fosters a sense of **productive peace**.

> **PRACTICAL THOUGHT:** A quiet spirit can exist in the middle of a noisy environment. It's about focusing on one voice—the Shepherd's.

## MARY AND MARTHA: ACTIVITY VS. DISTRACTION

In **Luke 10**, Martha is overwhelmed by her to-do list, while Mary opts to listen at Jesus' feet. The key? Mary wasn't just avoiding chores—she was avoiding **distraction**.

### 1. Activity Isn't the Enemy

Jesus isn't anti-effort. He's not telling Martha to neglect dinner. He's highlighting the difference between **serving with a quiet heart** and **serving with internal chaos**.

### 2. Choosing the Better Part

Mary chose to **focus** on Jesus. Even if Martha had continued her work, she could have done it with a spirit that was **tuned** to Him, rather than fretting about a million details.

> **LESSON:** We can be in full motion—at our jobs, in our homes—yet spiritually anchored if our hearts remain tuned to Jesus' presence.

## PRACTICING PRESENCE: HOW TO TAKE GOD INTO YOUR DAY

### 1. Micro-Prayers

Throughout your day, toss up short prayers: "Lord, help me with this call," or "Give me patience here, God." They're like tiny "inhalations" of grace that keep you connected.

## 2. Physical Reminders

A note on your desk, a Scripture on your phone lock screen—anything that gently **reorients** you to His reality.

## 3. Obedience to Small Nudges

Your coworker complaining? The Spirit might nudge you: "Shift the conversation," "Step away," or "Speak a word of hope." These micro-obedience's develop a lifestyle of living from the Shepherd's voice.

## 4. Scheduled Pauses

Every few hours, take a minute to breathe, pray, and **realign**. It's not about being hyper-spiritual, but about letting Jesus' voice cut through life's demands.

---

REMEMBER: You don't need perfect silence—just a quiet spirit that's open to God's gentle leading.

---

# EMBRACING THE SHEPHERD'S HEART

Jesus fully understands **human limitations**. He lived under them: working, traveling, cooking, socializing. John 10:9 is His promise that you can be **fully engaged** in life without disconnecting from Him. He's not a fragile presence that evaporates the moment you exit church doors.

- **Security for the Soul.** When you trust the Shepherd, you're not living in a fragile bubble. You can face chaos, tasks, even conflict, knowing He guides your responses.
- **Pasture in the Busy World.** "Find pasture" implies **sustenance and rest**. It means your soul can feed on His presence no matter where you are.

**This is real** freedom—**not** the absence of activity, but the presence of Jesus within every activity.

## A Prayer: Bringing God Into the Day

> **Lord,**
> *Thank You for inviting us to "come in and go out" under Your watchful care. We confess that too often we leave our "spiritual side" at church or in morning devotions. We want to carry Your presence into traffic jams, office meetings, family gatherings, and every mundane moment.*
> *Help us build a* **quiet spirit**—*attuned to Your voice amid life's noise. Show us how to obey those small nudges: stepping away from negativity, refocusing our restless minds, or sharing a timely word of encouragement.*
> *Thank You that we can find* **pasture** *in You, even in the busiest day. Teach us, like Mary, to choose connection with You over constant distraction, and empower us, like Martha, to serve from a place of peace rather than anxiety.*
> *We trust You, our Good Shepherd, to lead us every step of the way.*
> **Amen.**

## CONCLUSION: MOVEMENT WITHOUT LOSING CONNECTION

Yes, you'll still go to work, shovel snow, care for family, and call Grandma. But Jesus says, **"Come in and go out, and find pasture."** You're not leaving His presence behind—you're carrying it with you.

A quiet spirit doesn't need external silence, just **internal** focus on the Shepherd's voice. And that's the secret to bridging the gap between your "church self" and your "work self." **He** is Lord of both. The same Jesus who touches your heart during worship can guide you in a family gathering, grocery run, or workplace challenge. All it takes is a heart turned toward Him, open to those little prompts of grace that keep you anchored in His love.

### 1. Identify Your "Monday Moments"

Think back to a recent time you felt spiritually refreshed (like after church), then lost that peace almost immediately. What specific event or mindset pulled you out of that rest, and how might you invite the Shepherd's guidance next time?

### 2. Heeding the Nudge

Recall a situation (maybe at work or home) where you ignored a gentle internal prompt to step away from negativity or shift the conversation. How could responding differently acknowledge Jesus' leading and transform that moment?

# 44

# Silence the Negative Voices

We love formulas. Three steps to better finances, four ways to fix your marriage, five secrets to unstoppable faith. But if this book has one drumbeat, it's that Christology—doing what Jesus says—is the best methodology of all.

Jesus healed in many ways, each time giving specific instructions:

- "Wash in the Pool of Siloam."
- "Pick up your mat and walk."
- "Go, show yourselves to the priests."

From the outside, it might look random. But that's the point. Jesus's instructions weren't a burden, they were invitations—concrete ways to put faith into action. Because faith, in essence, listens.

## WHERE JAIRUS' STORY GUIDES US

One of my favorite examples is in Mark 5:37-41, where Jesus goes to raise Jairus' daughter from the dead. The house is in chaos: professional mourners wailing, friends and neighbors swirling with grief. Then there's this powerful moment in verse 40:

"But they laughed at him. After he put them all out, he took the child's father and mother and the disciples... and went in where the child was."

Jesus literally put out the mourners. He removed the noisy crowd of doubt. Their commotion wasn't helping faith one bit. Their negative energy tried to contradict His word that "the child is not dead but asleep." So, He told them to leave—and only then did He raise the girl.

## FAITH'S DIRECTIVE: FILTER OUT THE NOISE

In our modern era, "mourners" can be anything that feeds fear and unbelief. Social media—while it can be a platform for positivity—often devolves into a digital mourning session, saturating us with bad news, outrage, comparisons, and cynicism. Before you know it, your faith feels choked, not by some huge tragedy, but by an endless trickle of negativity.

- **Endless Scrolling:** Each flick of the thumb can bring another wave of gloom or gossip.
- **Fearful Headlines:** They stoke anxiety, making us question God's sovereignty.
- **Comparison Trap:** Seeing others curated "perfect lives" might spark insecurity: "Why not me, God?"

All that noise? They're mourners. Sometimes you need to "put them out" to hear Jesus clearly.

## CHRIST'S INSTRUCTIONS: DOING WHAT HE SAYS

Notice how the people who got healed or delivered in the Gospels never balked at Jesus' instructions. If He said, "Pick up your mat," they didn't argue. If He said, "Wash your eyes," they didn't demand a more convenient alternative.

Why? Because they recognized the authority in His voice. And because His instructions weren't complicated or manipulative. They were straightforward expressions of His power—an act of obedience that linked their faith to His promise.

Similarly, when He nudges you to shut off your phone or take a social media fast so you can better rest in His word—don't argue. It may feel odd or inconvenient, but if it clears the room of noise and commotion, that's precisely what your faith might need.

## MOURNER MANAGEMENT: PRACTICAL TIPS

### 1. Identify the Noisemakers

Make a quick list of your "mourners"—anything that consistently stirs doubt, fear, or negativity in your life. It could be social media, certain friendships, or even your own self-talk. Awareness is step one.

### 2. Set Boundaries

If your biggest mourner is doom-scrolling, commit to a social media pause or limit. If it's a friend who always speaks unbelief, consider having a frank conversation or at least balancing that relationship with other faith-building voices.

### 3. Open the Door to the Word

You're not just kicking out negativity; you're inviting in truth. Grab hold of a Scripture promise that counteracts the fear. Let that shape your mindset.

4. **Respond to His Promptings**

Take Jesus' lead. Sometimes He'll say, "Stand on the victory you already have." Other times He'll draw you closer, saying, "Come to Me with that burden." Either way, listen to His voice over the noise.

## REAL FAITH ISN'T AFRAID OF INSTRUCTION

Now, sometimes we get so allergic to "works" that we see any directive as legalism. But real faith isn't spooked by Jesus' instructions—it welcomes them. Why? Because we know He only directs us to do what sets us free. Think about Jairus' daughter: the miracle happened after the mourners were removed. Jesus didn't subject her parents to a thousand hoops; He just cleared the room so faith could flourish.

This is how Jesus still operates. He might say, "Cut out that endless negativity. Pick up your Bible instead of your phone every morning." Or, "Close the door on gossip and open your heart to encouragement." These are not burdens; they're simple instructions from the One who loves you.

## CHRIST: THE SOURCE, OBEDIENCE: THE OUTLET

**Here's the beautiful truth: Jesus is the living water**, and our obedience is simply the **cup** that allows us to experience Him. He remains the source of every blessing, every miracle, every spark of faith. When He says, "Put the mourners out," He's not assigning busywork. He's leading us to **resurrection life** in the very places we need it.

We're "simple creatures," and the Lord knows we thrive on **action steps**. The Gospel isn't always left at a lofty "just believe"—it often comes with tangible moves:

- "Come to the front if you believe."
- "Stretch out your hand."
- "Rise up and walk."

These aren't complications; they're the straightforward forms of obedience that help us interact with God's power in a very *human* way. The same Christ who tells us to **sit** at His feet in rest will also tell us to **rise** and walk when it's time. His instructions, while diverse, keep **Him** at the center.

We see this pattern repeated because **partnership** in the process often increases our revelation. When Jesus told a blind man to wash his eyes in the Pool of Siloam, the man listened—then saw. Faith becomes experiential as we follow through on the simplest directions, each step building our confidence for the next.

**Hebrews 11:6** reminds us that faith believes two things:

1. *God exists.*
2. *He rewards those who seek Him.*

If we'd never question that the world is full of "rewarders" (people paying wages, giving prizes, or awarding scholarships), why be hesitant to believe God rewards those who diligently seek Him? God's instructions, rooted in His goodness, make it **easier** to obey, not harder. You put the mourners out, not out of religious ritual, but because you trust His *intention* to bring life where there's been death or despair.

In short, we don't put out the mourners to prove we're "good Christians." We do it because we believe in the **loving Savior** whose every directive flows from an unfailing desire to bless and restore us. Obedience is simply our way of saying, "Yes, Lord—I believe who You are, and I trust what You say."

## A FINAL CHARGE: SHOW THE MOURNERS THE DOOR

As you pursue great faith, do a quick check: Who or what is mourning over your life's situation, telling you to give up hope? Put them out! Silence the voices of doubt and fear. If that means ignoring certain news feeds or cutting back on social media, do it. If it means letting go of toxic influences, go for it. Let Jesus lead you in this process.

When Christ says, "Be still," be still. When He says, "Step forward," step forward. His commands are not random chores; they're the lifeline that allows faith to breathe. And just like those He healed never protested His instructions, you'll find yourself looking back, grateful you followed through.

When you put out the mourners, your ears open wide to the voice of the One who raises the dead, calms the storm, and says to your heart: *"Do not fear; only believe."* That, my friend, is the sweet spot of great faith.

# 45

# Wisdom 101: Start with Common Sense

We often want **certainty** in life—an obvious neon sign from God about our next steps. But biblical wisdom usually involves moving forward with what's already clear or normal, **unless** the Lord explicitly redirects. Think of it like this: if you need medical help, see a doctor. If you want spiritual growth, attend church. If God has an **exception**—like miraculous healing or a unique path—He'll show up. Meanwhile, start with the **established** pattern.

## JESUS WORKED WITHIN THE NORMS

Sometimes we imagine divine wisdom as always zapping us with spectacular revelations. Yet **Jesus** often used everyday structures:

- **He attended synagogue** (Luke 4:16). No biblical law commanded synagogue attendance the way the temple was mandated, but it was an established Jewish custom. He didn't disdain it; He participated in local worship gatherings.

- **He engaged cultural practices** like feasts, dinners, weddings. He even turned water to wine at a wedding (John 2:1–11), meeting people **in** normal life.
- **He obeyed existing law**—He was "born under the law" (Galatians 4:4). He didn't upend every rule of Jewish life; He fulfilled and refined it.

**POINT: If the very Son of God could operate within earthly norms unless specifically led otherwise, how much more should we, in our quest for wisdom, start with what's already there?**

## FAITH DOESN'T MEAN IGNORING PRACTICAL STEPS

We sometimes think "real faith" equals ignoring doctors or skipping obvious resources. But that can slip into presumption. **Biblical faith** usually encourages reason and normal courses of action:

### 1. Consult the Doctor

If you're ill, going to a physician isn't a lack of faith; it's wise. If God wants to heal you miraculously, He can still do so. But you start with recognized means.

### 2. Attend Church or Seek Fellowship

Not sure where to connect spiritually? The straightforward answer is **church**—a community of believers. If God wants to lead you to something unique, He can, but begin with the normal path.

### 3. Use Common Sense

Faith doesn't bypass planning; it integrates God's leading **into** practical steps.

## WHY DOES GOD HONOR THIS "NORM-FIRST" STRATEGY?

**One might ask**: "Shouldn't we expect big miracles or radical leaps of faith?" Indeed, God can do the miraculous. But trusting God within the normal is still faith:

- **God Often Uses the Ordinary.** Example: Jesus multiplied bread and fish that a boy already had (John 6:9–13). He started with **something**. Faith acknowledges God's ability to work **through** the small, not always by conjuring something from thin air.

- **It's an Act of Humble Dependence.** We demonstrate faith by using the means God has already provided—like doctors, jobs, or communities—believing if a miracle or unique path is needed, **He'll** show it.

- **It Respects His Sovereignty.** We don't force God's hand by refusing normal help. Instead, we open ourselves to God's vantage: "Lord, I'll do what's standard unless You intervene differently." That mindset rests in His overarching wisdom.

## BIBLICAL PRECEDENT FOR "GOING BY THE NORM"

- **Naaman's Healing (2 Kings 5)**: Naaman sought healing from leprosy. The prophet Elisha told him to wash seven times in the Jordan River. That's a *relatively normal* act—no bizarre ritual. At first, Naaman was offended it wasn't grander. But in following the simple instruction, he got his miracle.

- **Paul's Advice on Illness (1 Timothy 5:23)**: Paul tells Timothy to take a little wine for his stomach. That's a practical measure, not a "pray and ignore your physical needs" approach.

**LESSON: The Bible frequently merges faith with down-to-earth steps, letting God insert an exception if He wishes.**

## RELATING TO OUR LIVES TODAY

### Scenario: Physical Ailment

You have a lingering headache or a more serious condition. **Wisdom** says: see a doctor, take medicine if prescribed, pray for healing. If God wants to do something beyond medical help, **He** can override. But start with the norm.

### Scenario: Spiritual Dryness

Feeling disconnected from God? The normal route: consistent prayer, Bible reading, and going to church. If He decides to whisk you away in a supernatural encounter, great—He's free to do so. But don't wait for a spectacle if you haven't embraced the basic avenues of growth.

### Scenario: Decision-Making

Unsure which job to take or which ministry to join? Examine your gifts, talk to mentors, pray, and maybe do a practical pros-and-cons list. If God wants to deliver a special dream or prophecy, **He** will. Meanwhile, you responsibly move forward with what's already revealed.

## LET GOD BRING THE EXCEPTION

**It's liberating** to approach life this way. We're not left paralyzed thinking, "I must conjure a miraculous path, or I'm lacking faith." Instead, we do the normal, the wise, the tested—and remain open to God's prompting if He desires a different route.

- **Trust**: This posture says, "Lord, I trust You enough to do the daily disciplines. If You want to redirect me, I'll follow."
- **Obedience**: Jesus Himself generally respected cultural norms—like synagogue worship—yet pivoted instantly when the Father led Him into miraculous territory.

## TYING THIS TO SECTION 3–THEOLOGICAL DEPTH & TRANSFORMATION

This is more than practical advice; it's a **theological** stance:

- **God's Providence**: Believing He orchestrates normal structures (like healthcare, community, jobs) for our benefit.
- **Human Participation**: Recognizing we're co-laborers with God, not passive spectators waiting for lightning-bolt revelations.
- **Deeper Transformation**: Often, consistently doing the ordinary with a faithful heart shapes our character, preparing us for any special assignment God might spring on us later.

In the same way Jesus claimed divinity in a vantage-laden manner (more powerful than a flat "I am God"), **God's** approach to guiding our day-to-day can be subtle yet potent. Our faith grows in the mundane, and if an exception emerges, we're ready to embrace it.

# CONCLUSION: WISDOM IN ACTION—DO WHAT'S NORMAL UNTIL GOD SAYS OTHERWISE

If you're unsure, **don't freeze** or hunt for a miraculous sign. Take the path Scripture and practical wisdom already highlight. Go to church if you're looking for community. Talk to a doctor if you're ill. Pray for guidance in job decisions but also apply basic reasoning.

**Should God** want something beyond the usual pattern—He'll let you know. This reflects true trust: you rely on God's established provisions, remain open to His leading, and let Him inject the exception if He chooses. That's biblical wisdom in a nutshell: **start with what's clear, stay attentive for God's nudge.**

## A Short Prayer

**Lord,**
*In moments of indecision, help me trust the normal paths You've given—church fellowship, professional counsel, simple acts of care. Teach me to rest in Your sovereignty, knowing that if You want to intervene supernaturally or redirect me, You will. May my faith shine through daily obedience, and may my heart remain open to any new route You provide.*
**Amen.**

### 1. Where in Your Life Are You Hesitating?

Identify a decision you've been postponing because you're unsure if you should wait for a miracle or take normal steps. What practical move can you make this week?

### 2. Which 'Normal' Options Have You Dismissed?

Maybe you're skipping doctors, mentors, or church attendance because you think "faith" forbids them. How might embracing these standard routes show trust in God's everyday provision?

### 3. How Open Are You to Exceptions?

When you do follow common-sense steps, do you still leave room for God to override with something special? What would that posture look like in your routine?

# 46

# Pray Boldly: Asking God Without Hesitation

In **Luke 11:1–4**, one of Jesus' disciples asks, *"Lord, teach us to pray."* Jesus responds with what we call the **Lord's Prayer**:

"Father, hallowed be your name, your kingdom come. Give us each day our daily bread. Forgive us our sins, for we also forgive everyone who sins against us. And lead us not into temptation."

This prayer is strikingly **simple** and **direct**—it doesn't begin with disclaimers about spiritual motives or advanced theology. Instead, it addresses **daily bread**, **forgiveness**, and **temptation**—*very* human needs. It's the ultimate reassurance that God is a **Father** who welcomes our everyday requests.

### THE PARABLE OF THE PERSISTENT FRIEND

Immediately after giving the Lord's Prayer, Jesus tells a story (Luke 11:5–8): a man needs bread to feed a guest, so he knocks on his friend's door at midnight. But the friend, already in bed, initially refuses. Jesus says:

> "**I tell you**, even though he will not get up and give you bread because of friendship, yet **because of your shameless audacity** he will surely get up and give you as much as you need" (Luke 11:8, NIV).

**KEY INSIGHT: The friend isn't swayed by relationship or pure goodwill. He's motivated by the man's persistence, his refusal to go away empty-handed.**

## "HOW MUCH MORE...": GOD IS NOT LIKE THAT RELUCTANT FRIEND

Jesus then flips the scenario: If even a **grumpy** neighbor—who's inconvenienced, not especially caring—will eventually help, **how much more** will God, **who is** loving and intimate, meet our requests?

### 1. God's Perfect Goodness

If the friend yields from sheer annoyance, your **Father** in heaven yields from a place of genuine love.

### 2. Confidence, Not Reluctance

Jesus deliberately contrasts *"despite no friendship"* with *"your Father who's all goodness."* The message: **go ahead and ask**—He's more willing than you think.

## ASK, SEEK, KNOCK

Luke 11:9–10: "**Ask** and it will be given to you; **seek** and you will find; **knock** and the door will be opened." Jesus doesn't complicate it with disclaimers about spiritual worthiness. He invites open, childlike requests. If the man in the parable—motivated by inconvenience—gave bread, **God**, in relationship with us, certainly gives.

**Key**: He doesn't say "pray only if you have a pure motive" or "be sure your request is super spiritual." The example was bread, a mundane need, and the impetus was "I have guests to feed—help me!" Jesus taught we can trust God with our everyday burdens.

## THE FATHER'S HEART FOR HIS CHILDREN

Jesus continues with a father-son analogy (Luke 11:11–13): If a child asks for a fish, would the father give a snake? Of course not. Then "how much more will your Father in heaven give...to those who ask Him?" (v. 13).

### 1. God's Parenting

This picture cements the idea of **God's approachability**. Earthly dads, even flawed ones, strive to provide good things. So, a **perfect** Father goes above and beyond.

### 2. Shift in Perspective

No strings attached—He's not verifying if your request is "spiritual enough." He just says, *"You're My kids. You need help. Ask Me."*

## NOT ABOUT "RIGHT MOTIVES," BUT ABOUT CONFIDENCE

Sometimes we spiritualize prayer: *"Pray only for God's glory; never for personal needs."* While glorifying God is essential, **Luke 11** reveals we can approach God about **basic** concerns—like daily bread or unexpected guests. God is not waiting for you to have a hyper-spiritual reason; He's teaching you to **trust** Him in everything.

- **Don't Over-Filter**: The man in the parable needed bread for an inconvenient reason—it wasn't a holy quest. Still, he asked with boldness.
- **God** doesn't require you to present the "perfect motive" first. Come as you are, confident in His fatherly heart.

## ENGAGING WITH GOD'S GENEROSITY

### 1. Start Simple

If you're hungry or worried about a bill, pray about it. If you need emotional support or solutions for a messy relationship, **ask**.

### 2. Expect a Good Outcome

This entire passage underscores God's willingness. You might not always get the exact item you envisioned, but you can trust the response will align with His loving fatherhood.

### 3. Keep the Relationship Front and Center

God's not an uninterested neighbor but a present Father. The entire vibe is personal: "your Father knows what you need." Confidence thrives when you remember who you're addressing.

## BALANCING BOLDNESS AND SURRENDER

While we ask, we also **surrender** the outcome to God's wisdom. He's a good Father, not a vending machine. But **Luke 11** leans heavily on the idea that we can be bolder than we often are. Sometimes we **downplay** prayer, feeling we might annoy God or think "He's not into trivial requests." Jesus' teaching says the opposite: *ask anyway—He's more than willing.*

## Practical Steps to Grow in Confident Prayer

### 1. Identify Real Needs

Don't over-spiritualize. If you're short on daily "bread," that's valid. Or if your relationship is cold, it's valid. Name it.

### 2. Bring It to Him

Pray specifically and plainly. "Lord, I'm anxious about this bill." "Father, please reignite my marriage."

### 3. Remind Yourself of God's Goodness

Reflect on Luke 11's analogies. If a cranky friend eventually helps, if an earthly dad meets his son's request, *how much more* will God come through?

### 4. Persist Even If It Feels Repetitive

The parable emphasizes shameless audacity. Keep asking, seeking, and knocking—knowing God's heart is open.

# CONCLUSION: YOUR FATHER DELIGHTS IN GIVING GOOD GIFTS

**Luke 11** teaches the Lord's Prayer, but it doesn't stop at a template. Jesus drives home the fatherly vantage of God—someone infinitely kinder than a sleepy neighbor, far more caring than any imperfect parent. And He invites us to pray **with confidence**. Even if your request feels mundane, remember that God's nature is to respond graciously.

**So go ahead—knock on the door.** Even if it's midnight, even if you're worried it's inconvenient. Jesus says, "Ask." If an uninterested friend can be moved by boldness, how much more your Father in heaven, whose love is unending?

## A Short Prayer

**Father,**
*Thank You for welcoming my every request—be it basic or deeply spiritual. Teach me to pray boldly, trusting Your goodness. May I remember You're not reluctant; You're eager to give good gifts to Your children. Help me approach You with the confidence Jesus showed in Luke 11, believing that even if my timing or motive isn't perfect, Your fatherly heart listens and responds in love.*
**Amen.**

# 47

# Heart Surgery: Let God Transform You From the Inside Out

We can rely on discipline or willpower for a while, but real transformation happens only when God changes our **heart**. It goes beyond external compliance—it rewires our desires from the inside out. That's powerful because it doesn't wear off like a forced routine. Once the heart is turned, the effort feels natural and energized by love rather than obligation.

**But here's the catch**: when we say, "Let God do it," we must remember He often acts **in** the normal. We can't just wait passively for some supernatural shift. **Faith** means trusting God enough to ask Him *and* trusting Him enough to act on it in everyday life.

### JESUS' TAKE: HARD HEARTS AND RELATIONSHIPS

In Mark 10:5, Jesus explains that Moses permitted divorce **"because of your hardness of heart."** He points not to mere circumstances but to an internal breakdown—the heart wasn't up to what marriage truly requires.

Similar things happen in friendships, spiritual dryness, or personal habits. When the heart's "hard," all the discipline in the world can't fix it permanently. We need a heart-level overhaul.

## THE IMPORTANCE OF PHYSICAL STEPS

We frequently separate the "spiritual" from the "physical." But **biblical wisdom** calls us to integrate both. For example:

- **Asking God**: "Lord, change my heart to desire better friendships,"
- **Then** physically **showing up** at social events or small groups—positions you to connect, trusting He'll move in that normal space.

**Faith** is acknowledging God can do the miraculous yet not confining Him only to miracles. He is **just as capable** of working through ordinary steps.

### 1. God in the Normal

Sometimes we imagine we're honoring God by "waiting" for a miracle, not doing anything mundane. But ironically, that might be a **lack** of faith—**disbelieving** He can use simple, everyday actions.

### 2. Belief in Action

When you pair prayer ("Lord, change my heart") with real steps (like going to that Bible study or apologizing to a spouse), you're demonstrating **you believe** God will meet you there.

## A RELATIONSHIP EXAMPLE: REKINDLING A MARRIAGE

Suppose you feel no spark with your spouse—just living as roommates. You pray, "God, transform my heart so I can love deeply again." That's awesome. But don't stop there:

> **Plan a date**, buy flowers, be vulnerable.
>
> **God** meets you in that normal action, bridging the gap between your prayer and your reality.

This synergy—your practical move + God's heart-shift—fuels genuine renewal. If you just prayed but never took physical steps, you might miss where God wants to do the heart work. Likewise, if you just forced date nights without prayer, you'd lean on willpower alone, risking burnout.

## TWO-SIDED FAITH: BELIEVING GOD IS BIG AND NEAR

Some people see God as so **lofty** they can't imagine Him operating in "smaller" human routines. Others see Him only in the mundane, forgetting the miraculous side. The sweet spot is:

1. **He's big enough** to do supernatural wonders,
2. **He's close enough** to transform us via everyday actions.

**That** posture invites God's presence at your job, in your friendships, or in your marriage—no matter how ordinary it seems.

## THE FREEDOM IN LETTING GOD BE PART OF BOTH

> **You pray**: "Lord, I want a transformed heart about finances,"
>
> Then you **commit** to a budget or talk to a mentor. If God wants to bring an "exception"—like a miraculous provision—He can. Meanwhile, you let Him move in your normal diligence.

This approach eliminates the false choice between "waiting idly for God to do something" vs. "forcing it all yourself." You **trust** God to do the heart-altering heavy lifting but also show that trust by **stepping out** in normal, practical ways.

## BIBLICAL PERSPECTIVE ON "CO-LABORING"

Throughout Scripture, God often partners with people:

- **Israel** marched around Jericho, then God brought the walls down (Joshua 6).
- **Naaman** dipped in the Jordan (2 Kings 5), and God provided healing.
- **The disciples** distributed the bread and fish after Jesus multiplied it (Mark 6).

In each instance, **God** did the miracle, but humans took a **basic action**—He works through faith that's willing to move.

## CONCLUSION: EMBRACE HEART CHANGE THROUGH PRACTICAL FAITH

If you want God to shift your heart—be it for a stale relationship, a yearning for friendships, or conquering a persistent habit—**invite** Him to do so, but **don't** ignore the small, obvious steps:

1. **Pray for desire**— "Lord, make me want what You want."
2. **Show up**—the date night, the friendship opportunity, the prayer meeting.
3. **Trust**—that God is fully present in these normal efforts, capable of infusing them with supernatural grace.

**When you pair** heart-level surrender ("Change me, Lord") with ordinary avenues of obedience, you harness the best of both worlds. That's not halfhearted—it's the place where spiritual life **blossoms**. Let Him change your heart but give Him the field in which to plant those seeds. The result? A transformation so real it feels natural, yet so deep you know it's only God.

**Amen** to that.

## Simple Prayer

**Lord,**
*I'm tired of forcing myself to do better without true heart change. I ask You to transform my desires as I do the simple steps I know—whether it's going on a date, attending church, or talking to a new friend. Meet me there, infuse the ordinary with Your power. I believe You're big enough for miracles **and** close enough to work in my daily routines.*
**Amen.**

## PRACTICAL EXERCISE: Pray and Act in Tandem

### 1. Pinpoint a Need

Take a moment to think of a specific area in your life where you long for heart change—maybe you're feeling relationally stuck, financially stressed, or spiritually dry.

### 2. Pray Specifically

Form a simple prayer: "Lord, give me desire for _____." Make it personal:

*Lord, give me desire for a healthier relationship with my spouse...*or
*Lord, give me desire for better financial stewardship...*

### 3. Plan One Tangible Step

Immediately decide on one small action that reflects your prayer. If you prayed for better marital connection, **schedule a date** this week. If it's finances, **create a simple budget** or cancel an unnecessary subscription.

### 4. Commit

Write down both your prayer and your planned action. Keep them in a visible place—like your phone notes or a sticky note on your mirror.

### 5. Reflect

After taking that step—whether it's going on the date or adjusting your budget—pause to notice if your heart feels even slightly more aligned with God's intention. Celebrate any sign of growth or renewed desire, however small.

# 48

# Jesus the Disrupter: Get Ready for Change

One thing is abundantly clear from the Gospels: **Jesus was a disruptor**. He consistently upended traditions, challenged power structures, and defied people's expectations. Yet as much as we respect the *idea* of change, most of us hate it. We gravitate toward the predictable—same time, same place, same people.

But when Jesus shows up, predictability goes out the window. Why? Because He demands something deeper than we're used to: **surrender**. The upheaval Christ brings isn't just about shifting routines; it's about **toppling walls and illusions** we've built. Letting them fall can be terrifying—but often essential for genuine growth.

## DISRUPTION IN ACTION: BIBLICAL SNAPSHOTS

### 1. Religious Elite

Jesus insisted on a deeper understanding of Scripture, offering grace to outcasts and turning their rigid legalism upside down. They hated this, calling it "misinterpretation" and eventually orchestrating His death.

2. **Disciples Leaving Their Nets (Mark 1:16–20)**

Peter and Andrew were fishermen, living in a predictable cycle of daily work. But Jesus' call "Come, follow me" shattered their normal. They left their nets *immediately*, trusting this holy disruption would lead to real purpose.

3. **The Rich Young Ruler (Mark 10:17–27)**

He wanted eternal life, but Jesus disrupted his comfortable worldview: "Sell your possessions and give to the poor." Faced with a radical shift, the young man walked away sad, unwilling to let Jesus tear down his walls of security.

## WHY THE THREAT?

They wanted God to fix things on *their terms* and only in approved ways. But Jesus refused such constraints. Real transformation meant letting illusions fall—illusions of perfect theology, rigid tradition, or personal security.

## WHY WE HATE DISRUPTION

It's easy to condemn the Pharisees or the rich young ruler. But **we** also resist upheaval:

1. **Loss of Control**

If Jesus disrupts your life, you can't cling to your old expertise or comfort.

2. **Fear of the Unknown**

A new path is risky—can we predict the outcome?

### 3. Walls Are Illusions

They look sturdy, but they keep us from trusting God fully. Sometimes God says, "Let them crash. They're not truly supporting you." If you're already hurting by clinging to the old, surrendering may bring needed healing.

> **BIG IDEA: Disruption isn't about chaos for chaos' sake. It's Jesus offering a genuine path forward that we'd otherwise miss if we remain locked behind "safe" routines.**

## THE HIDDEN GIFT IN UPHEAVAL

What is Jesus offering in the commotion?

### 1. A True Path Forward

Religious leaders wanted a Messiah who fit their mold. But Jesus brought raw, decisive truth about God's heart. Similarly, a job change or relational boundary might be the new path God's using to free you from a stagnant norm.

### 2. Healing and Restoration

Sometimes it takes upheaval to confront buried hurts or habits. The disciples discovered a far richer life than they ever imagined, but only because they let Jesus disrupt their day-to-day.

### 3. Confronting Life with God's Reality

David didn't defeat Goliath by mustering bravado—he relied on God's presence. That's not escapism; it's facing the challenge with the deepest reality: *God is with me.* If Jesus is flipping your world, it might be that He's freeing you from illusions that keep you spiritually stagnant.

## RESISTANCE AND APATHY: USUAL REACTIONS

- **Pharisees**: active resistance, orchestrating Jesus' downfall.
- **Others**: apathy—observing miracles but shrugging off His message.
- **Us**: ignoring the nudge to break a toxic pattern or staying safe in an unfulfilling status quo.

Jesus' disruption can feel scary—might cost a job, a relationship, a cherished dream—but the gain is real life. This isn't giving up; it's **surrender**—letting Christ do the work we keep trying to manage ourselves.

## A BIGGER PICTURE OF DISRUPTION

### 1. Disciples Freed for Purpose

Peter, Andrew, James, and John left normalcy to experience God's kingdom. They discovered miracles, purpose, and destiny they couldn't have tasted if they'd stayed in the boat.

### 2. Rich Young Ruler's Missed Opportunity

He wanted life on his own terms, leaving sorrowful instead of stepping into the **adventure** Jesus offered.

### 3. Modern Parallels

A sudden calling to switch careers, a wake-up call to reorder your priorities, or a gentle push to move beyond comfortable religion into active faith—these can be Christ's disruptions, leading to bigger opportunities for service and growth.

## REFLECTION: Where Do You Sense Holy Disruption?

- **Identify One Area**: Ask yourself, "Am I resisting a God-initiated shake-up in my relationships, career, or habits?"
- **Why the Resistance?** Pin down if it's fear of losing control, or fear of the unknown.
- **What's the Potential Gain?** Consider what blessings or growth might lie beyond that wall.

## A Short Action Step

**Write down** one "wall" you suspect is merely an illusion of safety. Pray specifically for courage to let God tear it down. Journal how that surrender might free you to walk more deeply in faith, just like the disciples who dropped their nets.

## A Prayer: Embracing the Holy Disruption

*Lord,*
*Forgive me for hating change even when it's Your way of guiding me to wholeness. Open my eyes to see where I'm clinging to false security. May I trust Your disruptions, believing You never tear down without rebuilding something far better. Help me, like the disciples, to drop my nets and follow—even if it disrupts my comfort. Tear down any self-made walls so I can live in the freedom You intended.*
*Amen.*

## CONCLUSION: LEANING INTO THE UPHEAVAL

**The world Jesus walked into wanted salvation but not disruption.** We're no different. Yet a surrendered heart sees that if Jesus is **disrupting** our lives, it's His grace at work—dismantling illusions, forging real transformation. Sometimes it stings, but it can also lead us toward richer faith.

Whether it's your job, your relationships, or your mindset, if Christ is prompting a shake-up, don't resist. Ask, "Is this Jesus, the Disrupter, offering a better path?" Because behind the chaos, He's always leading you out of stale religiosity and into genuine relationship with God. And that might cost you your old comfort zone—but it will give you far more: His abundant life.

# 49

# Jesus: The Author and Finisher of Your Faith

Picture a world-class orchestra. Each musician is talented, but the **conductor** is the one who brings the entire masterpiece to life—guiding volume, tempo, and unity so that the music soars.

Now consider **Jesus** as the conductor of our faith. Yes, He's the source—the One who gave us the instruments and the score—but He also directs the nuances: sometimes He cues you to **stand** on a truth you already possess; sometimes He beckons you to **run** into His arms, crying out like Bartimaeus or the woman with the issue of blood. The question is never "Which approach is correct?" but "Is Christ leading you in this moment—and are you listening?"

## STANDING OR GOING? IT DEPENDS ON THE CONDUCTOR

We've all heard teaching on "you're already healed, already blessed, already chosen—just believe it!" That's a powerful truth. Sometimes we desperately need that **reminder**. But there are also moments when that same statement can feel like a lead weight on our hearts—especially if we're struggling, still in pain or doubt, and someone quips, "You just need to believe harder!"

Why does it sometimes fall flat? Because the focus subtly shifts to **our faith** rather than on **Jesus**. We start measuring how strong we are instead of remembering how sufficient **He** is. Yes, Scripture says we've been healed, forgiven, chosen in Christ—but **how** we live that out can't be boiled down to a one-size-fits-all instruction.

**That's where Jesus comes in, directing your faith.** Maybe He'll whisper, "Stand on what I've accomplished." Or maybe He'll say, "Come to Me, ask again, pour out your heart." Both are valid if **He** is at the center.

- **Stand** like a soldier planted in Christ's completed victory, unshaken by circumstances.
- **Go** like a desperate child sprinting into her Father's arms, trusting He'll never reject her.

Both are "chef's kiss" moments when they're **initiated by Jesus**.

## "WHOEVER COMES TO ME, I WILL NEVER REJECT"

Remember **John 6:37**: "All those the Father gives me will come to me, and I will never reject them." Jesus is saying, "If you feel drawn to Me, it's because the Father is doing something in you—so come. I won't turn you away."

If you ever wonder if you should run to Him in prayer or stand on what's already done, ask yourself: **Are you drawn to Him right now?** If so, **go**—He will not drive you away. You're not messing up by asking again; you're entering deeper relationship.

On the flip side, maybe you sense a strong internal confirmation that God has already provided. You **know** He's calling you to stand. Then trust that. Either way, the question is: "Is Jesus at center stage, or am I stuck focusing on my own faith?"

## WHEN METHODS FADE IN HIS RADIANCE

Sometimes, if we're honest, we try to replicate what worked for someone else. We want that "five-step method" to guarantee our miracle. But the Gospels show us that Jesus rarely repeated the same procedure. He spat in mud to heal blindness one day, then simply spoke a word the next. The woman with the issue of blood said, "I'll just touch His garment," but you can't find a single verse where Jesus taught, *"And thou shalt be healed by grabbing my robe."*

**God's Spirit** breathes life into each situation. Adam didn't take a crash course in "Becoming a Living Soul 101." God simply **breathed** into him, and Adam became alive. That's how personal and tailor-made our God is. When you see that, you realize formulas and methodologies fade in the brightness of **His** presence.

*"It is written in the Prophets: 'They will all be taught by God.' Everyone who has heard the Father and learned from him comes to me."* – John 6:45

**"Learning from Him"** in the Greek implies absorbing key facts through experiential knowledge. It's not just head-knowledge. It's a lived, relational discovery of who He is. That's the difference between reading about the sun and feeling its warmth on your face.

## BELIEF IN HIS GOODNESS: EXPRESSION, NOT REDUCTION

Sometimes we fear that emphasizing God's goodness reduces the seriousness of our faith. But believing God is good doesn't shrink truth; it **amplifies** it. It's like sunlight to the sun—**the brightness is the very point**. The sun is meant to shine. God's goodness is meant to be displayed, experienced, and yes, even marveled at.

Faith *expresses* that goodness: "Lord, I see You for who You are—faithful, kind, fiercely loving. Help me to trust You." The more we see His heart, the more naturally we respond in faith. It's not about working ourselves into an emotional frenzy; it's about letting His character reshape our perspective.

**PRACTICAL POINTERS: Staying in Step with the Director**

1. **Ask the Right Question**

Instead of asking, "Do I have enough faith?" ask, "Where is Jesus leading me right now?" Are you sensing a nudge to rest in His finished work? Or do you feel drawn to pour out your heart at His feet?

2. **Check Your Center**

Is Christ truly at the center of your approach? If you're fixated on the method—be it declarations, petition, or something else—maybe it's time to refocus on **Him** rather than how you execute the technique.

3. **Embrace Your Own Journey**

The woman with the issue of blood had a unique approach, so did Bartimaeus, so did Naaman. Don't fall into the trap of formula envy. If God is breathing life into your path—walk it confidently.

4. **Reflect on His Goodness**

Spend time meditating on His character. Are you convinced He is for you and never rejects the seeker? The deeper that truth sinks in, the more natural your faith response will become.

## FINAL THOUGHTS: FAITH IS A RELATIONSHIP, NOT A CHORE

Faith isn't a chore list: "Check off daily confessions, stand unwavering, never ask, never doubt." Faith is dynamic because it flows from **relationship** with a living Person who wants to direct every note of your spiritual journey.

When you find yourself wondering, "Should I stand on victory, or should I run to Jesus?"—remember you're free to do both, as long as **He** is the reason. Sometimes the Spirit draws you near for deeper communion. Other times, He'll remind you of a promise already stamped with "Paid in Full" at Calvary.

**Either way, Jesus is the One orchestrating your faith's growth.** He's not merely the wellspring; He's the loving hand that guides the path, the subtle voice that corrects, and the sure presence that lights your way.

Let the Director do His job. Let Him cue you when to rest, when to ask, when to declare, and when to draw near. In every scenario, it's all about His radiance—the One who said, *"I will never reject you,"* and backed up every word He ever spoke. That's the anchor of your faith: **Him.**

# 50

# "Grace That Changes Everything"

God's grace isn't merely *leniency*; it's *unmerited favor*, lavishly poured out regardless of our prior devotion or confessions. We see Jesus demonstrating it all over the Gospels: healing, delivering, and blessing people "free of charge." Yet, *some* worry that such boundless grace tempts us to complacency or sin.

But is that really the case? The New Testament paints a different picture—**grace** freely given, yes, but also **powerful** enough to transform the hearts of those who truly encounter it.

## JESUS HEALING WITHOUT CONDITIONS

Throughout Jesus' ministry, He healed people before they called Him "Lord" or properly recognized His messianic role.

### 1. God Reigns on the Just and Unjust

Matthew 5:45 reminds us God "makes His sun rise on the evil and on the good." The same generosity that sends rain for everyone can also bring healing or provision for those who haven't even professed faith.

## 2. Unconditional Compassion

Jesus repeatedly met needs without interrogating motives. That's **grace** in action—a generosity that operates on *His* goodness, not our worthiness.

---

> **KEY THOUGHT: If we see a "one-size-fits-all" approach that requires us to prove we deserve grace, that's not biblical. Jesus bestows blessings freely, trusting that those touched deeply will respond with gratitude and faith.**

---

# THE TEN LEPERS: GRACE FOR ALL, BUT ONE RETURNS

A powerful example of unconditional favor is **Luke 17:11–19**—the healing of ten lepers.

### 1. All Ten Healed

Lepers, outcasts of society, couldn't approach people closely without crying "Unclean!" Jesus didn't demand they first hail Him as Messiah. He healed them all—no strings attached.

### 2. Only One Came Back

Nine took their miracle and kept going, presumably with no further contact. But one returned and thanked Jesus, praising God with a loud voice. Jesus asked, "Were not all ten cleansed? Where are the other nine?"

### 3. A Deeper Interaction

The one who returned shows how grace *truly hits the heart*. He not only received physical healing but also recognized the Healer. That's worship, gratitude, and real transformation.

> INSIGHT: Did Jesus regret healing the other nine? There's no hint of that. He let grace flow freely, yet only one responded. Grace was not diminished by those who misused it.

## THE WOMAN WITH THE ISSUE OF BLOOD: A DIFFERENT TOUCH

In **Mark 5**, we see a crowd pressing in on Jesus. Many touched Him physically, but only one woman drew healing power from Him. She had been bleeding for 12 years, deemed "unclean."

### 1. A Crowd vs. One True Contact

Jesus noticed: "Power has gone out from me." Everyone else was jostling Him, but her touch was *faith-filled*—and it led to immediate healing.

### 2. A Heart Response

She didn't do a theological dance. She simply believed Jesus was powerful and good. Her "touch" stands out from the rest. She experienced grace physically (her ailment was cured) *and* spiritually (He called her "Daughter," affirming her worth).

> TAKEAWAY: Grace is available to all, but it doesn't equally impact every person's heart. Some remain at surface level, while others truly connect and find lasting change.

## GRACE VS. EXTERNAL JUDGING

We often look at someone's outward response to "too much grace" and worry: "See, they're taking advantage; it must be the grace message that's flawed." But Jesus Himself never withheld goodness for fear of misuse. He consistently **operated in full grace**. If some choose to remain ungrateful or lax, that doesn't negate the authenticity of grace—nor does it tarnish the depth of those who do respond.

> **External Actions Aren't Always Proof.** People might speak "God loves me!" but keep living recklessly. That only shows they never truly *encountered* or *internalized* His love. A label doesn't guarantee transformation.

## TRUE GRACE PRODUCES A HEARTFELT RESPONSE

### 1. No Diminishment if Misused

The fact that nine lepers didn't return didn't stop Jesus from healing them in the first place. Grace wasn't "tainted" or "less real" because they chose not to worship.

### 2. God Trusts the Encounter

Grace is meant to reveal God's heart so profoundly that recipients *want* to come back and give thanks. That's how sincere devotion arises—from a grateful response, not enforced obligation.

## JESUS: THE FULL EMBODIMENT OF GRACE

Christ's life epitomizes everything we've said:

> **He gave Himself** for humanity while we were still sinners (Romans 5:8).

- **He healed** freely, **fed** crowds, **forgave** sinners, and **welcomed** the unworthy.
- People weren't forced to call Him Lord first—He loved them into glimpsing the Father's goodness.
- Those truly touched became passionate followers and worshipers, not rule-checkers.

If that's how God in the flesh operated, then shouldn't we also trust that unfiltered grace can transform hearts more effectively than partial, conditional grace?

## PRACTICAL TAKEAWAYS

### 1. Resist Judging Grace by Outliers

Don't assume the message of grace is flawed just because some appear to misuse it. The same sun that causes flowers to bloom might mean nothing to a closed bud—but the sun remains unchanged.

### 2. Look for Heart-Level Change

True grace reveals itself in responses like gratitude, worship, and devotion, as seen in the one leper who returned. Focus on fostering genuine encounters with God, rather than policing externals.

### 3. Keep Pouring Out Grace

If Jesus kept healing, feeding, and loving, we shouldn't dim the grace message to avoid "misuse." Stay faithful in presenting God's radical kindness; trust that the hearts truly touched will show it.

## REFLECTION QUESTIONS

### 1. Where Have You Withheld Grace?

Think of a time you hesitated to show or declare God's goodness, worried someone might exploit it. Did that strategy help them grow spiritually?

### 2. Identify a "Leper" Moment

Recall a situation where Jesus blessed you before you had it all figured out. How did that unmerited favor spark gratitude or obedience in you?

### 3. Prayer Challenge

Next time you see someone who seems to "take advantage" of grace, pray specifically: "Lord, may they truly **encounter** You." Let that remind you not to water down grace but to trust God's Spirit to convict and transform.

## CONCLUSION: MORE THAN CHANGED CIRCUMSTANCES—CHANGED HEARTS

Jesus never toned-down compassion or withheld miracles for fear that someone might remain ungrateful. He healed the ten lepers with no strings attached, fully aware not all would respond in worship. Yet, for the one who did, that moment was a life-changing encounter.

So, if you find yourself tempted to scale back on proclaiming God's radical love—don't. *Grace isn't about demanding a certain outcome; it's about revealing **Who** God is.* And when that revelation hits the heart, the fruit is unmistakable: a shift from simply *receiving* something from God to *responding* in deep gratitude and devotion.

That's the hallmark of **true grace**—it elicits a heartfelt response. It's not cheap or irresponsible; it's the blazing goodness of God in action, capable of transforming even the most distant soul. Spread it wide, and let Jesus handle the rest. Because hearts truly touched by grace don't settle for a mere "fix"—they come back, they worship, they follow.

# 51

# Faith in the Real World
# How to Be Social

When it comes to faith and social engagement, most believers gravitate toward one of two extremes:

1. **Over-Socializing**

We hang out with anyone, anytime, adopting the stance, "Jesus ate with tax collectors and sinners; I'm just shining my light." But often we end up **compromising** our values, letting "bad company" dull our testimony. Our original desire to share faith gets lost in the crowd.

2. **Over-Restraint**

Out of fear we'll slip into sin or lose our testimony, we avoid almost all social activity, keeping our faith quarantined. We might quote "bad company corrupts good morals" and become a **hermit**, failing to engage nonbelievers. The result? We never let our light shine, missing the chance to show God's love in real relationships.

> **KEY THOUGHT:** Both extremes often stem from unbelief—a lack of trust in God's ability to guide and protect our walk. Truly walking by faith means letting the Holy Spirit steer us, whether to pull back or step forward.

## JESUS' MODEL: TIMES TO ENGAGE, TIMES TO WITHDRAW

Jesus balanced a remarkable social life with moments of solitude:

### 1. He Dined with Sinners

In Mark 2:15-17, Jesus reclined at the table with tax collectors and "sinners." He wasn't afraid of being "tainted." Instead, He brought transformation to the meal. That's courageous, faith-based engagement.

### 2. He Withdrew to Pray

Frequently, Jesus "went off to a solitary place" (Mark 1:35; Luke 5:16). Even when crowds pressed in, He retreated for fellowship with the Father. He knew when to **recharge** and avoid burnout.

> **PRACTICAL LESSON:** If the Son of God needed discernment—sometimes stepping into the crowd, other times stepping away—how much more do we?

## THE ROOT ISSUE: LACK OF FAITH IN GOD'S GUIDANCE

**The Overly Social** among us might fear missing out if we slow down, or believe we can handle all influences without consequence—never pausing to ask God, "Should I be here?"

- **We might compromise** our values or hide our faith so well that nobody knows we're Christian. That defies the original purpose of *"I want to be a light."*

**The Overly Restrained** among us might fear we'll instantly fall into sin if we interact with nonbelievers, forgetting God's capacity to keep us. We assume we must hide away, or we'll fail.

- **We might miss** the chance to love people tangibly, failing to emulate Christ's own pattern of entering broken spaces to bring hope.

---

**ANSWER: Both groups must trust God enough to let the Holy Spirit direct each social step—whether it's a green light to go or a red light to pause.**

---

## MODERN SNAPSHOT: OLIVIA'S DILEMMA

**Over socialization**: Take Olivia. She's a friendly extrovert who loves attending concerts, game nights, and after-work socials. She justifies it by saying, "Jesus hung out with all sorts of people." Yet deep down, she realizes she sometimes joins gatherings that compromise her values—she's ended up in gossip or borderline behavior, leaving her feeling guilty afterward.

One night, a coworker invites her to a **house party** known for heavy drinking. Olivia prays, "Lord, is this wise?" She senses a nudge to **skip** it, something she's rarely done. Initially, she worries about missing fun or dissing her coworkers. But trusting God, she declines, opting for a chill evening with a Christian friend instead. The result? She feels peace, sees she didn't "die of boredom," and recognizes God's faithfulness in guiding her to healthier social rhythms.

Here we see how **real** faith requires giving God the final say in our social decisions—trusting Him to fulfill our emotional and relational needs, not just our outward sense of "I must be a light." The next time Olivia gets an invite, God might say, "Yes, go," if it's a chance to share His love without moral compromise.

## MODERN SNAPSHOT: DANIEL'S HESITATION

**Over restraint:** Daniel grew up in a strong Christian home where he was taught to be cautious about "worldly influence." As an adult, he's remained deeply committed to his faith—but somewhere along the way, that commitment turned into near-complete isolation.

He skips work parties, avoids group dinners where alcohol might be served, and keeps most of his conversations at the surface level unless he's with fellow believers. His coworkers like him—but they don't really know him. And they certainly don't know his faith.

One day, a colleague from work invites him to a book club that meets at a local café—nothing sketchy, just people from different backgrounds discussing life and culture. Daniel hesitates. It's not a Bible study. He wonders if it's even worth attending. But as he prays, he feels a gentle nudge: *"Go. You don't need to preach. Just be present."*

Nervously, he goes. The conversation is thoughtful, not hostile. He doesn't feel pressure to argue—just to listen. A few weeks in, someone brings up faith in passing and then says, "Daniel, you're religious, right? I'd love to hear your take on that sometime." That moment humbles him.

It's not about pushing an agenda. It's about trusting God to lead the conversation in His time. Daniel's presence, not his avoidance, opened the door.

Here we see how real faith meant trusting God **not only to keep him grounded**, but to use him in spaces he once feared. His obedience didn't dilute his faith—it displayed it.

# STEPS TO TRUST GOD WITH YOUR SOCIAL LIFE

### 1. Ask for His Leading

Before saying yes or no to an invitation, pray: "Lord, do I go? Do I stay? Guide me." Wait quietly for a sense of peace or caution.

### 2. Check Motives

Are you entering a scene because you trust God can use you there, or to feed a fear of missing out or an ego-boost?

Conversely, are you avoiding it out of wise caution or out of fear that God can't protect you?

### 3. Practice Discernment

If you do go, **stay alert**. Don't bury your light or get swept into sin. If you sense it's spiraling, trust God enough to exit.

### 4. Balance Engagement with Solitude

Carve out "withdrawal times" like Jesus did—prayer, worship, fellowship with believers—so your tank isn't empty.

# WHY TRUE FAITH IS FOUND IN BOTH DIRECTIONS

- **Faith** might call you outward: "Don't be so isolated. I can protect your testimony; go show grace and truth among nonbelievers."
- **Faith** might also call you inward: "Slow down. Not every party is your mission field. Let me fill that need for connection."

**Either** direction demands trust. If we rely on God's promise to keep us from falling (Jude 1:24), we can follow His cues without panic.

## REFLECTION QUESTIONS

### 1. Identify Your Tendency

Are you more prone to over-socialize, risking compromise, or to isolate out of fear of stumbling? Why do you think that is?

### 2. Listen for God's Nudge

Next time an invitation arises or an opportunity to engage nonbelievers presents itself, commit to pausing. Ask, "Lord, is this for me?" and wait for peace or caution.

### 3. Balance "Go" and "No"

Think of one scenario you should say "no" to, trusting God you won't miss out. And one scenario you sense He's calling you to "go" and represent His love. How can you obey each directive?

### A Prayer for Trust in Social Engagement

> *Lord,*
> *We confess that sometimes we either hide away in fear or dive into every social scene without listening to You. Teach us that true faith isn't in extremes but in trusting You to guide each step. Help us know when to pull back for our spiritual health and when to step forward as a light to the world. May we rely on Your voice rather than our comfort or our assumptions. Amen.*

## CONCLUSION: FAITH FOR REAL RELATIONSHIPS

Jesus was neither a recluse nor an unrestrained socialite. He was led by the Spirit in every interaction—sometimes at a party, sometimes on a mountain alone. **That's the model** for believers: a dynamic walk of trust, not fear. If we yield our social decisions to God, we'll discover fresh opportunities to shine His goodness without losing ourselves.

So next time you're torn—**Stay in or go out?** —remember it's not about which is "more spiritual." Its about which choice aligns with **God's** current leading. That's real faith in action—a faith that shapes your relationships and daily life into a mission field or a quiet place of rest, all under the Shepherd's guiding hand.

# 52

# Obedience is the Most Spiritual Thing You Can Do

We sometimes think "spiritual" acts revolve around prayer, praise, or worship—activities we link to the **supernatural**. Meanwhile, tasks like cleaning the house, going to the gym, or working on a budget feel **less** spiritual. But here's the truth: **anything** God instructs you to do is profoundly spiritual, because it flows from **Him**, who is Spirit (John 4:24).

> **KEY INSIGHT: When God speaks, He's not dividing life into "spiritual vs. physical." His realm encompasses all you do. So, if He says, "Go to the gym for your health," that command is as spiritual as any worship service.**

## HOLY HABITS VS. LEGALISM

When we talk about forming good habits—like exercising or organizing our homes—some fear slipping into a **legalistic** mindset: "Oh, so I have to do these chores to please God?" That's not the point. The point is:

1. **God's Directives Are Inherently Spiritual**

If the Holy Spirit nudges you to adopt a healthier lifestyle or become more orderly, obeying that nudge is an act of faith, not a box to check.

2. **Legalism vs. Grace**

Legalism enforces rules without the relational aspect of God's guidance. **Grace** recognizes God's voice behind the task, fueling you with His power to carry it out. You're not simply "doing chores"; you're aligning with His will.

## THE GYM EXAMPLE: WEIGHT LOSS AS A DIVINE DIRECTIVE

Imagine you've prayed about losing weight, wanting a healthier body to serve God better. Some might expect a miraculous meltdown of pounds, but the Lord might say, "Go to the gym three times a week." Instantly, that routine becomes **spiritual**. Why?

- **Obedience Beats Presumption.** Presuming God will supernaturally remove weight while ignoring His practical command is like ignoring the instructions Jesus gave some blind men while healing others instantly. He uses **different methods** for different people.
- **Partnership with God.** You do your part (hitting the gym), trusting that He backs you—giving grace to sustain you, build character, and protect you from discouragement.

---

**CONCLUSION: The gym is not "less spiritual" than a prayer meeting if God is the One directing you there.**

## ANOTHER EXAMPLE: CLEANING YOUR HOUSE OR MANAGING YOUR SPACE

Some believers shrug off tidiness, insisting they're "too spiritual" for domestic details. But if God leads you to cultivate a more orderly environment—maybe to free your mind for prayer, to offer hospitality, or to reflect discipline—then that's **holy** ground.

### 1. Martha and Mary Revisited

We often think Mary "did the spiritual act" by sitting at Jesus' feet, while Martha did the "practical." But if the Lord instructs you to get your house in order, that's no less spiritual than listening to a sermon.

### 2. Spiritual Fruit in Physical Tasks

Patience, diligence, and stewardship can flourish in you by cleaning or organizing regularly—an unseen formation of godly character.

## JESUS' VARIED METHODS: ONE SIZE DOES NOT FIT ALL

Throughout the Gospels, Jesus healed differently from person to person:

- Some blind individuals He touched directly.
- Others He told to wash in the Pool of Siloam (John 9:7).
- Lepers He sometimes healed with a word; other times told to show themselves to the priest (Luke 17:14).

---

**LESSON: God might supernaturally deliver you from a habit instantly, or He might say, "Form a new routine," or "Seek wise counsel." Any approach He chooses becomes the holy pathway for you.**

---

## OBEDIENCE: THE ULTIMATE SPIRITUAL ACT

If prayer, worship, and Bible study are spiritual because they come from God, then so is cleaning, exercising, budgeting—**if He's telling you to do it**. Ultimately, **obedience** is the apex of spirituality because it's our direct response to God's **living** voice (John 14:15).

### 1. Faith = Following His Voice

True faith says, "Lord, if You're in this, it's no small matter." You trust He won't leave you hanging—He'll supply grace.

### 2. Don't Downplay Simple Directives

Something as mundane as "Get to bed earlier" could be God's word for you today, shaping your health and mental clarity. Ignoring it might stifle further guidance.

## BALANCING DISCERNMENT AND GRACE

Of course, **discern** whether it's truly God prompting you or just your own impulse. But if consistent prayer and Scripture confirm a directive—like stewarding your body, mind, or home—**go for it** wholeheartedly. Don't reduce it to an unspiritual chore; see it as the **sacred step** He's leading you into.

### Avoid:

- **Legalistic Pride**: "I follow all these routines—look how spiritual I am." That's about self-righteousness, not reliance on God.
- **Hyper-Spiritual Excuses**: "God will do it for me, so I won't try." That's presumption. Obedience demands action steps—like going to the gym or cleaning up.

## A Real-Life Snapshot: Sandra's Budget

Sandra prayed for financial breakthrough, wanting to give more to missions. She hoped for a miraculous debt cancellation. Instead, she sensed God saying, "Sit down weekly, track expenses, and cut unnecessary spending." At first, she felt underwhelmed—like that was "less spiritual." But once she committed to it, she experienced peace and a sense of God's presence during her budgeting sessions.

Over months, her debt shrank, and she found extra room to give. She realized this "boring" budgeting was **charged** with divine purpose, transforming her heart toward generosity, not just her finances.

## REFLECTION QUESTIONS

### 1. Identify a 'Mundane' Command

What's one ordinary area—health, finances, housekeeping, scheduling—where you sense God prompting a change? Have you shrugged it off as "not spiritual enough"?

### 2. Check Your Motivation

Are you resisting simple directives because you want a "flashier" miracle? How might obeying the small prompt lead to bigger growth?

### 3. Obedience as Worship

Next time you do that task—gym workout, budget meeting, house cleaning—dedicate it to the Lord: "God, I'm doing this because I believe You asked me to. May this glorify You."

### A Prayer: Embracing All That God Says

*Lord,*
*Forgive me for measuring spirituality by how "churchy" something looks. Teach me that once a command comes from You, it's holy ground, whether it's praying for hours or scrubbing a kitchen floor. Open my ears to hear Your everyday directives. Grant me the grace to obey wholeheartedly, trusting You to back me up. Help me realize that the simplest habit—when done in obedience—is as sacred as any act of worship.*
*In Jesus' name, Amen.*

## CONCLUSION: TRANSFORMING THE MUNDANE INTO HOLY GROUND

When God leads you to the gym, it's not "less spiritual" than a worship session—because He's the One calling the shots. When He says, "clean your house" or "rework your budget," that directive carries His **Spirit**. **Real** spirituality isn't about chasing only "supernatural" events; it's about **obeying** whatever the Father says—even if it looks ordinary.

So don't downplay the simple tasks He assigns. **Obedience** is the ultimate spiritual act, because it flows from a living God who empowers each step. Embrace those daily habits with fresh reverence and watch how an everyday routine becomes a divine partnership, shaping you for God's bigger purposes.

# 53

# God's Word Works—
# Let It Do Its Job

Ever browsed the self-help section of a bookstore? It's overflowing with motivational books—how to get fit, get wealthy, get enlightened. And that's not *bad*. Sometimes you need a kick in the pants or a practical framework. But let's be honest: **self-help** relies on **you** to power the change.

- A self-help book says: "Apply these seven habits."
- If you don't apply them, it all stays in your head—**no transformation.**
- **You** do the heavy lifting, or it doesn't get done.

We're not here to bash self-help. We're just exposing its limit: **it's only as strong as your own ability to act.**

## SCRIPTURE: FIRE AND HAMMER

**The Bible** is different. It doesn't merely provide principles for you to master. It's described as *"a fire...and like a hammer that breaks a rock in pieces"* (Jeremiah 23:29). Think about that metaphor:

1. **Fire** consumes and refines on its own. It doesn't wait for someone to "activate" it—it just **is**.
2. **A Hammer** exerts force that can shatter obstacles. Its effectiveness isn't entirely dependent on the rock cooperating.

So yes, the Bible urges us to respond—to obey, to believe. But even before we do, **it** is doing something. **It** can break through hardened hearts. **It** can burn away lies. This is power beyond mere human resolve.

## SEEDS THAT BEAR FRUIT INSTANTLY

Look at **Colossians 1:6**:

*"...the Gospel is bearing fruit and growing throughout the whole world—just as it has been doing among you since the day you heard it."*

Since the **day they heard** it, the message had been actively bearing fruit. No extensive "implementation" plan was required before it started working. Hearing the Word sparked **immediate** growth—like a seed germinating the moment it touches fertile soil.

**That's** the revolutionary part: Scripture isn't idle until we muster the will to apply it. From the day we *truly hear*, it goes to work within us.

## DANIEL'S INSTANT ANGELIC RESPONSE

In **Daniel 10**, the prophet prays, and an angel later tells him:

*"From the first day that you set your heart to understand... your words were heard, and I have come because of your words." (Daniel 10:12)*

God didn't hold off until Daniel completed a 7-step plan for spiritual success. The moment Daniel prayed; heaven was mobilized. The Word of God and prayer converge with **God's power**—not a series of life-hacks.

## THE POWER TO SUBDUE, LIKE A BRIDLE

I once found myself in rehab, facing addiction head-on. One day, we had an equine therapy challenge: get a horse into an 8x8 box, using only what was around us. I tried everything—food, coaxing, even brute force. Nothing worked. Finally, I spotted a **bridle** hanging on the fence, slipped it on the horse, and led it easily into the box.

That bridle had a **strength** of its own. I didn't have to do a million tasks—just use it. **God** spoke to me in that moment, implying, "If you surrender to Me, I'll show My power. You don't need to generate it on your own."

**That** is how the Word works: it subdues our strongest inner "horses" (fears, addictions, pride) if we'll just let it do its job.

**Not "You-Centric"— "God-Centric"**

Self-help can be helpful, but it's **you-centric**. It tells you how to harness *your* untapped abilities. Scripture, on the other hand, is **God-centric**:

- **His** power,
- **His** willingness,
- **His** unstoppable Word.

We don't read the Bible merely to find new rules or personal development tips. We look to see **what God has done and is willing to do**.

## A PERSONAL GOD IN ACTION

The Word's living power is rooted in **relationship**—the Holy Spirit uses it to transform hearts, break chains, and spark faith. You hear the Word, it penetrates, and things begin to shift even before you fully grasp it.

- **Ephesians 6:10** says, "Be strong in the Lord and in **His** mighty power." Notice it's **His**, not ours.
- It's not about revving up your willpower but leaning into **God's** supernatural capacity to change you from the inside out.

## WHY IT MATTERS

Too often, we open the Bible as if it's another self-help manual, scanning for bullet points: "What do I do today?" But Scripture begs a deeper question: **What is God up to?** Because once you see that, your hope skyrockets. You realize you're not alone in the trenches of life—**He** fights with you.

**If you rely on yourself alone**—no matter how disciplined—you eventually hit the end of your rope. But if the Word of God is truly alive (Hebrews 4:12 calls it "living and active"), it means:

1. **It can stir your heart** even when your energy is low.
2. **It can confront your doubts** even when you're not sure you want to believe.
3. **It can speak to your situation** without requiring you to be some spiritual juggernaut.

## INVITATION: LET THE WORD ACT UPON YOU

**So how do we let Scripture do its work?** We stop treating it like it's passively waiting for our expertise. We receive it. We read not just to glean advice, but to encounter the **living God** behind the words.

- **Pray** before you read: "Lord, make Your Word alive in me."
- **Listen** for that nudge, that unexpected phrase or verse that grabs you.

- **Trust** that from the day you hear it, it's already bearing fruit—even if you don't see the leaves just yet.

## A Prayer for Active Transformation

*__Lord,__*
*Thank You that Your Word is not a self-help script but an active force—fire that refines, a hammer that breaks down strongholds. Forgive us for limiting Scripture to a "to-do list." We ask that You do what only __You__ can do: stir our hearts and produce lasting fruit the moment we truly hear and believe. Like Daniel, we want to set ourselves before You, trusting that heaven moves on our behalf. And like the bridle subduing a powerful horse, may Your Word subdue every inner obstacle we face. Let Your power be the driving force in our transformation. In __Your__ mighty name, we pray.*
*__Amen.__*

# CONCLUSION: POWER THAT DOESN'T WAIT ON YOU ALONE

Self-help can sharpen your mind, refine your habits, or boost your motivation—but it demands **you** be the prime mover. **God's Word** doesn't rely on your might. It's living, potent, and able to **initiate** freedom in places your own willpower can't reach.

From the day you hear it, something begins to shift. **That's** the difference: you're not left straining to conjure change by your own strength. The Bible reveals a God ready to act in you, through you, and for you—no cosmic pep rally required.

So yes, glean practical wisdom from self-help. But when you need a **fire** that refines your soul and a **hammer** that breaks down what you thought was unbreakable, turn to the Word that carries **God's** power. Let it do the heavy lifting. You won't regret it.

1. **Where Do You Rely on Your Own Power?**

Think of a specific habit or struggle you've tried to fix using self-help or sheer willpower. How might letting Scripture "do its own work" change the approach you've been taking?

2. **Identify Your 'Rock':**

Jeremiah 23:29 describes God's Word like a hammer that breaks rock. What feels "rock-like" in your life—hard, immovable—that you suspect only God's power can break? Write it down, then pray for Scripture to act on that very area.

3. **Pray Before Reading:**

Next time you open the Bible, pray, "Lord, let Your Word act in me." Jot down any unexpected shifts—small or large—that happen over the next few days, trusting the Word will spark change even before you see it.

# From Encounter to Understanding

*(Transition from section 3 to section 4)*

The transformative power of Scripture is remarkable—how it reshapes our identity, shifts our focus to Jesus, and renews our hearts through genuine encounter. But like any profound relationship, our connection with God's Word grows deeper when we learn to listen well and understand accurately.

Have you ever had a conversation where you completely misunderstood what someone was saying, only to have an "aha moment" later when you grasped their actual meaning? That shift in understanding changes everything. Similarly, learning to interpret Scripture correctly doesn't diminish its power—it amplifies it, helping us hear God's voice with greater clarity.

Many believers hesitate to engage with Bible study mechanics, fearing it might reduce God's living Word to a sterile academic exercise. But that's like saying learning to read music would somehow make a beautiful symphony less moving. The truth is, understanding the structure helps us appreciate the beauty even more.

In this section, we'll explore practical study techniques that honor the text and its Author. You'll discover how context shapes meaning, how to avoid common interpretive mistakes, and how to confidently approach challenging passages. These aren't dry academic exercises—they're keys that unlock deeper understanding and more authentic encounter.

Because when we learn to read Scripture as it was intended to be understood, we're not diminishing its spiritual power—we're positioning ourselves to experience it more fully.

31 Then their eyes were opened, & they knew him, and he vanished out of their sight.

32 And they said betweene themselues, Did not our hearts burne within vs, while hee talked with vs by the way, and when hee opened to vs the Scriptures?

33 And they rose vp the same houre, and returned to Ierusalem, and found the eleuen gathered together, and them that were with them,

34 Saying, The Lord is risen in deede, and hath appeared to Simon.

35 Then they told what things were done in the way, and how hee was knowen of them in breaking of bread.

36 ¶ And as they spake these things, Iesus himselfe stood in the mids of them, and said vnto them, Peace be to you.

37 But they were abashed and afraid, supposing that they had seene a spirit.

38 Then he said vnto them, Why are ye troubled? and wherefore doe doubts arise in your hearts?

39 Behold mine hands and my feete: for it is I my selfe: handle me and see: for a spirit hath not flesh and bones, as ye see me haue.

40 And when he had thus spoken, he shewed them his hands and feete.

41 And while they yet beleeued not for ioy, and wondered, he said vnto them, Haue ye here any meate?

42 And they gaue him a piece of a broyled fish, and of an hony combe.

43 And hee tooke it, and did eate before them.

44 ¶ And hee said vnto them, These are the words, which I spake vnto you while I was yet with you, that all must bee fulfilled which are written of mee in the Law of Moses, and in the Prophets, and in the Psalmes.

45 Then opened hee their vnderstanding, that they might vnderstand the Scriptures,

46 And said vnto them, Thus it is written, and thus it behooued Christ to suffer, & to rise againe from the dead the third day:

47 And that repentance, & remission of sinnes should be preached in his Name among all nations, beginning at Hierusalem.

48 Now ye are witnesses of these things.

49 And behold, I doe send the promise of my Father vpon you: but tarie ye in the citie of Hierusalem, vntill yee bee endued with power from on high.

50 ¶ Afterward he led them out into Bethania, and lift vp his hands, and blessed them.

51 And it came to passe, that as he blessed them, hee departed from them, and was caried vp into heauen.

52 And they worshipped him, and returned to Hierusalem with great ioy.

53 And were continually in the Temple, praysing, and lauding God. Amen.

# THE HOLY GOSPEL OF IESVS CHRIST ACCORDING TO IOHN.

## CHAP. I.

1 In the beginning was the Word, and that Word was with God, and that Word was God.

2 This same was in the beginning with God.

3 All things were made by it, and without it was made nothing that was made.

4 In it was life, and that life was the light of men.

5 And that light shineth in the darkenesse, and the darkenesse in comprehended it not.

6 ¶ There was a man sent from God, whose name was Iohn.

7 The same came for a witnesse, to beare witnesse of that light, that all men through him might beleeue.

8 Hee was not that light, but *was sent* to beare witnesse of that light.

9 ¶ This was that true light, which lighteth euery man that commeth into the world.

10 ¶ He was in the world, and the world was made by him: and the world knew him not.

11 He came vnto his owne, and his owne receiued him not.

12 But as many as receiued him, to them he gaue prerogatiue to be the sonnes of God, *euen* to them that beleeue in his Name.

13 Which are borne not of blood, nor of the will of the flesh, nor of the will of man, but of God.

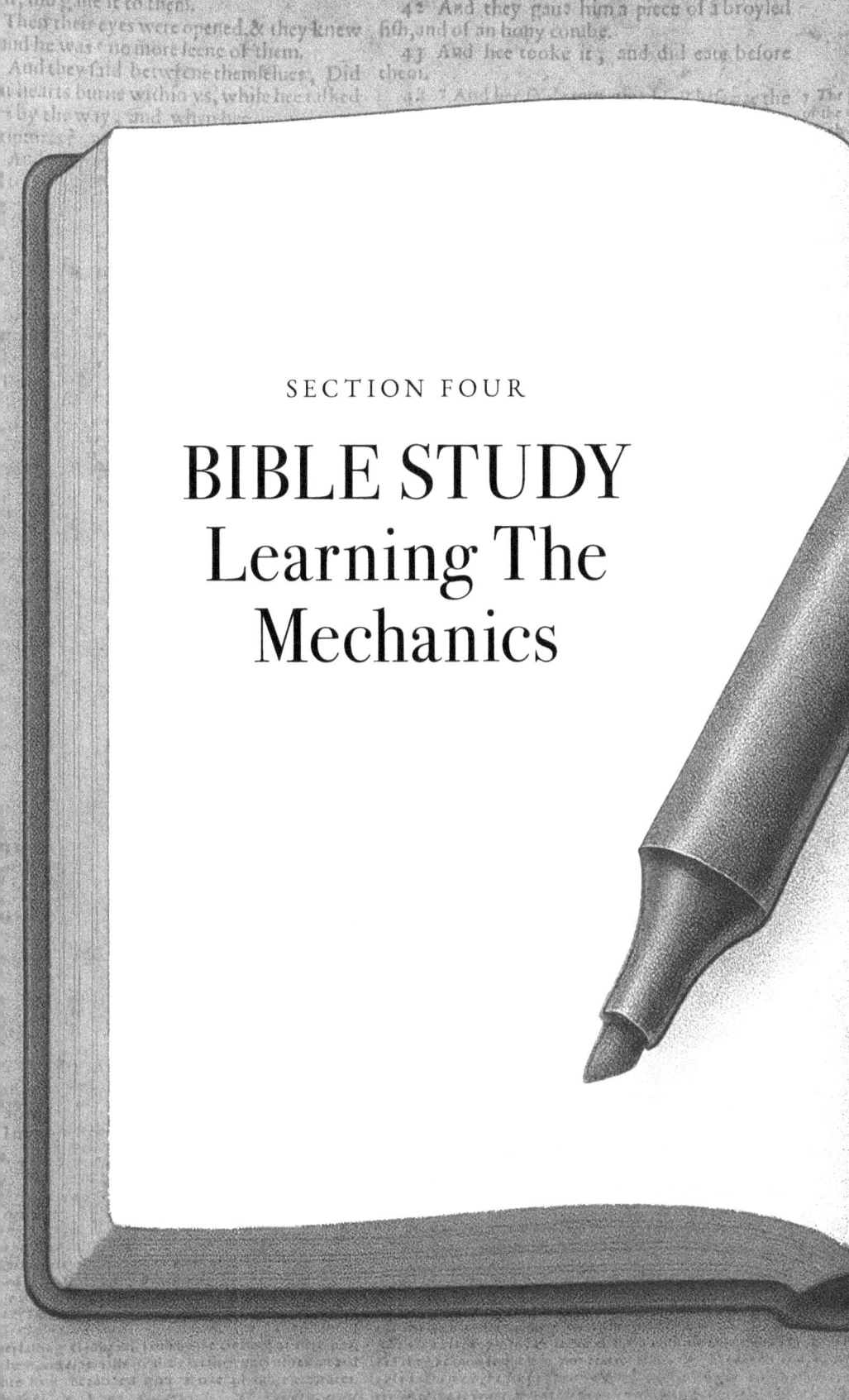

SECTION FOUR

# BIBLE STUDY
# Learning The Mechanics

# 54

# A Bible Study: "It Will Not Be Forgiven"

**Understanding the Unpardonable Sin** *(Matthew 12:22–37, Mark 3:22–30, and Hebrews 6 & 10)*

## STEP 1: Context Is Crucial

Before diving directly into Jesus' words about an unforgivable sin, we need the broader setting in Matthew's Gospel. In **Matthew 12:22–24**, Jesus heals a demon-oppressed man who is both blind and mute. The public reaction is immediate:

> *Then a demon-oppressed man who was blind and mute was brought to Him, and He healed him, so that the man spoke and saw. And all the people were amazed, and said, "Can this be the Son of David?" But when the Pharisees heard it, they said, "It is only by Beelzebul, the prince of demons, that this man casts out demons." (Matthew 12:22-24, ESV)*

Notice two things:

1. **A Public Healing:** Jesus' miracle takes place in front of onlookers who openly wonder if He is the Messiah ("Son of David").

2. **A Public Accusation:** The Pharisees respond not with silence or private skepticism but by publicly declaring that Jesus' power comes from "Beelzebul" (a name associated with Satan).

This immediate context of public debate, in the presence of a crowd, becomes the backdrop for Jesus' strong warning. It is not an isolated theological statement but a response to a very real and open challenge to His identity and the Spirit's work in Him.

## STEP 2: The Judicial Statement

After the Pharisees attribute His work to demonic power, Jesus addresses their accusation. First, He shows the logical inconsistency of Satan fighting Satan (Matthew 12:25–26). Then He says:

*"...if it is by the Spirit of God that I cast out demons, then the kingdom of God has come upon you."* (Matthew 12:28)

Jesus identifies the true source of His power: **the Holy Spirit**. Immediately following this, He issues a solemn warning:

*"Therefore, I tell you, every sin and blasphemy will be forgiven people, but the blasphemy against the Spirit will not be forgiven."* (Matthew 12:31)

Here, Jesus moves from the Pharisees' words to a "judicial fact": blaspheming the Holy Spirit is an offense "that will not be forgiven." A few verses later, He repeats:

*"...whoever speaks against the Holy Spirit will not be forgiven, either in this age or in the age to come."* (Matthew 12:32)

### Key Observations:

▸ **Future Passive Verb**: "Will not be forgiven" (Greek: *ouk afēthēsetai*) indicates a divine withholding of forgiveness.

- **Public Context**: This warning arises in direct response to a **public** accusation against the Spirit's work in Jesus.

## STEP 3: The Public Charge—Not Merely Ignorance

In the verses we just saw, the Pharisees do not claim ignorance or confusion. They have witnessed a clear miracle, recognized by the crowds as evidence of messianic authority, yet they audibly label it as satanic. This is not a private error or a quiet doubt; it is a deliberate, public statement.

- **Matthew 12:24**: "It is only by Beelzebul, the prince of demons, that this man casts out demons."

- **Mark 3:30** (the parallel passage) clarifies the reason for Jesus' warning: "For they were saying, 'He has an unclean spirit.'"

### Mark's Parallel (Mark 3:22-30)

Mark confirms the same scenario, but also adds that this sin is an "eternal" one:

*"Whoever blasphemes against the Holy Spirit never has forgiveness, but is guilty of an eternal sin." (Mark 3:29)*

Just like in Matthew's account, it is triggered by the scribes publicly declaring, "He is possessed by Beelzebul" (Mark 3:22). When multiple Gospel writers highlight the same event and tie it to the same warning, we see the seriousness of the charge.

## STEP 4: Understanding "Blasphemy Against the Spirit"

The Greek word for "blasphemy" (βλασφημία, *blasphēmia*) can mean speaking evil of or slandering. In Matthew 12 and Mark 3, it involves more than a careless slip of the tongue. The Pharisees publicly ascribe God's redemptive work to the power of Satan—an act of **malicious defamation**. They see truth but label it as evil.

### Why Public?

One critical point is the emphasis on the **public** nature of their accusation. In these passages:

- **A Public Miracle:** The healing of a demon-oppressed man is seen by onlookers.
- **A Public Response:** The crowds wonder if Jesus is the Messiah.
- **A Public Accusation:** The Pharisees speak out loud, declaring the power is from Satan.

By doing so, the Pharisees are not just rejecting truth for themselves; they risk turning others away from recognizing the Holy Spirit's authentic work. Jesus' severe warning addresses this overt, intentional smear of God's Spirit in a public forum.

## STEP 5: Additional References That Illuminate

Although Luke 12:8–10 and Hebrews 6 & 10 do not use the identical phrase "blasphemy against the Holy Spirit" in the same narrative context, they echo similar principles:

### Luke 12:8–10

Jesus speaks of acknowledging Him before men, then adds:
> *"...everyone who speaks a word against the Son of Man will be forgiven, but the one who blasphemes against the Holy Spirit will not be forgiven." (Luke 12:10)*

Again, we see a distinction between rejecting Christ in ignorance versus a deeper, more willful offense against the Spirit—an offense Jesus says will not be forgiven.

## Hebrews 6:4-6; 10:26-29

- **Hebrews 6:4–6**: Describes those who have "tasted the heavenly gift" and "shared in the Holy Spirit," yet then fall away in such a way that "it is impossible to restore them again to repentance."

- **Hebrews 10:29**: Warns of those who have "outraged the Spirit of grace," trampling underfoot the Son of God.

While the context in Hebrews does not explicitly say "blasphemy against the Spirit," it similarly paints a picture of someone who has experienced genuine revelation of God's power but then publicly and decisively repudiates it. The idea is the same: a willful turning of the truth into a lie, such that no avenue for repentance or forgiveness remains.

## Why Does This Matter?

These cross-references help us see that blasphemy against the Spirit is not a casual, accidental sin. Rather, it arises in moments of clear revelation—where one knows the truth yet *intentionally* calls it false or evil, often in full view of others.

## STEP 6: The Judicial Fact— "It Will Not Be Forgiven"

Returning to **Matthew 12:31–32** (and **Mark 3:29**), Jesus' language is stark:
*"Whoever speaks against the Holy Spirit will not be forgiven, either in this age or in the age to come." (Matthew 12:32)*
Some interpret this warning primarily as the sinner's inability (they **cannot** repent anymore). Others see it as God's judicial act

(He **withholds** forgiveness). The Greek text uses a **future passive**—"will not be forgiven." That is, it depicts an action **done to** the person rather than an action the person does themselves.

- **The Person's Condition**: Other Scriptures, like Hebrews 6:6 or 10:29, depict someone who is hardened and will not repent.
- **God's Judicial Response**: Here in Matthew 12 and Mark 3, Jesus explicitly states that forgiveness **will not be granted** for this sin.

Both perspectives appear in the broader biblical witness, yet Matthew 12 is explicitly **God's refusal** to extend forgiveness to those publicly attributing the Spirit's work to Satan.

## STEP 7: Why This Is "Unpardonable"

**From Scripture alone**, here is why this sin is singled out:

- **A Final and Public Rejection of Truth**: The religious leaders are not guessing or speculating. They observe a legitimate miracle of God's Spirit and still declare, "This is from Satan."
- **Denying the Only Source of Grace**: The Holy Spirit reveals and testifies to Christ (John 16:8; Matthew 12:28). If one brands the Spirit's testimony as satanic, they are effectively cutting themselves off from any channel that would lead them to repentance.
- **God's Judicial Pronouncement**: Jesus does not say, "It will be difficult to be forgiven." He says, *"It will not be forgiven"*—a definitive, uncompromising statement.

## STEP 8: The Public Dimension—A Critical Element

As we have seen in Matthew 12 and Mark 3, the context involves onlookers. The Pharisees make their accusation in front of the crowd asking if Jesus might be the "Son of David." Their goal seems to be to **turn the public** against Jesus. This aspect highlights:

> **The High Stakes**: They are leading others astray, suppressing the Spirit's testimony in a group setting.

> **The Severity of Jesus' Warning**: By publicly labeling the Holy Spirit's work as evil, they risk not just their own fate but that of those who might have believed.

Although not every passage on hardened unbelief mentions a "crowd," Matthew 12 and Mark 3 specifically emphasize the community context. This public element intensifies the seriousness of the charge.

## STEP 9: Distinguishing Passive vs. Active—A Limit in Contextual Gathering

Scripture often gives complementary angles on the same reality, but they do not always merge seamlessly:

1. **Matthew 12:31–32 / Mark 3:29 – Passive (He Withholds Forgiveness)**

   > Jesus declares that blasphemy against the Spirit "will not be forgiven" (future passive). This indicates a **judicial refusal** from God's side.

   > The Pharisees have publicly slandered the Spirit's work, and Jesus proclaims that forgiveness is withheld—divine judgment is pronounced.

2. **Hebrews 6:6 / 10:29 – Active (They Cannot Repent)**
   - These passages describe people who "fall away" (6:6) or "outrage the Spirit" (10:29) after having known the truth.
   - The text emphasizes **the sinner's inability** to turn back: "It is impossible...to restore them again to repentance" (Hebrews 6:4–6).

## Why This Distinction Matters

- **Matthew/Mark** highlight the **passive** refusal of God to forgive.
- **Hebrews** highlights the **active** hardening of the individual, rendering them incapable of repentance.

These are **complementary** but **not identical** pictures. One focuses on God's declared judgment (the sin "will not be forgiven"); the other on the sinner's inner state ("impossible to restore... to repentance"). While they align in describing a grave condition, **they address two different dimensions** of a similar problem. When we try to force them into a single neat formula, we risk missing each passage's distinct emphasis.

## STEP 10: Why It Is Forgivable to Reject Jesus at First, But Not the Holy Spirit

### 1. Ignorance vs. Willful Hardness

Throughout the Gospels, we see examples of people rejecting Jesus **ignorantly** rather than through open-eyed defiance. For instance:

- **Luke 23:34**: "Father, forgive them, for they know not what they do."

**1 Timothy 1:13**: Paul confesses he was a "blasphemer" but received mercy because he acted "ignorantly in unbelief."

When someone initially rejects or misunderstands Jesus out of ignorance, there remains hope. As soon as they are enlightened to the truth (John 16:13), genuine repentance and forgiveness are available (1 John 1:9).

### 2. The Holy Spirit as God's "Final" Testimony

The Holy Spirit uniquely testifies to who Christ is (Matthew 12:28; John 15:26). When the Spirit reveals the truth about Jesus with undeniable power, and someone **knowingly** calls that work "evil," they have shut themselves off from the very avenue meant to bring them to life (John 16:8). It is "unforgivable" because the person **attacks** the final, clear witness to Christ. Hebrews 10:29 describes it as having "outraged the Spirit of grace," effectively burning the bridge to repentance.

### 3. How Jesus Forgives "Words Against the Son of Man"

Jesus Himself says in Matthew 12:32 that speaking against the "Son of Man" can be forgiven, while blasphemy against the Spirit cannot. Why? Because **speaking against Jesus** might happen from a place of genuine confusion—people may not fully grasp who He is. But once they encounter the Spirit's miraculous revelation—and still publicly denounce it as demonic—they have **crossed a line** beyond ignorance into defamation of God's direct testimony.

## SUMMARY AND CONCLUSION

Putting all these steps together, we see that in **Matthew 12:22–37** and **Mark 3:22–30**:

1. **Jesus performs a public miracle**—casting out a demon by the Spirit of God.
2. **The Pharisees openly ascribe** that Spirit-empowered work to "Beelzebul," effectively calling light "darkness."
3. **Jesus warns** there is a sin—blasphemy against the Holy Spirit—that "will not be forgiven" (future passive), indicating a **divine refusal** to pardon such slander.

Meanwhile, **Hebrews 6:4–6 and 10:29** describe a state of **active**, willful rejection in which the sinner **cannot** repent. These passages complement but do not perfectly overlap with the Gospel accounts. One speaks of **God's withholding** of forgiveness, the other of **the sinner's inability** to repent.

Finally, Scripture distinguishes between those who reject Jesus out of ignorance and those who knowingly defame the Spirit. The former can be forgiven upon recognizing who Christ truly is; the latter irrevocably scorns God's clear testimony and thereby severs the path to mercy.

**In short:** The unpardonable sin, as per Matthew 12 and Mark 3, is this public, deliberate blasphemy against the Holy Spirit—attributing His undeniable work in Jesus to Satan. It remains unforgiven because it assaults God's final avenue of revealing truth and bringing about repentance.

# 55

# Bible Study: Understanding John 3:1–15

> "No one can see the kingdom of God unless they are born again (from above)." *(John 3:3)*

John 3:1–15 records a late-night conversation between **Nicodemus**, a Pharisee and ruler of the Jews, and **Jesus**. It culminates in one of the Bible's most famous pronouncements: *"No one can enter the kingdom of God unless they are born of water and the Spirit."* (3:5). Many Christians assume we fully "get" this passage—Nicodemus asks about Jesus' authority, Jesus replies about being "born again," end of story. But **applying our mechanics** (context checks, cross-examination, coherent conversation flow) can reveal deeper nuances: *What triggered Jesus' statement?* **Is** He expanding Nicodemus' observation or **correcting** it? And how does this passage fit into **John 3's** wider context?

1. **Zoom Out—Context of John 3**

**Overall Setting:**

- John 2 ends with Jesus performing signs at the Passover (2:23), and many believe, but Jesus *"would not entrust himself to them"* (2:24).

▸ John 3 then opens: *"Now there was a Pharisee..."* (3:1). Nicodemus, a Jewish leader, comes "by night," presumably to investigate Jesus more privately.

**Mechanic:**

▸ **Ask:** "What themes did John just set up? Why mention Jesus refusing to entrust Himself to sign-based faith?" Nicodemus is likely emblematic of those intrigued by miracles but not yet understanding who Jesus **truly** is.

### 2. Nicodemus' Opening Observation (v. 2)

Nicodemus addresses Jesus:
*"Rabbi, we know that you are a teacher come from God, for no one can do these signs... unless God is with him." (3:2)*

**Is Nicodemus correct?** Partly: he sees Jesus' miracles as divine authentication. **But** the question is, does he grasp Jesus' full identity? Probably not. He calls Him "teacher" (a big compliment from a Pharisee), but:

▸ **He might** be regulating Jesus: "You do signs, so you're clearly a teacher from God."

▸ **He might** be missing Jesus as far more than a teacher—He's the **Son** who reveals the Father (cf. John 1:14–18).

**Mechanic:**

▸ Zoom in on Nicodemus' words. He sets a partial observation: "You do signs, must be from God." Is Jesus going to expand that or correct it?

3. **Jesus' Response— "Unless One Is Born Again (From Above) …" (vv. 3, 5)**

**John 3:3**: *"Truly, truly, I say to you, unless one is born again (from above) he cannot see the kingdom of God."*

- **Does Jesus even address Nicodemus' compliment?** Not directly. Instead, He shifts to discussing a radical condition for seeing God's kingdom.

## Mechanic:

- **Check** the conversation's logic: Nicodemus states, "We know you are from God." Jesus replies with a statement about "no one seeing the kingdom without new birth." This can feel abrupt if we read it moralistically. Possibly, Jesus is **correcting** or **expanding** Nicodemus' limited viewpoint about who truly perceives God's reign.

**Verse 5** reiterates it: *"Unless one is born of water and the Spirit, he cannot enter the kingdom of God."*

This intensifies the necessity: it's not about verifying Jesus as teacher; it's about a **spiritual rebirth** from above.

A critical nuance is that the Greek for "born again" can also be translated **"born from above."** Christians historically popularized "born again," partly due to Nicodemus' confusion (*"Enter the womb again?"*). But **Jesus'** point is that this new birth originates **"from above,"** linking to **His** own heavenly origin.

1. **John 3's Theme**: John emphasizes Jesus as the One "from above"—Nicodemus says He's a "teacher from God," but Jesus clarifies He's more: truly **"from above,"** requiring us to be "born from above" too.

2. **John the Baptist's Testimony** (later in John 3:31): *"He who comes from above is above all."* This cements the central focus on **Jesus'** heavenly origin.

3. **Why it Matters**: "Born **from above**" highlights the **divine** source of new life—Jesus' cross and mission are from God, so are those born of the Spirit. **"Born again"** can make us think mostly about our change in status, whereas **"born from above"** underscores **God's** initiative and Jesus' elevated identity.

In short, if we took Nicodemus' womb-based interpretation ("enter again?") as correct, we'd ironically shape our translation around his misunderstanding. **But** the text's message is that Nicodemus *doesn't* understand. Jesus says, "from above," echoing John's wider theme of Jesus being the One from heaven.

4. **Nicodemus' Confusion— "How Can a Man Be Born When He Is Old?" (v. 4)**

Nicodemus, literal-minded:
*"Can he enter a second time into his mother's womb?"* (3:4)
Clearly, he's perplexed. Jesus isn't giving a normal "lesson in religion." He's speaking of a **spiritual** (or heavenly) dimension. Possibly, Nicodemus was expecting a theological Q&A about Jesus' credentials. Instead, he's confronted with talk of being "born from above."

**Mechanic:**

> The confusion signals that Jesus' statement doesn't flow from Nicodemus' perspective. He's shifting the conversation from "You do signs, so you must be from God" to "Even to see God's kingdom, a radical heavenly birth is needed." That's a **correction** more than an elaboration on Nicodemus' opening compliment.

## 5. Jesus Explains "Born of Water and the Spirit" (vv. 5–8)

Jesus unpacks it:

*"That which is born of the flesh is flesh, and that which is born of the Spirit is spirit." (3:6)*

*"The wind blows where it wishes... you hear its sound, but you do not know where it comes from or where it goes..." (3:8)*

He's distinguishing **two realms**—flesh vs. Spirit. Nicodemus, an expert in Jewish law, presumably knows prophecies like Ezekiel 36:25–27 about God giving a new heart and a new Spirit. Jesus is pointing to that deeper transformation, not just "sign-based recognition." So, yes, Nicodemus sees Jesus is from God, but Jesus says: *"Real participation in God's kingdom requires a Spirit-wrought new birth from above."*

### Mechanic:

> Cross-reference with Ezekiel 36:25–27 (water & Spirit imagery). Jesus is possibly referencing that prophecy. "Born from above" is a fulfillment of what OT hinted at—a new creation.

## 6. Nicodemus Still Stunned— "How Can This Be?" (vv. 9–10)

Nicodemus: *"How can these things be?"* (3:9)

Jesus gently rebukes: *"Are you the teacher of Israel and yet you do not understand these things?"* (3:10)

**Meaning**: Nicodemus should recall OT promises about spiritual renewal (Jer. 31:33, Ezek. 36:26–27). He's a revered teacher in Israel, but he's missing the spiritual significance behind Jesus' words. **He's** the one who saw Jesus, but it's incomplete. Jesus' emphasis is that intellectual acknowledgment of "signs" or "teacher from God" is insufficient. One needs **inner, Spirit-led transformation** from above.

**Mechanic:**

> ▸ If Nicodemus were simply correct that "Jesus = teacher from God," Jesus might have said "Yes, correct." Instead, He's correcting Nicodemus: "You must be born from above to see the kingdom."

### 7. Verses 11–15: Jesus Cites Heavenly Authority & the Bronze Serpent

**John 3:11–13**: Jesus references speaking of "heavenly things" (3:12). He alone has come down from heaven (3:13). So, He's not just a teacher validated by miracles—He's from above, the Son of Man.

**John 3:14–15** references Moses lifting the bronze serpent (Numbers 21:4–9). Just as the serpent was lifted up to save Israel from deadly serpents, so the Son of Man must be "lifted up" (crucified/exalted) so that those who believe may have eternal life. This is a direct link to:

1. The cross event: Jesus will be "lifted up."
2. The offer of salvation to those who look upon Him in faith.

**Mechanic:**

> ▸ This cements the context: Nicodemus sees Jesus as a teacher, but Jesus reveals a **heavenly** origin and a future "lifting up" parallel to Moses' serpent. He's expanding Nicodemus' minimal "We know you come from God" statement into "I'm the Son of Man who descended and will be lifted up for eternal life."

## 8. The Larger Context of John 3:16–35 (Briefly)

Though we focus on 3:1–15, **verses 16–35** continue clarifying Jesus' identity as God's Son. John 3:16–17: *"God so loved the world..."* frames the Son's mission to save, not condemn. John the Baptist (3:26–36) exalts Jesus as "above all." All synergy points to:

1. Jesus isn't merely a God-approved miracle worker—He's the **Savior** who must be lifted up.

2. Nicodemus is confronted with a radical call: be "born from above" to truly see or enter God's kingdom.

## Mechanic:

> Zoom out: The rest of John 3 underscores the same revelation. If Nicodemus doesn't grasp "born from above," he also misses Christ's central role in salvation.

## 9. Coherence Check—What Initiates Jesus' Response?

**Nicodemus**: *"Rabbi, we know you're a teacher from God..." (3:2)*
**Jesus**: *"Truly, truly... unless one is born from above he cannot see the kingdom." (3:3)*

**Is Jesus expanding or correcting?**

> **He's correcting/redirecting** Nicodemus from "You do miracles, so you must be from God" to a deeper reality: *"You must be spiritually reborn from above to perceive God's kingdom."*

> Nicodemus' opening sets Jesus up to reveal that He's more than a teacher validated by signs—He's the Son from heaven, destined to be lifted up, and only those born of the Spirit can grasp this.

**Mechanic:**

> If it were an "expansion" of Nicodemus' statement, Jesus would say, "Yes, I'm a teacher from God." Instead, He flips it: "Unless you're born from above, you can't even see the kingdom."

## CONCLUSION

**John 3:1–15** revolves around Nicodemus' partial observation— *"We know you're a teacher from God."* Jesus neither simply confirms nor denies that; He **transcends** it. He presents a far more **profound** revelation: to truly see or enter God's kingdom (and to understand who Jesus is—**the Son who must be lifted up**), one must be born **from above**.

**Key Takeaways:**

1. **Initiation**: Nicodemus politely recognizes Jesus as a miracle-backed teacher.

2. **Jesus' Response**: Shifts the conversation to the necessity of spiritual rebirth **from above—correcting** Nicodemus' limited vantage.

3. **Wider Context**: The allusion to Moses' bronze serpent (3:14–15) and the later verses (3:16–35) clarify Jesus is the **Son** from heaven, crucified ("lifted up") for eternal life.

4. **"From Above," Not Merely "Again"**: As we saw, "born from above" better captures the heavenly origin Jesus insists upon. Nicodemus' womb-based misunderstanding is exactly that—a misunderstanding. Scripture's emphasis is that Jesus is from above, so must His followers be if they want to see the kingdom.

5. **Mechanic**: This consistency ensures no random moral lesson but a revelation of Jesus' identity and the heart of salvation. "Miracles prove I'm from God," says Nicodemus. Jesus counters with "You can't see the kingdom *unless* the Spirit regenerates you **from above**, and you look to Me as the One lifted up for eternal life."

Thus, John 3:1–15 **isn't** merely explaining new birth in a vacuum; it's Jesus **correcting** Nicodemus' superficial acknowledgment. Rather than a teacher validated by signs, Jesus is **the** heavenly Son, requiring a Spirit-induced transformation to perceive Him rightly—and that transformation stems **from above**, paralleling Christ's own heavenly origin.

# 56

# Bible Study: Reading Matthew 24 with Care

**STEP 1: Zoom Out—What Triggers Jesus' Words?**

At the start of Matthew 24, **Jesus stuns His disciples** by declaring the Temple's impressive buildings will be destroyed:
*"Do you see all these things? ...not one stone here will be left on another." (Matthew 24:2)*
They're shocked, naturally asking (Matthew 24:3):
*"When will these things happen? And what will be the sign of your coming and of the end of the age?"*
**But notice**: the disciples don't conceive of a scenario in which the Temple's fall *isn't* the grand finale. To them, the Temple's destruction feels *apocalyptic*, so they fold both ideas—Temple destruction **and** end of the age—into a single question. It's as though they say:

1. *"When will the Temple be destroyed?"*
2. *"This must be the same as Your coming and the end, right?"*

They see them as **one event**, while Jesus will later clarify these are **two distinct things**.

**Mechanic:**

1. **Read** the disciples' question slowly. Are they asking one question or two?
2. **Note** how their assumption (*Temple collapse = end of the age*) shapes Jesus' corrective reply.

## STEP 2: Recognize the Disciples' Shock

The disciples were just **marveling** at the Temple architecture (Matthew 24:1). This wasn't some casual interest; first-century Jews saw the Temple as central to their faith and national identity. **Hearing** it'd be destroyed would feel like the **end of the world**. Naturally, they ask, *"When?"*

**Mechanic:**

- In your mind, picture the disciples' reaction. They're devout Jews, convinced of the Temple's sanctity. This is an existential crisis for them.
- This *emotional driver* behind their question explains why they assume destruction of the Temple = the end of everything.

## STEP 3: Jesus' Loving Clarification

Jesus responds with a layered explanation. On one hand, He addresses the **Temple's fall**—which indeed occurs in A.D. 70. On the other hand, He speaks of His **future, ultimate return**. In so doing, He's gently **untangling** their assumption that these events must coincide:

1. **Temple's Fall:**
   - *"When you see Jerusalem surrounded by armies..." (Luke's parallel, Luke 21:20)*
   - *"Pray that your flight will not take place in winter or on the Sabbath..."* (Matthew 24:20)
   - *"...this generation will certainly not pass away until all these things have happened."* (24:34)

2. **End of the Age:**
   - *"...they will see the Son of Man coming on the clouds..."* (24:30)
   - *"...about that day or hour no one knows, not even the angels in heaven, nor the Son..."* (24:36)
   - He emphasizes suddenness and unpredictability.

**Mechanic:**

- Look for **clues** Jesus gives for each scenario. One (Temple destruction) is **localized**, with an urgent call to flee Judea. The other (His return) is **global** and beyond anyone's scheduling.
- Note how He *deliberately* distinguishes "this generation" timing from "no one knows the day or hour."

## STEP 4: One Question, Two Answers

What initiates Jesus' entire discourse is their combined question. The disciples **assumed**: "If the Temple is destroyed, that's obviously 'the end.'" Jesus essentially says:

*"That destruction is coming—and within your generation. You'll see it and some of you can survive it by fleeing. But the ultimate end—My second coming—operates on a different timetable."*

He's **loving them** by clarifying that the Temple's demise, as devastating as it will be, isn't the grand cosmic finale. They **can** (and should) flee to the mountains; it's not an *inescapable apocalypse*.

**Mechanic:**

- **Ask**: "Would Jesus use two drastically different sets of instructions (flee vs. no one knows the day or hour) if these were the same event?" Of course not. He's addressing two related but distinct crises.

- Recognize that the disciples' shock is what drives the conversation. Jesus gently shifts them from *"end-of-the-world panic"* to *"a catastrophic, but survivable, historical event—and then a future final return."*

## STEP 5: How This Affects the "Signs"

Jesus lists so-called **signs**: wars, earthquakes, false messiahs, etc. We often treat these as universal indicators of the **end of the age**. But now we see:

1. **Some signs** specifically relate to the Temple's fall (e.g., local Judean warnings).
2. **General distress** (wars, earthquakes) characterizes human history, not necessarily pinpointing a final countdown.

He also underscores *suddenness* for the **final** event: *"No one knows... not even the Son."* (v. 36) That's quite a contrast from the **Temple destruction** He knows will happen in "this generation."

**Mechanic:**

- Note how the disciples' question merges the two events. By paying attention to their confusion, we see why Jesus lumps together near and far references—He's **addressing their assumption** while also teaching about ultimate readiness.

### STEP 6: The Readiness Emphasis for Both Scenarios

Interestingly, Jesus closes with parables (Matthew 25) about readiness—**virgins keeping their lamps**, the **talents** parable, etc. This theme of watchfulness applies:

- **In the near term** (Temple fall): They needed practical readiness—when Rome besieged Jerusalem, believers who took Jesus' words seriously could escape.
- **In the long term** (His final return): We can't pin down the date, so we must live in daily faithfulness.

**Mechanic:**

- Draw parallels between the immediate instruction to flee (a literal readiness) and the spiritual readiness for Christ's ultimate return. Both revolve around *"Don't be caught off guard."*

### STEP 7: Conclusion—Understanding the Trigger Explains the Answer

Because the disciples' question was fueled by their shock that the Temple could be destroyed, Jesus addressed *that event* **and** their assumption that it signaled the *end of the age*. By doing so, He clarified two timelines:

1. **Temple Destruction** (which He *did* know the approximate timing of—within "this generation").
2. **Second Coming** (which even He, in His earthly ministry, declared unknown: *"nor the Son…"*).

**Key Takeaway:**

- The disciples basically asked one question, fusing Temple destruction with the world's end.

- Jesus' answer divides that fusion—He predicts a near, historical devastation but also points forward to a distant, cosmic culmination.

- *Signs* apply more directly to the first crisis (though they echo on as general reminders), while the final return remains date-unknown, requiring constant vigilance.

**Mechanic for Application:**

- When a biblical passage seems confusing, **zoom back** to see *what question or situation sparked it*. Often, the key to interpretation is in that initial trigger.

- **Don't** assume one-size-fits-all. Jesus gave specific instructions (flee Judea) for a historical event *and* broad readiness instructions (watch, be faithful) for His return.

## EPILOGUE: LIVING IN THE TENSION

**Matthew 24** can be perplexing if we flatten it into purely "end-time signs" or purely "first-century events." The disciples' question is the hinge: they see Temple destruction as the final curtain. Jesus gently corrects them, weaving immediate and ultimate concerns together. For us, the lesson is:

1. **Recognize historically fulfilled prophecy** (the Temple fell in A.D. 70).

2. **Stay watchful for the final day**—no exact timetable, but the call to faithfulness stands.

3. **Embrace Jesus' love** in clarifying that not all disasters equal "the end." Some judgments are real and near, but life and mission continue until He truly returns.

**So**: read Matthew 24 with the disciples' shock in mind, see how Jesus answered *that* question, and appreciate the brilliant way He addresses both a near historical crisis and the far-off culmination of all things. We're reminded that no matter the era, **our stance is humble readiness**—since whether it's A.D. 70 or the final day, His word stands:

*"Heaven and earth will pass away, but my words will never pass away."* (Matthew 24:35)

# 57

# Bible Study: The Parable of the Ten Minas (Luke 19)

"Sometimes we fixate on the details, but Jesus told this parable to refute a faulty assumption."

### STEP 1: Zoom Out—What Prompted the Parable?

*"While they were listening to this, he went on to tell them a parable, **because** he was near Jerusalem and the people thought that the kingdom of God was going to appear at once." (Luke 19:11)*

- The parable arises **directly** from the crowd's mistaken assumption: *"The Kingdom is about to appear right now!"*
- In their eyes, once Jesus gets to Jerusalem, He'll presumably reveal Himself as King and overthrow Rome or usher in a political reign immediately.

**Mechanic:**

- Always **ask**: "Why did Jesus start telling a story at this exact moment?"

- The text explicitly says it's **because** they believed in an imminent kingdom. That's the key to understanding everything else.

## STEP 2: The Parable's Setup—A Delayed Kingdom, Not Immediate

*"A man of noble birth went to a distant country to have himself appointed king and then to return." (Luke 19:12)*

### 1. A Distant Country

- Right away, Jesus' story contradicts their assumption of instant enthronement. The man **goes away** first, implying delay.
- This stands in direct tension with their *"It's going to happen at once!"* mind-set.

### 2. They Hated Him

- *"His subjects hated him."* (v. 14)
- This, too, clashes with the crowd's assumption that everyone wants this man to be king. In reality, there's **rejection**—a parallel to how Jesus will be rejected in Jerusalem.

### Mechanic:

- **Compare** the crowd's assumption ("We're all in! The Kingdom is now!") to Jesus' parable details (a long trip, hatred from subjects). The story is a direct corrective.

# STEP 3: The Servants and Their Instructions—Obedience vs. Lip Service

*"So, he called ten of his servants and gave them ten minas. 'Put this money to work,' he said, 'until I come back.'" (Luke 19:13)*

- **Command**: "Invest until I return." Even though the nobleman is "hated," some servants *do* obey.

- Interestingly, these "subjects who hate him" can still comply with the king's orders—showing that external "hate" doesn't necessarily translate to total disobedience.

- Meanwhile, one servant claims to *fear* the master but disobeys the direct command by hiding the mina.

## Mechanic:

- **Notice** the dichotomy: Some who "hate" him fulfill the charge (earning more money). Another servant, who *say* he's mindful of the master, he ends up disobeying.

- Jesus is highlighting the difference between **true obedience** and **empty excuses** or **lip service**.

### New Mechanic: Actions Speak as Loudly as Words

Ironically, when we study Scripture, we often fixate on the **words** while missing the **actions**. Yet here, **behavior** reveals as much as the dialogue:

- The **king's** action of rewarding obedient servants with "ten cities" or "five cities" spotlights his willingness to bless those who truly follow his instructions—*regardless* of initial appearance.

- The **last servant** acts so contemptuously that he doesn't even attempt a bare minimum, simply wrapping the mina in a cloth. While claiming he "fears" the master, his action proves otherwise. This disparity shows how little he values the master's command, underscoring why judgment follows.
- This dynamic clarifies Jesus' broader message: outward talk means nothing if it isn't backed by real obedience—especially for those claiming to be His people (Israel). They might profess reverence but behave in a way that treats God's gifts with apathy.

**Mechanic to Remember:**

- *Don't just ask what the characters say, watch what they do.* Very often, Jesus' point emerges in the contrast between claimed loyalty and actual performance.

## STEP 4: The Ending–Judgment and No Immediate Kingdom

The parable climaxes with the master's **return**:

1. **Reward for the obedient:**
   - *"Well done, my good servant! Because you have been trustworthy..."* (v. 17)
   - They're given authority over cities, hinting at future blessing rather than an immediate rule right now.

2. **Rebuke for the disobedient servant:**
   - He's stripped of his mina. It's given to the one who already has ten, illustrating that **false "fear"** (or superficial reverence) doesn't cut it.

3. **Judgment on enemies:**

   - *"Those enemies of mine who did not want me to be king... bring them here and kill them..."* (v. 27)

   - It's a stark, ominous warning: outright refusal of His kingship leads to ultimate condemnation.

**Mechanic:**

- Ask: *"What's the final picture? Immediate kingdom or delayed accountability?"* The parable's storyline is that the king will return eventually for **reckoning**. Meanwhile, the "immediate kingdom" assumption is shown to be wrong.

## ADDITIONAL INSIGHT: THE LAST SERVANT, CONTRASTS, AND MATTHEW 21

A striking feature in **Luke 19** is the servant who *claims* to fear his master but disobeys by hiding the mina. Meanwhile, other subjects outwardly appear to "hate" the nobleman yet follow his instructions. This **upside-down contrast** mirrors a similar teaching in **Matthew 21:28–31**, the parable of the two sons:

1. **First Son**: *"I will not,"* but later obeys.
2. **Second Son**: *"I will, sir,"* but never does his father's will.

When Jesus asks, *"Which of the two did what his father wanted?"* (Matthew 21:31), the crowd replies, *"The first."* They basically confirm that true obedience matters more than polite lip service. Likewise, in Luke 19:

- **Subjects who "hate"** the nobleman ironically do what he commands (investing the mina).

- The final servant spouts reverent-sounding words about fear and caution but ends up disobeying.

In both cases, Jesus then issues a **judgment** statement. In Matthew 21:31, He famously says, *"the tax collectors and prostitutes are entering the kingdom of God ahead of you,"* showing that those who appear far off may actually do God's will, whereas those boasting of righteousness might refuse it. Here in **Luke 19**, the master responds, *"I will judge you by your own words,"* (v. 22)—the servant's self-justification condemns him.

This shared theme across the Gospels emphasizes that **lip service, outward respect, or religious veneer** cannot replace the genuine obedience Jesus demands. God's Kingdom welcomes repentant hearts that truly follow the King—even if at first, they seemed resistant—while those who only say "yes" but never actually obey face judgment.

## STEP 5: What's the Core Lesson?

**They thought the kingdom was happening *now* just because Jesus was near Jerusalem.** In the parable:

- **Nobleman Goes Away**: Jesus is signaling a delay; He won't seize an earthly throne immediately upon arrival in Jerusalem.

- **Rejection**: Many actively reject this future king, paralleling Israel's ultimate rejection of Jesus at the cross.

- **Servants**: Some externally appear to hate the master yet obey; one claims fear (or respect?) but disregards instructions. Jesus thereby shows obedience and disobedience can't always be judged by surface sentiment.

- **Ultimate Judgment**: The real "kingdom manifestation" happens *later*, when the master returns as a king who rewards faithful servants and condemns enemies.

**Mechanic:**

> Keep returning to **Luke 19:11**: *"He told them this parable **because** they thought the kingdom of God was going to appear at once."* That's your interpretive anchor. If your reading of the parable doesn't address that, you've missed the point.

## STEP 6: Ruling Out What This Passage Isn't About

### 1. It's Not Primarily About Stewardship

> While the parable uses financial language (minas, investments), the main thrust is about **delayed kingship** and **true vs. false obedience**—not a general lesson on money management.

### 2. It's Not "Savior vs. Saved"

> The parable's tone is more confrontational, detailing *subjects who hate him* and a servant who *says* one thing but does another.

> It highlights impending **judgment** for rejecting the rightful king, more than a sweet dynamic of personal salvation.

**Mechanic:**

> **Ask**: "Does the parable's focus tie back to the crowd's erroneous assumption about immediate kingdom triumph?" Yes—so it's far more about the kingdom's timing, acceptance or rejection of the king, and ultimate accountability than about financial stewardship.

## STEP 7: Conclusion

**The Ten Minas parable** is Jesus' direct response to people expecting **instant glory** and a swift, earthly regime in Jerusalem. By weaving a story of a nobleman's delayed enthronement, widespread rejection, and eventual triumphant return, Jesus warns that:

1. The kingdom **won't** manifest fully the moment He enters Jerusalem.
2. **Rejection** of the king has dire consequences.
3. **True obedience** might come from unexpected quarters, while some who claim reverence are disobedient.
4. **Judgment** (not immediate coronation) awaits at the final return.

So, **Luke 19:11–27** isn't just a moral lesson on wise investing; it's an **ominous prophecy** addressing the false belief in an instant kingdom. Jesus is gently but firmly reshaping their perspective, showing that He'll be rejected by many, that the full manifestation of His reign awaits a future time, and that there will be accountability for both outright hostility and hollow lip service. The parable's entire structure exists **to correct** the notion that "the kingdom of God was going to appear at once."

# 58

# "Take Up Your Cross"— Embracing His Cross, Not Ours

A Bible Study: "Take Up Your Cross"—Embracing His Cross, Not Ours (Luke 9:18-23, Mark 8:27-34, Matthew 16:13-24, and John 6:53-68)

## STEP 1: Luke—A Confession Redefined (Luke 9:18-23)

1. **Who Do You Say I Am? (vv. 18–20)**

**Text Recap**
- Jesus, while praying alone, asks the disciples, "Who do the crowds say I am?" They offer speculation—John the Baptist, Elijah, or a prophet. Then He turns it on them: "But what about you?" Peter answers, "God's Messiah."

**Mechanic:**
- This is massive—Peter declares Jesus is the long-awaited Christ. Yet the disciples still carry expectations of a conquering King, not a crucified one.

### 2. A Suffering Messiah (vv. 21–22)

- Jesus immediately tells them not to publicize this yet—because their understanding is incomplete. Then He says something unthinkable: "The Son of Man must suffer... be killed... and rise on the third day."

**Mechanic:**

- Right after Peter's bold confession, Jesus redefines what it means to be the Christ. He will not triumph by overthrowing Rome—but through death.

### 3. "Take Up Your Cross Daily" (v. 23)

- Jesus then says to all: "Whoever wants to be my disciple must deny themselves and take up their cross daily and follow me."

**Mechanic:**

- This comes directly after the revelation of His death. "Daily" underscores that acknowledging a crucified Messiah is not a one-time epiphany—it's a daily reorientation. We don't get to reshape Him into something more palatable.

**Luke's Focus**

Luke roots the cross in Jesus' identity. There is no version of Him apart from suffering. To follow Jesus is to accept Him as He is.

## STEP 2: Mark—The Blunt Prediction And Peter's Rebuke (Mark 8:27–34)

1. **Peter's Confession in Caesarea Philippi (vv. 27–30)**

    > Peter again speaks on behalf of the disciples: "You are the Messiah." Jesus tells them not to share this yet.

2. **Plain Teaching of Death (vv. 31–32)**

    > "He began to teach them that the Son of Man must suffer... be killed... and after three days rise again." Mark adds: He spoke plainly—no metaphors or parables.

**Mechanic:**

---

> The moment He's acknowledged as Christ, He removes all ambiguity about what that means.

3. **Peter's Outburst and Jesus' Sharp Rebuke (vv. 32b–33)**

    > Peter pulls Jesus aside and rebukes Him. Jesus responds: "Get behind me, Satan!"—because Peter's objection opposes the entire mission.

**Mechanic:**

---

> Peter's resistance is not just wrong—it's satanic. To oppose the cross is to stand in opposition to God's redemptive plan.

4. **"Take Up Your Cross" (v. 34)**

    > Jesus turns to the crowd: "Whoever wants to be my disciple must deny themselves and take up their cross and follow me."

**Mechanic:**

- This directly answers Peter's protest. Jesus doesn't soften the message—He sharpens it. If you want Him, you don't get to strip away the cross. You accept the Messiah as crucified.

**Mark's Focus**

Mark delivers it brisk and bold: this is who Jesus is. The cross is non-negotiable.

## STEP 3: Matthew—Good Intentions, Bad Discipleship (Matt. 16:13-24)

1. **The Confession (vv. 13–16)**
   - Peter's bold proclamation: "You are the Messiah, the Son of the living God." Jesus affirms him, noting that the Father revealed this.

2. **The Turn (v. 21)**
   - "From that time on..." Jesus starts teaching clearly that He must go to Jerusalem, suffer, be killed, and be raised.

**Mechanic:**

- This signals a shift. From this moment forward, the cross is front and center.

3. **Peter's Interference (vv. 22–23)**
   - Peter pulls Jesus aside: "Never, Lord! This shall never happen to you!"
   - Jesus responds: "Get behind me, Satan!"

**Mechanic:**

> Peter's motives are sincere but misaligned. His instinct is to protect Jesus from suffering. Jesus calls that satanic—not because Peter is evil, but because he's thinking in human terms, not divine.

### 4. "Take Up Your Cross" (v. 24)

> Then Jesus tells the disciples: "Whoever wants to be my disciple must deny themselves and take up their cross and follow me."

**Mechanic (with a logic test)**

> If Jesus were just moralizing about daily hardships, the sequence wouldn't make sense. Peter says, "Don't die," and Jesus replies, "Carry your own burdens"? Disjointed.
>
> It only makes sense if Jesus is saying: "You can't stop Me from dying. In fact, if you follow Me, you embrace My crucified identity."

**Matthew's Focus**

The disciples are not invited to carry their own crosses—they're challenged to embrace His.

## STEP 4: Parallel To John 6—A Test Of True Followers (John 6:53-68)

### Reference

Jesus says something equally scandalous: "Unless you eat the flesh of the Son of Man and drink His blood, you have no life in you." Many walk away—it's too much.

He turns to the Twelve: "Will you leave too?" Peter replies: "You have the words of eternal life."

**Mechanic:**

Both moments—John 6 and "take up your cross" in the Synoptics—present hard teachings that sift followers. These aren't moral slogans; they're moments of theological rupture. People must accept Him as He is or walk away.

## STEP 5: Why Getting This Right Matters

### 1. It's Not a Slogan About Our Burdens

Reinterpreting "take up your cross" as personal hardship turns the focus inward and dulls the shock. The Gospels are ruthlessly focused on Christ, not our generic pain.

### 2. We Risk Diminishing the Atonement

Jesus' cross is not a metaphor. It's the atoning sacrifice for humanity's sin. Equating it to "daily struggles" dilutes its singular power.

### 3. We Misread the Text's Logic

This isn't a life-principle lesson. It's a correction to the idea that Jesus should avoid suffering.

### 4. We Lose the Discipleship Challenge

Jesus isn't asking us to find our cross. He's asking if we'll follow Him—the crucified One. "Take up your cross" means: Don't try to reshape Christ. Receive Him as He is.

5. **The Cross Belongs to Christ**

Scripture never says, "Like Jesus had His cross, you have yours." The cross is not a mere symbol; it's the site of divine judgment and mercy. God does not allow what is holy to become common. Calling your hardship "your cross" seems devout but treats the most sacred event—Jesus' crucifixion—as ordinary. The Bible guards the cross by narrowing it entirely to Christ's sacrifice, not broadening it to everyone's burdens. When Jesus says "take up your cross," He's confronting us with His cross—asking if we'll embrace Him as the crucified Messiah.

## STEP 6: Conclusion—Embrace His Cross, Not Yours

Across Luke 9, Mark 8, and Matthew 16, the pattern is unmissable:

- The disciples declare Jesus is the Messiah.
- Jesus declares He must die.
- Peter resists.
- Jesus insists the cross cannot be avoided.
- Then comes the challenge: Will you still follow Me—like this?

This isn't about our crosses. It's about His—and whether we will accept Him on His terms.

# 59

# Cross-Examining Jesus' Words

*Avoiding Harmful Assumptions in Matthew 7:13 (With a Cross-Reference to John 10)*

### STEP 1: Recognize the Need for "Cross Examination"

When we hear Jesus say, *"Enter through the narrow gate... for wide is the gate... that leads to destruction"* (Matthew 7:13), we often assume we know exactly how it applies to us. After all, we're believers, right? Jesus came to save us. So, we plug ourselves in as the audience, and the lesson becomes: "Hey, believer—make sure you pick the narrow gate!"

But wait. Was Jesus addressing faithful disciples here, or a broader crowd that might reject Him? In a courtroom analogy, it's like hearing one side of the testimony ("Enter the narrow gate!") but never letting the opposing counsel cross-examine. We walk away with a single perspective—an entrenched interpretation that may not hold up under deeper scrutiny.

**Mechanic:**

1. **Stop**: Instead of taking a verse at face value, pretend you're cross-examining the text.

2. **Ask**: "Who's on the stand? What's the context? To whom is Jesus speaking? Did He repeat these words in private to His Twelve disciples—His core believers?"

## STEP 2: Identify the Audience—Is It Really "Us Believers"?

A crucial question is: *Who was listening when Jesus spoke of the narrow gate and the broad road to destruction?* The Sermon on the Mount (Matthew 5–7) was primarily directed at a large, mixed crowd. It wasn't a private sermon to a group of committed Christ-followers. By the end of the Gospels, we see that many of these hearers *reject* Jesus outright.

- If He's warning about "destruction," He's addressing people who may or may not heed His teaching.
- The Gospels conclude that the Jewish leadership and many in the crowds turned against Him (Matthew 27, John 19).

**Mechanic:**

- **Check** the immediate setting of the Sermon on the Mount (Matthew 5:1–2, 7:28–29). "Crowds" frame the beginning and end.
- **Cross-examine**: "If He's speaking to a mixed group of potential followers and skeptics, can we assume this is a direct admonition for all longtime believers?"

## STEP 3: Observe the Tone Toward the Disciples—Is It the Same?

When alone with His closest disciples, Jesus' tone is often reassurance (e.g., John 14–17). He calls them friends, prays for them, comforts them:

*"I no longer call you servants... I have called you friends..."* (John 15:15)

Does He threaten them with "destruction" if they don't squeeze through a narrow gate? Not in the same way. Instead, He warns them of persecution from the world, encourages them to abide in Him, and promises the Holy Spirit.

**Mechanic:**

- **Compare** Matthew 7:13 with, say, John 14:1–3 or John 17:6–12—very different posture.
- **Ask**: "If 'narrow gate' is a broad crowd warning, does that match the tender approach He takes with His core disciples?"

## STEP 4: Consider Cultural and Historical Context

In 1st-century Judea, people heard Jesus' radical teaching about the Kingdom of Heaven. Many found it compelling, but others wanted a Messiah who would overthrow Rome, not call for inner repentance. The "wide" and "narrow" gates are a stark image:

- **Narrow Gate**: A challenging way that might involve self-denial, a genuine heart change, or repenting from mere external religion.
- **Wide Gate**: The "easy" route—maintaining the status quo, relying on cultural expectations, or outright dismissing Jesus.

**Mechanic:**

- **Place** yourself in their shoes: If you were a Jew in Jesus' day, uncertain about His claims, this might be a call to decide: follow His radical Kingdom message or stick with the comfortable, popular path.

- **Don't** automatically assume Jesus is telling seasoned Christians, "You might lose salvation if you don't fit through this gate."

## STEP 5: The Trap of "Knowing Too Much"

We know the end of the story—Jesus' crucifixion, resurrection, and the birth of the church. We read Paul's letters and think, "Oh, wide gate = unsaved, narrow gate = saved." But the original audience, including the disciples, did not yet fully grasp Jesus' mission or final atonement:

> *"They did not understand any of this... it was hidden from them." (Luke 18:34)*

**Mechanic:**

- **Cross-examine**: "Am I reading in my modern theology or letting the text's historical moment speak first?"
- It's not wrong to see the ultimate meaning of salvation here but be mindful that the crowd wouldn't have fully parsed 'penal substitution' or 'justification by faith alone.'

## STEP 6: Test the Interpretation—Does It Fit the Rest of Scripture?

If we interpret *"Enter through the narrow gate"* as a direct, ongoing threat to every Christian— *"Watch out or you'll be destroyed!"*—that can conflict with other New Testament passages that offer assurance for genuine disciples (Romans 8:1, John 10:28). Scripture does include warnings but typically aimed at those who are superficial or only appear to follow Jesus.

**Mechanic:**

- **Look** for any repeated phrase about "narrow gate/broad gate" in Jesus' private talks with the Twelve. It doesn't show up.
- **Separate**: Are you already a committed follower? Or are you in the uncertain crowd, still deciding whether to receive Christ?

## STEP 7: A Helpful Cross-Reference—John 10

We can find a parallel idea to "narrow vs. broad" in John 10, where Jesus describes Himself as the **door** (or "gate") for the sheep:

*"Very truly I tell you, I am the gate for the sheep... All who have come before me are thieves and robbers, but the sheep have not listened to them." (John 10:7–8)*

1. **Narrow Concept**: Jesus is the *only* legitimate entry for the sheep— "the door." That's a one-way-in image, reminiscent of the "narrow gate."

2. **Broad Concept**: Thieves and robbers who try multiple illegitimate ways—jumping over the fence, forcing entry. That's akin to the "broad road" of Matthew 7:13, where many find themselves on a path that doesn't lead to authentic life.

**Mechanic (Cross-Reference Use):**

- **Focus** on words like "door/gate," "thieves/robbers," "only legitimate way." Notice how John 10 parallels the idea of exclusivity: "one door" = narrow, while many attempts to sneak in = broad and illegitimate.
- **Ask**: "Does John 10 confirm Jesus' consistent teaching on legitimate vs. illegitimate approaches to God?" Yes, He alone is the way—He's not scolding the faithful who trust Him, but warning about false claims and false ways to God.

Thus, cross-referencing John 10 clarifies the metaphor: *There's only one rightful gate—Christ Himself. Any other path or multiple 'broad' methods are illegitimate.*

## STEP 8: The Courtroom Strategy—Don't Let the Witness "Leave the Stand"

Imagine you're the defense attorney: the witness says, *"Enter the narrow gate or face destruction."* Before you let that stand as final:

1. **Question**: "To whom is Jesus speaking—committed disciples or a mixed crowd?"
2. **Question**: "Where else does Jesus talk about gates or entrances?" (John 10)
3. **Question**: "Does He treat all hearers the same, or does He speak differently to the Twelve vs. the masses?"
4. **Question**: "Is this a universal condemnation for all believers, or a challenge to uncommitted listeners to trust the one and only legitimate 'door'?"

**Mechanic:**

> By cross-examining in this way, you avoid a simplistic reading that lumps every Christian into "you might be destroyed if you're not careful." Instead, you see Jesus calling people to choose His path (narrow/true) over the status-quo path (broad/false).

## STEP 9: A Balanced Application—What It Means for Us

So, does this verse apply to us at all? Yes, in principle:

- **For those not yet truly committed**: The "narrow gate" is Jesus Himself. Life in Him might seem restrictive or counter-cultural at first—repentance, humility, following His commands—but it leads to real life.

- **For believers already walking with Christ**: The direct threat of "destruction" isn't typically Jesus' warning to His devoted disciples. Instead, we find comfort and assurance in passages like John 10, where He is our Good Shepherd, and we enter safely through Him.

## Mechanic:

- **Identify** where you stand. Are you among the uncertain crowd or already sheep inside the fold?
- **Cross-reference** John 10: "I am the door." Are you resting in that knowledge, or do you still think there might be a broader, easier path to God?

## STEP 10: Final Thought—How Cross-Examination Prevents Misuse

Matthew 7:13 can become a fear-inducing verse if preached without context: *"If you're not squeaky clean, you'll be destroyed!"* But cross-examining the text—checking the audience, tone, cultural setting, and parallel passages (John 10)—shows Jesus calling people to enter true life through Him rather than the popular but empty alternatives of the day.

1. **We Avoid Harmful Assumption**: We don't automatically transfer crowd warnings to the faithful.

2. **We Use Helpful Cross-Examination**: Considering John 10's "door" imagery confirms that Jesus is describing Himself as the *exclusive* way into the fold; the "broad ways" are false and cannot save.

The overarching principle:

- **Yes**, Christ is the only door, the narrow gate, the one legitimate route to life.
- **No**, we shouldn't interpret every strong warning as aimed at faithful disciples who might lose their footing.

By combining audience analysis, historical context, and cross-referencing with John 10, we handle the text responsibly affirming the unique, exclusive nature of Jesus' invitation without scaring believers into thinking they're forever on the brink of destruction.

# 60

# When the Bible Interprets Its Own Story

*Learning from Ishmael in Genesis 16:12  
(And Paul's Explanation in Galatians 4)*

### STEP 1: Ask: "Does This Story Appear Again in Scripture?"

Genesis 16:12 describes Ishmael as *"a wild donkey of a man,"* living in hostility toward his brothers. Many have heard the claim, *"Ishmael fathered the Arab people of today,"* and so the text is taken as a prophetic statement about modern ethnic tensions.

**But is that the primary message Scripture itself wants to convey?** Before we finalize any interpretation, **we check**: Does this story resurface later in the Bible? If yes, do the authors provide their own explanation?

**Mechanic:**

1. **Scan the rest of Scripture** for references to Ishmael (Hagar, Sarah, Abraham's two sons).
2. **Take note** if a New Testament writer—like Paul—explicitly revisits the event. Often, that's where Scripture clarifies its intended takeaway.

## STEP 2: Recognize Paul's Explicit Interpretation in Galatians 4

We find the *most extensive commentary* on Sarah, Hagar, Isaac, and Ishmael in Galatians 4:21–31. Paul digs into the story, not to address ethnic origins, but to illustrate a **theological truth** about living under slavery (the Law) vs. living in gospel freedom.

> *"These things are being taken figuratively: The women represent two covenants. One covenant is from Mount Sinai... This is Hagar... corresponds to the present city of Jerusalem... She is in slavery with her children... but the Jerusalem that is above is free, and she is our mother." (Galatians 4:24–26, NIV)*

Notice that Paul re-frames the entire Hagar/Ishmael scenario around the **Law vs. Promise** dynamic, contrasting children "born according to the flesh" and "children of the promise."

### Mechanic:

- **Mark** every instance Paul refers to Hagar and Sarah, or Isaac and Ishmael.
- **Ask**: "What is Paul doing with these references? Is he focusing on genealogical facts or spiritual allegory?"

## STEP 3: Compare the "Likely Conclusion" vs. the "Biblical Point"

Yes, historically, many believe Ishmael's descendants eventually populated Arab regions. That may be true—**but** the text itself never stresses, *"And behold, from Ishmael sprang the Arab peoples."* Instead, Scripture is silent on that big genealogical conclusion.

Meanwhile, Paul's commentary is loud and clear:

- Ishmael = children of bondage (Hagar).
- Isaac = children of promise (Sarah).

**Mechanic:**

- **List** what the text says vs. what we assume or insert.
- **Identify** if the biblical author is interested in genealogical details or if they're unveiling a deeper spiritual truth.

## STEP 4: Notice Paul's "Hard Stop" on Our Inferences

In Galatians 4, Paul specifically states, *"These things are being taken figuratively"* (v. 24). He's not presenting a DNA chart for the Middle East; he's offering a **metaphor** about slavery vs. freedom, flesh vs. promise. Then he concludes:

*"Therefore, brothers and sisters, we are not children of the slave woman, but of the free woman." (Galatians 4:31)*

He directly **applies** the story to believers in Christ: if you're in Jesus, you're an heir of the promise like Isaac, **not** an enslaved child-like Ishmael. He's driving home a point about **spiritual liberty**—*not* genealogical predictions.

**Mechanic:**

- **Circle** or **highlight** every time Paul references slavery/freedom in this section.
- **Ask**: "Does that match the genealogical theme we sometimes impose?" Likely not—Paul's all about who's under the Law vs. who's in Christ.

## STEP 5: Why This Matters—It's Not "Semantics"; It's Vital

Some might say, *"Okay, so we read Ishmael as father of the Arabs—what's the harm?"* The harm lies in **missing** the profound revelation

Paul offers about freedom in Christ. Fixating on genealogical theories distracts from the Scripture's deeper spiritual message:

1. **Freedom in Christ**: If we see Ishmael as a symbol of bondage to Law, we realize we're called to a better way—living under grace like Isaac, not under the "fleshly" system.
2. **Relational Outcome**: The text is trying to teach us about God's promise vs. self-effort, not about current ethnic tensions.

**Mechanic:**

- **Compare** the fruit of each interpretation: Does focusing on "Ishmael = Arabs" transform your spiritual life? Probably not. Does focusing on Paul's allegory about grace vs. law free you to live boldly in Christ? Absolutely.

## STEP 6: When the Bible Interprets Itself, Our Add-Ons Lose Priority

We often say, *"All Scripture is God-breathed."* (2 Timothy 3:16). So, if the Holy Spirit-inspired authors interpret a passage, that's our top-tier reading. Our own guesses—no matter how historically plausible—**cannot supersede** the explicit meaning Scripture gives.

**Mechanic:**

- **Rank** biblical interpretations: #1 = Scripture's own direct commentary on a story.
- **Check** if Paul or another author has weighed in. If they have, that's the final word on what the text aims to convey.

## STEP 7: Apply the "Does This Story Reappear?" Filter in Your Study

This principle isn't just for Ishmael. Any time you see a major figure or event in the Old Testament, ask:

1. "Does this reappear later—maybe in the Prophets or the New Testament?"
2. "Does the text explicitly reinterpret or draw a theological lesson from it?"

Examples:

- **The manna in the wilderness** reappears in John 6, where Jesus calls Himself the "true bread from heaven."
- **Jonah** reappears in Matthew 12:40, with Jesus referencing Jonah's three days in the fish as a sign of the resurrection.

**Mechanic:**

- **Stay alert** for cross-references.
- **Use** a Bible concordance or study Bible notes to see if a story is discussed elsewhere.

## STEP 8: Summarize the Mechanics—Finding the Bible's Own Interpretation

1. **Spot the Original**: Read Genesis 16 carefully—note Ishmael's introduction, the prophecy over him, and the tension with Isaac (Genesis 21, too).
2. **Hunt for a Reprise**: In the New Testament, check if Jesus or Paul references that story. (Galatians 4 is the big one for Ishmael.)

3. **Observe the Shift**: Paul transforms the narrative from genealogical to allegorical, emphasizing the difference between bondage (Hagar/Ishmael) and freedom (Sarah/Isaac).

4. **Elevate Scripture's Emphasis**: If Paul invests time explaining the meaning—**that** is what the Holy Spirit wants us to glean, not a side detail about modern ethnic lines.

## STEP 9: Conclusion—Embrace the Bible's Intent

**Does the Bible hint that Ishmael might be father to Arab nations?** Possibly. But that's never the theological point it develops. **Paul's explicit teaching** is about living under the law vs. under grace. God's Word aims to free us from bondage—He uses the Ishmael/Isaac story to illustrate that.

1. **Less Important**: A genealogical claim—**who** Ishmael's descendants might be today.

2. **Central Lesson**: Ishmael represents a system of **fleshly striving** and **slavery** to the old covenant; Isaac stands for **promise, grace, and freedom**.

When we reduce Ishmael to a modern ethnic origin story, we might feel we've found some factual insight, but we forfeit the **spiritual** insight: *Are we living under bondage or in the freedom of the new covenant?* That's the question Galatians 4 wants us to wrestle with.

---

> **REMEMBER: The best reading is the one Scripture itself endorses. If Paul's detailed interpretation is present, we follow his lead. That's how we avoid letting our personal inferences overshadow the life-giving revelations God intended.**

---

# 61

# "Faith Without Works Is Dead"

## Walking Through the Mechanics *(James 2:14-26)*

### STEP 1: Look for the Claim James Is Addressing

The first key to unpacking James 2 is paying attention to **how** James introduces his topic. Let's zero in on verse 14: *"What good is it, my brothers and sisters, if someone **claims** to have faith but has no deeds? Can such faith save them?"* (James 2:14, NIV)

- **Notice the Word "Claims"**: James isn't talking about genuine faith yet. He's talking about a *person who says* they believe—someone who slaps a "Faith" label on themselves.

- **Immediate Cue**: James' tone is confrontational from the start: *"What good is it?"* He's forcing us to test whether that claim holds water.

### Practical Mechanic:

- **Circle or highlight** the phrase "if someone claims" in your Bible or notes.

- **Ask**: "Is James discussing *real* faith, or a claim that needs verification?"
- **Conclude**: The rest of the passage will revolve around verifying (or refuting) that *claim*.

## STEP 2: Identify the Rhetorical Questions

James continues by asking:
"Can such faith save them?"

He's setting up a test. Is the *claim* enough, or do we need evidence? James is basically saying, *"Is that so-called faith actually alive, or just lip service?"*

### Practical Mechanic:

- Whenever an author uses rhetorical questions, **stop** and consider: "What point are they trying to make? Why pose the question this way?"
- Here, James wants us to feel the tension: *"Claimed faith"* vs. *"Can it really save?"*

## STEP 3: Check James' Real-Life Example

Immediately after posing these questions, James presents a scenario:
"Suppose a brother or a sister is without clothes and daily food. If one of you says to them, 'Go in peace; keep warm and well fed,' but does nothing about their physical needs, what good is it?" (James 2:15–16)

1. **Observe the Setup**: It's practical, almost painfully simple. Someone is cold and hungry.

2. **Spot the Claim**: "Go in peace"—words that *sound* caring.

3. **Contrast**: The talk does not match the action. Nothing is done to help.

This example models James' main contention: **words alone aren't enough.** Just like with faith, if you claim to have it but show nothing for it, James pronounces it "dead."

---

PRACTICAL MECHANIC: **Ask**: "Why did James pick such an everyday example?" **Answer**: Because it reveals hypocrisy in a common scenario—if we won't help a need we clearly see, maybe our 'faith' is just talk.

---

### STEP 4: Notice James' Repeated Phrase: 'What Good Is It?'

He uses this phrase in verse 14 and again in verse 16— *"what good is it?"* This repetition is a big hint:

- James wants us to question the *usefulness* or *effectiveness* of faith that's merely declared but never displayed.

- *"What good is it?"* is also rhetorical, hinting that the answer is "It's no good at all."

**Practical Mechanic:**

---

- When you see a repeated phrase, **take note**. Biblical writers often repeat key lines to hammer home a single theme. Here, James's repeated question keeps pointing us to the *lack of benefit* in empty words.

## STEP 5: Observe the Confrontational Tone

James doesn't tiptoe around. He's blunt. Verse 17 sums it up:
"...faith by itself, if it is not accompanied by action, is dead."

**But what exactly is 'dead?'** It's the *faith*—the claimed faith—that has no life to it. James is not undermining genuine faith; he's exposing a *fake version* of faith that lacks works.

---

> **PRACTICAL MECHANIC: Identify the Tone**: James is direct, almost combative. In Scripture, an author's forcefulness usually signals how urgent or rampant the problem is among the recipients. **Ask**: "Why so strong?" Likely because this issue—people claiming faith but living otherwise—was a major concern in the early church (and still is!).

---

## STEP 6: Examine How James Argues with a Hypothetical Opponent

In verse 18, James stages an imaginary conversation:
"But someone will say, 'You have faith; I have deeds.' Show me your faith without deeds, and I will show you my faith by my deeds." (James 2:18)

Here's James's *testing approach* in action: *"Alright, you claim to have faith—prove it."* He sets up two "speakers":

1. **Person A**: "You have faith; I have works."
2. **James**: "Show me your faith without works, and I'll show you mine by my works."

**Practical Mechanic:**

---

> - **Watch for Dialogue**: When authors bring in a "someone says..." scenario, it's meant to highlight the tension in a debate.

> **James's Logic**: Faith is invisible until it's manifested through action. If you have *real* faith, it *will* come out in how you live.

## STEP 7: Cross-Reference: Moral Unbeliever vs. Immoral Believer?

There's an age-old debate: *Does God prefer a moral unbeliever or an immoral believer?* James cuts through this by essentially saying an "immoral believer" is an oxymoron. Genuine faith transforms a person. If you remain consistently immoral with no repentance or change, you are contradicting the very nature of belief.

**James's Style**:

> He refuses to allow a split between "faith" and "action." Any so-called believer living in willful, ongoing immorality is *not* a case of "faith that's just a little behind on good works." James would say, "That's *dead* faith. It's not legit."

## STEP 8: Check the Biblical Examples—Abraham and Rahab

To back up his point, James cites two Old Testament characters:

1. **Abraham (James 2:21–24)**

    > He believed God (Genesis 15:6), and that belief was shown when he was willing to act in obedience (Genesis 22).

    > James's point: Abraham's *faith* wasn't just a label. He walked it out.

2. **Rahab (James 2:25)**

    > Rahab believed that Israel's God was real and powerful (Joshua 2:9–11). She *proved* it by risking her life to hide the spies.

    > Again, that's living faith in action.

**Practical Mechanic:**

- When a passage references biblical examples, **take time** to read those original stories. Look for the *action* that validated their *belief.*

- James sees faith and works as a single, seamless whole—the root (faith) always produces fruit (works).

## STEP 9: Compare James and Paul—Builder vs. Tester

Some claim James and Paul are at odds: Paul says we're saved by grace through faith alone (Romans 3:28; Ephesians 2:8–9), while James says faith without works is dead. Are they contradicting each other?

- **Function Difference**: *Paul is the builder*: He constructs the doctrine of salvation by grace through faith. *James is the tester*: He evaluates claims of faith. Once the "chair" of salvation is built, James sits in it to see if it holds weight.

- Both men agree: Genuine faith, once built, *will demonstrate* itself in the life of a believer.

**Practical Mechanic:**

- Always look at **the author's purpose**: Paul's letters often address legalism—people trying to *earn* salvation by works. James addresses complacency—people claiming salvation but not living it out.

## STEP 10: Synthesize the Whole Passage—It's About Authenticity

By now, you can see James 2 is all about testing the authenticity of faith. He's not cheapening faith or promoting a "works-based" gospel. He's safeguarding true biblical faith from empty talk.

1. **James' Opening Words**: "What good is it if someone *claims*...?" That sets the tone: James is dissecting *false claims*.

2. **The Rhetorical Questions**: They challenge us to see that "faith" without tangible expression is worthless.

3. **The Real-Life Example**: If you see a needy person but only say kind words, that's not love in action.

4. **Hypothetical Dialogue**: Show me your faith! Faith by itself can't be seen unless it's accompanied by a changed life.

5. **Biblical Proof**: Abraham and Rahab—living faith always bore tangible fruit.

6. **James & Paul**: Different angles on the same truth—Paul builds the case for salvation by faith alone; James tests that faith by seeing if it's truly alive.

## CONCLUSION: FOLLOWING JAMES' MECHANICS YOURSELF

James 2:14–26 lays out a simple but piercing test for faith:

- **Step into James' shoes**: Ask, "What good is your claim?" whenever you hear someone (including yourself) say they believe.

- **Look for evidence**: Is there any real outworking of that belief in daily life—love, obedience, moral transformation?

- **Remember the Big Picture**: Faith and works aren't two separate concepts; they're inseparable aspects of a true, living relationship with God.

By walking through James' logic—his opening questions, his examples, his blunt scenarios, and his rhetorical challenges—we see how we're meant to read Scripture:

1. Identify the author's tone and target.
2. Look for repeated phrases or rhetorical techniques.
3. Cross-reference biblical stories that provide real-life proof.
4. Make sure you grasp the larger biblical unity (how James complements Paul).

Ultimately, James is protecting the integrity of **faith**—far from belittling it. He's telling us: if the box says "faith," open it up and check the contents. If there's *nothing* inside, it's dead. But if it's genuine, then that faith isn't just enough—it will be more than enough, because it naturally springs into action.

# 62

# When We Stretch the Text Too Far

### 1. A Common Trap: "Expanding" Beyond the Context

In many church circles, you'll hear someone quote a single verse—maybe 1 Timothy 4:1 about "doctrines of demons"—and then launch into a long, winding exposition about Satan's strategies, the Garden of Eden, and spiritual warfare in general. While there's nothing wrong with recognizing those themes elsewhere in Scripture, the problem arises when we **completely overlook** the fact that **Paul already explains** what he means just two verses later (1 Timothy 4:3–5). The text itself clarifies these "doctrines of demons" as **forbidding marriage** and **requiring abstinence from certain foods**—a very specific distortion that was cropping up among certain false teachers in Timothy's day.

**The irony?** We can miss the simplest explanation because we're too busy weaving a grand, all-encompassing theory. It's like driving yourself in circles searching for the exit—even though the big "EXIT" sign is right there, plain as day.

## 2. How the Text Actually Interprets Itself

Observe how Paul's statement flows in *1 Timothy 4:1–5*:

"Now the Spirit expressly says that in later times some will depart from the faith by devoting themselves to deceitful spirits and teachings of demons... *[how so?]* ...by forbidding marriage and requiring abstinence from foods that God created to be received with thanksgiving..."

In other words:

- **Paul states the problem**: Certain teachings are demonically influenced.
- **He identifies the concrete examples**: Opposing marriage and declaring certain foods off-limits.
- **He refutes them**: Reminding believers that God created these good gifts to be received with gratitude (vv. 4–5).

**That's the immediate context.** Yet if we only read verses 1–2, ignoring verses 3–5, we can spin up an entire system of speculation— **Who are these demons? Are they controlling the culture? Is this about end-times conspiracies?** On and on we go, and we end up with a "doctrine" that the text itself never taught. We miss Paul's main point because we want it to be bigger, more mysterious, or more universal than it is.

### 3.1. We Love Big Explanations

Christians (and humans in general) are natural storytellers. We prefer sweeping narratives to simple, direct statements. So, when we see "teachings of demons," we sometimes assume Paul must be speaking of a cunning, invisible infiltration of every corner of society. But in **this** context, he's talking about a **real, first-century group** pushing strange ascetic rules. Yes, it's spiritually dangerous— but it's also more straightforward than we might realize.

Moreover, when we look at Paul's more explicit warnings about "church infiltration," they often describe those who "spy out" believers' freedom (Galatians 2:4) and try to "enhance" faith by adding unnecessary moral requirements—essentially a religiosity that perverts the gospel. It's reminiscent of the Judaizers, who insisted on extra rules for salvation. Paul describes such false religiosity as "having a form of godliness but denying its power" (2 Timothy 3:5), urging us to have nothing to do with people who push such distortions. In other words, the real-life infiltration he warns about is a moral and doctrinal rigidity that misunderstands God, rather than the kind of cosmic infiltration we might imagine the moment we see the word 'Satan.' Jumping straight to a grand demonic conspiracy can cause us to lose the intensity and direction of 1 Timothy 4:1–5, where Paul's focus is on a localized, misleading ascetic movement.

### 3.2. We Confuse Peripheral Truths with the Main Text

Many of the themes introduced (Satan as father of lies, the serpent deceiving Eve, etc.) are *true biblical concepts.* They're found in **other passages**. But if we jam all of that into 1 Timothy 4 without pausing to see what Paul explicitly says, we disrespect that text's own boundaries. We end up mixing contexts in a way that might overshadow the simpler, more direct message.

### 3.3. We Miss the Immediate Authorial Intention

Paul was writing to Timothy—who was dealing with specific false teachings in Ephesus. By reading past verses 3–5, we can see how the apostle corrects those teachings. When we parachute in a hundred other biblical references without first letting Paul finish his point, we dilute the focus. We risk turning a localized warning into a vague, universal monster in our minds.

## 4. Learning from This "What Not to Do" Example

So, returning to the example "Bible study" on 1 Timothy 4:1-2, it had many well-intended biblical truths—yes, the devil is a liar; yes, false teachers exist; yes, seared consciences matter—but it jumped around so much that it only **lightly touched** verses 3-5 (which contain the clarifying meaning). This is classic over-expansion: we end up making a big, fuzzy lesson on "doctrines of demons," forgetting the text is primarily calling out ascetic mandates (no marriage, no certain foods) *right there in the next lines.*

### A quick self-check:

- Do I usually skip the "next verses" to hunt for my own favored cross-references?
- Am I trying to prove a broad concept when the text itself is narrower?
- Am I ignoring the immediate, obvious meaning—like forbidding marriage—because it's less thrilling than a cosmic-level storyline?

## 5. Practical Tips to Avoid Overstretching Scripture

- **Read the Surrounding Verses First.** Don't just grab one or two verses. Familiarize yourself with the immediate context—often the "puzzle piece" you need is *literally* in the next few lines.
- **List What the Text Explicitly Says.** If a passage straightforwardly identifies certain practices ("forbidding marriage, abstaining from foods"), start there. Resist the urge to chase a bigger idea until you've honored the plain sense.

- **Look for Internal Explanations.** Many passages come with a built-in definition. Paul warns about "teachings of demons" and then gives examples in the **same breath** (verses 3–5). Notice when the text interprets itself—it often does!

- **Cross-Reference Cautiously.** Yes, the Bible is interconnected. But cross-referencing should **augment**, not **displace**, the immediate meaning. If referencing other books or themes takes you far away from the author's central point, check if you're forcing a grand unification.

- **Respect Distinct Situations.** 1 Timothy's context differs from, say, Ephesians or John 8 or Genesis 3. While all Scripture harmonizes in the big picture of God's redemptive story, not every concept is equally relevant in every passage.

## A Quick Note on "Last Days"

Sometimes, when Paul (or other biblical writers) mentions "the last days" (1 Timothy 4:1, 2 Timothy 3:1), readers assume he's predicting a distant, end-of-the-world scenario. This can lead to the idea that Paul's warning about "some departing from the faith" only matters for a future era. But the term "last days" doesn't necessarily hinge on chronological timing—it often describes our place in God's overarching salvation plan.

- Placement in God's Plan: Scripture portrays the coming of Christ as inaugurating the "final stage" of salvation history. In that sense, we're already in the last days—God's redemptive work through Christ and the church is the climactic phase before the ultimate fulfillment of His kingdom.

- Present Tense Reality: When Paul says that in the "later times" certain people will fall away, he's not relegating this danger to a far-off future. Rather, he's reminding Timothy (and us) that these patterns of deception can surface at any point in the church age—a reality already unfolding in Ephesus during Paul's lifetime.

So, Paul's use of "last days" or "later times" does not undercut his relevance to the immediate situation. It's more like a statement of where we are in the big picture of God's plan and what believers can expect as the gospel spreads—false teachings, distortions, and spiritual opposition may appear anytime within this final, climactic era. By shifting our focus from pure chronology to God's ongoing story, we can see how Paul's words still speak powerfully to the church of every generation.

## 6. A Final Encouragement

Over-stretching Scripture usually springs from **good intentions**. We love God's Word, and we want to see it all knit together. But ironically, we can end up distorting a passage when we keep piling on bigger themes. The simplest course is often the best: **start with what the text explicitly says**, then widen out slowly if the immediate context invites it.

**With 1 Timothy 4:1–5:**

- Paul isn't giving a universal treatise on demonology.
- He's warning Timothy about specific false teachers who forbid marriage and certain foods.
- That's it, in a nutshell—no guesswork needed.

So next time you're tempted to jump from 1 Timothy 4:1 to a dozen other passages on spiritual warfare, pause. Ask: "Does the next verse or two clarify this point already? Am I listening to Paul on his own terms?" You might find the answer is simpler and clearer than all the extra leaps we sometimes take.

**REMEMBER: Over-elaboration can be just as misleading as under-explaining. In our zeal to honor Scripture, let's not overshadow the text with our own broad brushstrokes. The Bible has a marvelous, cohesive story to tell, but each passage has its own place in that story—so let's give it the space to speak plainly before we start filling in every possible blank.**

# From Pieces to Pattern

*Transition chapter from section 4 to section 5)*

Armed with practical study techniques and interpretive principles, you've learned to approach individual passages with greater confidence and clarity. You've discovered how to examine verses in context, consider the author's intention, and avoid common misunderstandings. These skills are invaluable—but there's still one more perspective that will transform how you view Scripture.

Imagine trying to appreciate a magnificent mosaic by studying each individual tile in isolation. You might admire the craftsmanship of each piece, but you'd miss the breathtaking image they create together. Similarly, we can become so focused on understanding individual passages that we lose sight of the grand narrative unfolding across Scripture.

Many believers experience the Bible as a collection of disconnected stories, commands, and promises. They know the individual pieces but struggle to see how they fit together into a coherent whole. It's like having all the puzzle pieces scattered across the table without the picture on the box to guide assembly.

In this final section, we'll step back to view the entire landscape of Scripture—not just individual trees, but the whole forest. You'll discover how seemingly disconnected passages are part of one unfolding story of redemption. You'll see how various themes and concepts form patterns that reveal God's character and plan more fully than any single verse could.

Because when we grasp Scripture's overarching narrative, individual passages take on deeper meaning, apparent contradictions find resolution, and God's redemptive purpose emerges with stunning clarity.

31 Then their eyes were opened, & they knew him, and he vanished out of their sight.

32 And they said betweene themselues, Did not our hearts burne within vs, while hee talked with vs by the way, and when hee opened to vs the Scriptures?

33 And they rose vp the same houre, and returned to Ierusalem, and found the eleuen gathered together, and them that were with them,

34 Saying, The Lord is risen in deede, and hath appeared to Simon.

35 Then they told what things were done in the way, and how hee was knowen of them in breaking of bread.

36 ¶ And as they spake these things, Iesus himselfe stood in the mids of them, and said vnto them, Peace be to you.

37 But they were all afraid, supposing that they had seene a spirit.

38 Then he said vnto them, Why are ye troubled? and wherefore doe thoughts arise in your hearts?

39 Behold mine hands and my feete, for it is I my selfe: handle me and see, for a spirit hath not flesh and bones, as ye see me haue.

40 And when he had thus spoken, he shewed them his hands and feete.

41 And while they yet beleeued not for ioy, and wondered, he said vnto them, Haue ye here any meate?

42 And they gaue him a piece of a broyled fish, and of an hony combe.

43 And hee tooke it, and did eate before them.

44 ¶ And hee said vnto them, These are the words which I spake vnto you while I was yet with you, that all must bee fulfilled which are written of mee in the Law of Moses, and in the Prophets, and in the Psalmes.

45 Then opened he their vnderstanding, that they might vnderstand the Scriptures.

46 And said vnto them, Thus it is written, and thus it behoued Christ to suffer, & to rise againe from the dead the third day,

47 And that repentance & remission of sinnes should be preached in his Name among all nations, beginning at Hierusalem.

48 Now ye are witnesses of these things.

49 And behold, I doe send the promise of my Father vpon you: but tarie ye in the citie of Hierusalem, vntill yee bee endued with power from on high.

50 ¶ And he led them out into Bethania, and he lift vp his hands, and blessed them.

51 And it came to passe, that as he blessed them, hee departed from them, and was carried vp into heauen.

52 And they worshipped him, and returned to Hierusalem with great ioy.

53 And were continually in the Temple, praysing, and lauding God. Amen.

# THE HOLY GOSPEL OF IESVS CHRIST ACCORDING TO IOHN.

### CHAP. I.

5 And that light shineth in the darkenesse, and the darkenesse comprehended it not.

6 ¶ There was a man sent from God, whose name was Iohn.

7 The same came for a witnesse, to beare witnesse of that light, that all men through him might beleeue.

8 Hee was not that light, but was sent to beare witnesse of that light.

9 This was that true light, which lighteth euery man that commeth into the world.

10 He was in the world, and the world was made by him, and the world knew him not.

11 He came vnto his owne, and his owne receiued him not.

12 But as many as receiued him, to them he gaue power to be the sonnes of God, euen to them that beleeue on his Name.

13 Which were borne, not of blood, nor of the will of the flesh, nor of the will of man, but of God.

1 IN the beginning was the Word, and the Word was with God, and the Word was God.

2 The same was in the beginning with God.

3 All things were made by him, and without him was made nothing that was made.

4 In him was life, and the life was the light of men.

SECTION FIVE

# Seeing the Big Picture

# 63

# How to Read the Gospels

*We've Been Reading the Gospels Too Small*

Many of us have been taught to read the gospels through a specific lens—one that places the church at the center and views Jesus primarily as the founder of Christianity. This approach seems natural, especially for believers who identify Jesus as Lord and Savior. After all, isn't establishing the church precisely what Jesus came to do?

Yet this church-centric reading, while understandable, often causes us to miss the immediate and explosive drama at the heart of these texts. Before Jesus was the head of the church, He was Yahweh incarnate walking among His covenant people—those who claimed exclusive devotion to Him for centuries. This divine visitation created a crisis of recognition that reverberates through every page of the gospels.

## THE PROBLEM OF APPLICATION-FIRST READING

For many of us raised in church settings, we've been conditioned to approach the gospels with a particular lens: *What is the moral lesson here? How should I apply this to my life?* This application-first approach seems natural and beneficial. After all, shouldn't Scripture guide our daily lives and behaviors? Pastors regularly conclude sermons with "application points," Bible studies often end with "action steps," and devotional materials frequently focus on how biblical passages can be immediately implemented in daily life.

Yet this approach, while well-intentioned, can inadvertently flatten the profound narrative of the gospels into mere moral directives. When we rush to application, we often miss the explosive confrontation at the heart of these texts: God Himself has come in the flesh to His covenant people—those who claim devotion to Him—and how that encounter unfolds reveals something profound about both God and humanity.

Consider how often we teach Bible stories: "Jesus healed on the Sabbath to show us that helping people is more important than religious rules." While not incorrect, this reduction misses the deeper drama. What does it reveal about religious devotion when those who claim to love God most are angered by God healing on a day designated to honor Him? This isn't merely about moral priorities—it's about exposed hearts.

The application-first approach often creates a troubling dynamic where we position ourselves as the heroes of these stories while distancing ourselves from those who failed to recognize Jesus. We imagine we would have been among those who followed Him rather than those who rejected Him. This comfortable assumption allows us to extract moral lessons without confronting the more disturbing possibility: that our own religious devotion might be similarly disconnected from genuine relationship with God.

## THE IMMEDIATE CONTEXT: JESUS' MISSION TO ISRAEL

A fundamental error in our reading of the gospels stems from anachronistically imposing church-centric thinking onto texts that were primarily addressing an immediate crisis within Israel. We often forget that Jesus himself explicitly stated, "I was sent only to the lost sheep of Israel" (Matthew 15:24). This wasn't merely a strategic starting point but defined the primary context of his earthly ministry.

When we consider the actual spiritual landscape Jesus entered, we gain crucial perspective. The Pharisees weren't merely cartoon villains but respected spiritual leaders who had earned their cultural authority through genuine service to Israel. In an era of foreign occupation and cultural dissolution, they had helped Israel maintain its distinct identity by making Torah accessible and applicable to everyday life. They weren't rejected by the populace because, quite simply, they met real spiritual needs.

Much like how today's popular pastors translate ancient texts into practical guidance, the Pharisees developed systems that helped ordinary people live out their faith amid complex circumstances. Their influence wasn't maintained through coercion but through providing genuine spiritual value—offering clarity where there was confusion, structure where there was uncertainty, and consistency where there was change.

This context makes Jesus' confrontations with them far more dramatic than we often recognize. He wasn't challenging fringe extremists whom everyone already distrusted; He was questioning leaders who had earned their credibility through decades of helping people navigate their faith. For the average Israelite, the choice wasn't between an obviously corrupt religious system and Jesus—it was between trusted spiritual guides who had proven their commitment to Israel's traditions and this new teacher making extraordinary claims.

When we understand this reality, we can better appreciate why people didn't immediately abandon the Pharisees to follow Jesus despite His miracles and compelling teaching. The religious establishment represented stability, familiarity, and communal identity during a time of foreign occupation. Following Jesus meant risking not just theological disagreement but potential community exclusion and identity crisis.

This perspective transforms how we read the gospels. The tension wasn't simply between "bad religious leaders" and Jesus—it was between an established system that provided genuine value and a radical new reality that threatened to upend everything people thought they understood about God and faithfulness. In this light, the resistance to Jesus becomes more comprehensible, and the decision to follow Him appears even more costly and significant than we often recognize.

## THE DISCIPLES' REALITY: UNDERSTANDING WITHOUT HINDSIGHT

When we read the gospels from our modern perspective, knowing the full story and its outcome, we often miss the immediate lived reality of the disciples. For them, following Jesus wasn't the beginning of "Christianity" as we conceptualize it—it was a profound spiritual crisis within their Jewish identity and worldview.

The disciples weren't experiencing a smooth transition to a new religious paradigm. They were witnessing their entire understanding of God, scripture, and covenant being fundamentally reoriented in real time. Even when Jesus spoke plainly to them, the gospels repeatedly show them misunderstanding his parables, mission, and predictions about his death. They struggled to reconcile what they were witnessing—miracles no mere human could perform—with Jesus' predictions of his coming crucifixion. They believed he was "the One," but their expectations of what "the One" would do (overthrow Rome, establish God's sovereign rule) were being systematically dismantled.

Given this context of overwhelming cognitive and spiritual upheaval, it is frankly nonsensical to suggest that Jesus was simultaneously laying out detailed church government structures through veiled comments. As Jesus himself acknowledges in John 16:12, "I have much more to say to you, more than you can now bear." The disciples were already struggling to process the immediate implications of who Jesus was and what his appearance meant for Israel's covenant relationship with God.

Paul himself later acknowledges that the church was a "mystery" revealed after Jesus' resurrection (Ephesians 3:1-6), not something Jesus was explicitly establishing in his teaching to Israel. This doesn't diminish the importance of the church, but it recognizes the actual historical and narrative progression as it unfolded for those experiencing it without the benefit of hindsight.

When we impose our church-centric reading on texts like Matthew 18, interpreting them primarily as instructions for church governance and discipline, we anachronistically flatten the text and miss the immediate drama. Jesus' disciples weren't ready to conceptualize a primarily Gentile church that would exist centuries later; they were struggling to understand why their Messiah spoke of his coming death rather than his coronation. Their plate was more than full with the immediate revelation unfolding before them. The magnitude of spiritual upheaval that Jesus' arrival caused cannot be overstated—we truly cannot fathom it from our modern perspective.

The religious leaders of Jesus' day weren't simply confused about His identity. The narrative reveals something far more unsettling: many recognized something profoundly true about Him yet actively resisted this truth to protect their religious systems and status. The issue wasn't intellectual misunderstanding but heart-level resistance.

Nicodemus acknowledges, "Rabbi, we know that you are a teacher who has come from God. For no one could perform the signs you are doing if God were not with him" (John 3:2). This statement reveals that at least some religious leaders recognized divine authority in Jesus, yet many still opposed Him. This wasn't mere confusion—it was active resistance to a truth they partially recognized but found threatening to their religious identity and authority.

Imagine a marriage where one spouse meticulously maintains all the external signs of commitment—wears the wedding ring, speaks respectfully in public, remembers anniversaries—yet their heart has grown distant and self-protective. The external signs of devotion mask an internal disconnection. This is precisely what the gospel narrative exposes about religious devotion apart from genuine relationship.

## GRACE AS EXPOSURE: REVEALING THE TRUE NARRATIVE

What makes Jesus' approach so profoundly intelligent is that He didn't primarily rely on direct confrontation or accusation to reveal the true condition of Israel's relationship with God. Any religious leader can say, "You're hypocrites." What Jesus understood was that grace—not condemnation—would most effectively expose what truly lived in people's hearts.

When God incarnate appears among His covenant people, we might expect a seamless, joyful reunion—like a husband returning home to a welcoming embrace. Instead, Jesus' acts of grace created immediate tension and resistance. This unexpected friction reveals the core narrative of the gospels: God has come to His people who claim to worship Him, but their response to His grace exposes that their devotion has become hollow religious performance rather than genuine relationship.

The older brother in the Prodigal Son parable perfectly illustrates this dynamic. His true heart condition is not exposed by any rule he breaks or by direct confrontation. It's his reaction to the father's grace toward his wayward brother that reveals everything. His outrage exposes that his "faithfulness" was never about loving the father but about securing his position and status. Without the father's celebration of the younger son, this heart condition might have remained hidden indefinitely—even from the older son himself.

When Jesus heals on the Sabbath, the religious leaders' anger reveals something far deeper than mere rule-following. As Jesus points out, they themselves "break" the Sabbath to circumcise (John 7:23), showing their selective application of principles. The issue wasn't about consistent interpretation of the Law—it was about who had the authority to interpret. Their resistance exposed that they weren't truly concerned with honoring God through Sabbath observance; they were concerned with maintaining their position as the authoritative interpreters of God's will. Jesus's act of grace threatened not just their interpretation but their very status as interpreters.

This approach bypasses natural defenses. When confronted directly about hypocrisy or false devotion, people can argue, rationalize, or deflect. But when confronted with grace that doesn't fit their spiritual accounting system, their true heart response emerges unfiltered. Grace creates a crisis of recognition precisely because it doesn't play by established religious rules—it exposes whether we truly love God or merely the religious systems we've built around Him.

The genius of Jesus' approach is that He didn't merely tell people their devotion was hollow—He created situations where they would demonstrate it themselves through their responses to grace. The ultimate question of the gospel narrative thus becomes painfully clear: are we serving God, or are we serving ourselves in God's name? The answer is revealed not in our religious knowledge or performance, but in how we respond when God extends grace in ways that threaten our religious identity and status.

This pattern permeates the entire gospel narrative. The cosmic drama isn't merely whether people recognize Jesus intellectually, but whether those who claim to love God can recognize Him when He appears in unexpected ways and extends grace that challenges their religious frameworks. The religious leaders' resistance to Jesus wasn't primarily intellectual confusion—it was heart-level protection of religious identity and authority when confronted with grace that threatened both.

This reframing fundamentally transforms how we read the gospels. They aren't primarily instruction manuals for Christian living but the unfolding story of what happens when God personally appears among those who claim to worship Him—and how grace, not confrontation, most effectively reveals the true state of that relationship.

## THE IRONY AT THE CENTER: WHO REALLY LOVES GOD AND WHY

One of the most striking aspects of the gospel narrative is its profound irony: those considered furthest from God often recognized and honored Him most authentically, while those claiming closest relationship often resisted Him most strongly.

At its core, the story becomes about who really loves God and why they love Him. The narrative reveals a crucial distinction: Those who genuinely love God remember that He is the source of their meaning and value—not that they are somehow special in themselves. No amount of religious knowledge, doctrine, or external adherence can salvage the relationship when it shifts from gratitude toward God to entitlement and arrogance.

Consider the contrast between Simon the Pharisee and the "sinful woman" in Luke 7. Jesus points out that Simon didn't offer even basic hospitality—"You gave me no water for my feet"—while this woman lavished honor on Him. The religious leader who should have recognized God's presence failed to show even common courtesy, while the outcast demonstrated profound reverence.

This wasn't an isolated incident. When Matthew the tax collector throws a banquet to honor Jesus, the narrative isn't merely showing that Jesus "associated with sinners." It's highlighting that tax collectors—despised as traitors and thieves—recognized something in Jesus worthy of honor and celebration that the religious elite missed entirely.

This pattern repeats throughout the gospels:

- A Roman centurion shows faith "not found in all Israel" (Matthew 8:10)
- A Samaritan woman recognizes Jesus as Messiah while religious leaders plot against Him (John 4)
- Zacchaeus responds with immediate, radical generosity while the religious crowd grumbles (Luke 19)

Look closely at these examples. Zacchaeus celebrates by hosting Jesus and giving half his possessions to the poor. The woman who kisses Jesus' feet does so with tears of gratitude, washing his feet with her hair. Matthew the tax collector throws a banquet to honor Jesus. What do these responses reveal? They show that those who truly love God are the ones who recognize Him as the source of their pardon, status, and meaning. Their love flows from gratitude for grace received rather than pride in religious accomplishment.

The narrative consistently shows that religious knowledge, practice, and identity can become obstacles to genuine relationship with God when they become ends in themselves rather than expressions of love for Him. It warns us not to be arrogant, assuming that our initial awe of God can't be lost and replaced by entrenched entitlement and our own perceived spiritual heroics.

This irony creates a profound challenge for those of us embedded in religious systems. It suggests that our very religiosity—our biblical knowledge, our church involvement, our theological precision—can become the greatest barrier to recognizing God's actual presence and activity. The more invested we are in our religious identity, the more threatened we might feel by God acting in ways that don't conform to our expectations or that extend grace to those we deem unworthy.

## THE PARADOX OF SPIRITUAL PRIVILEGE

Perhaps the most sobering aspect of the gospel narrative is the paradox it reveals those most vulnerable to spiritual ruin are precisely those who appear most spiritually privileged. Jesus declares this explicitly when He tells the religious leaders, "Therefore I tell you that the kingdom of God will be taken away from you and given to a people who will produce its fruit" (Matthew 21:43).

This statement would have been shocking to its original hearers. The religious leaders believed their special status as God's people was secure. Yet Jesus reveals a profound truth: they were only God's people because He made them His people, and it remains His prerogative to redefine the boundaries of His kingdom.

The narrative reveals a crucial distinction: God's commitment to Israel was not obligatory but faithful. He wasn't fulfilling His promises because He had to, but because faithfulness is His character. This understanding transforms everything about religious identity. It means that privileges—whether those of ancient Israel or the contemporary church—are always gifts given in grace, never status earned through merit.

In this light, Paul's warning to Gentile believers in Romans 11 takes on profound significance for all who engage with the gospel narrative. When Paul tells the Gentile Christians, "Do not be arrogant...

for if God did not spare the natural branches, he will not spare you either" (Romans 11:20-21), he's applying the very lesson that the gospel narrative reveals about Israel's response to Jesus.

Paul specifically warns against the tendency to read Israel's story with a sense of superiority—as if we would have recognized Jesus had we been there, as if we are somehow spiritually more discerning than those who missed Him. This attitude reveals we've missed the most profound lesson of the gospels: that spiritual privilege provides no guarantee against spiritual blindness when entitlement replaces gratitude.

Consider how Paul deliberately emphasizes Israel's spiritual advantages before discussing their stumbling: "Theirs is the adoption to sonship; theirs the divine glory, the covenants, the receiving of the law, the temple worship and the promises. Theirs are the patriarchs..." (Romans 9:4-5). He's not describing spiritual nobodies who lacked revelation or knowledge. Israel had extraordinary spiritual privileges—far greater than the Gentile believers to whom Paul was writing, who were relative newcomers to the covenant story.

Yet despite these advantages, many in Israel didn't recognize God when He stood before them. Not because they lacked information or revelation, but because their approach to that revelation had transformed from humble gratitude into entitled status. They had begun to believe that their spiritual privileges were evidence of their own special status rather than expressions of God's faithfulness.

Paul sees this as a sobering warning for the church. In 1 Corinthians 10, he makes a similar point, noting that Israel "were all baptized into Moses in the cloud and in the sea. They all ate the same spiritual food and drank the same spiritual drink; for they drank from the spiritual rock that accompanied them, and that rock was Christ. Nevertheless, God was not pleased with most of them" (1 Corinthians 10:2-5). The parallel to Christian baptism and communion is unmistakable—Paul is warning that participation in sacred rituals provides no guarantee of genuine relationship with God.

This reframing addresses the natural question: If we're not reading the gospels primarily for moral application, what are we reading them for? The answer is that we're reading them for the most crucial spiritual lesson of all—that genuine relationship with God is never straightforward, never guaranteed by religious knowledge or practice, and constantly threatened by the subtle shift from gratitude to entitlement.

The gospel narrative, read properly, instills the very humility and gratitude that protects against this danger. It reminds us that we are favored only because God favors us, that we receive grace only because He gives it, that our spiritual identity is never earned but always received. It warns us against the comfortable assumption that we would have recognized Jesus when those before us did not and challenges us to examine whether our own religious devotion might contain the same fatal disconnect that plagued Israel despite all their spiritual advantages.

The irony becomes clear: the more spiritual privilege one has, the more vulnerable one becomes to the temptation of entitlement. Hence, those in spiritual leadership should be the humblest, recognizing the thin line between privilege and entitlement, between grace received and arrogance assumed.

## BEYOND APPLICATION TO TRANSFORMATION

This narrative approach doesn't simply give us moral directives to follow. It places us within the story, forcing us to ask whether we might be the religious devotees who would miss God standing right before us. This is infinitely more challenging than being told what to do or not do—it requires ongoing discernment rather than mere compliance.

When we read the gospels primarily for application, we often position ourselves as the heroes of the story—identifying with Jesus or the disciples while distancing ourselves from the "bad" religious leaders. The narrative approach forces us to consider whether we might be more like the Pharisees than we care to admit.

The question becomes not simply "What should I do?" but "Who am I becoming in relation to God?" Not "Am I following the rules correctly?" but "Is my heart truly surrendered to God, or am I using religious observance to maintain control while appearing devoted?"

Consider how Peter's denial unfolds after his confident assertion, "Even if all fall away on account of you, I never will" (Matthew 26:33). The narrative doesn't just teach "don't be overconfident." It reveals how easily religious devotion can mask our true heart condition even from ourselves. Peter genuinely believed in his own devotion until the moment of testing exposed what truly lived in his heart.

This pattern of self-deception appears throughout the gospels. The rich young ruler believes he has kept all the commandments until Jesus' challenge reveals his attachment to wealth (Mark 10). The disciples argue about who is greatest even after Jesus repeatedly teaches servant leadership (Luke 22). These episodes don't merely provide moral lessons about humility or generosity; they expose how easily we can maintain external religious compliance while our hearts remain unchanged.

## THE FALSE SECURITY OF RELIGIOUS KNOWLEDGE

One of the most unsettling aspects of the gospel narrative is how it challenges the value of religious knowledge divorced from relationship. The religious leaders possessed extraordinary knowledge of Scripture. They had memorized vast portions of the Law and the Prophets. They devoted their lives to understanding and applying these sacred texts.

Yet this knowledge didn't lead them to recognize God standing before them. In fact, Jesus suggests their knowledge had become an obstacle: "You have let go of the commands of God and are holding on to human traditions" (Mark 7:8). Their interpretation of Scripture had become so rigid and self-referential that it couldn't accommodate God acting in unexpected ways.

This presents a profound challenge to contemporary church culture, which often prizes biblical knowledge and theological precision. The gospel narrative suggests that such knowledge, while valuable, provides no guarantee of genuine relationship with God. In fact, it can create a dangerous sense of spiritual security while masking heart-level disconnection from God.

Jesus' parable of the two sons (Matthew 21:28-32) illustrates this dynamic. The son who says he will obey but doesn't represent those whose verbal affirmation of faith isn't matched by their hearts. The son who initially refuses but then obeys represents those whose hearts ultimately surrender despite their initial resistance. Jesus concludes by telling the religious leaders that tax collectors and prostitutes are entering God's kingdom ahead of them—not because these "sinners" have more religious knowledge, but because they recognized their need and responded to God's grace.

This doesn't devalue Scripture or theological understanding. Rather, it suggests that such knowledge fulfills its purpose only when it leads to genuine relationship with God rather than becoming an end in itself or a source of religious identity and status.

## THE HAZARDS OF APPLICATION-FIRST READING

When we read the gospels as narrative rather than primarily for application, the most profound lessons emerge with clarity. Our tendency to focus on application stems from a fundamental misunderstanding:

the assumption that devotion to God equals relative obedience—that repeating God's words or maintaining correct positions automatically constitutes genuine relationship with Him.

We often believe the connection between external compliance and internal devotion is straightforward. We take moral stances ("God doesn't approve of this behavior"), defend doctrinal positions ("baptism must be performed this way"), and attend religious services—all assuming these actions naturally reflect or produce genuine devotion to God.

What the gospel narrative reveals, however, is that this connection is not straightforward at all. You can comply externally while your heart remains completely disconnected. You can defend correct doctrine while opposing the very God that doctrine describes. You can maintain perfect religious attendance while remaining a stranger to genuine relationship with God.

But the narrative exposes an even greater danger: the very act of defending moral stances or engaging in doctrinal debates can reinforce the hardening of your heart. Consider the Pharisees—each time they stood up for Sabbath regulations or purity laws, they were hardening their hearts against the God those very laws were meant to honor.

This reveals the profound irony at the heart of religious devotion: you can defend God against God. You can cite Scripture to resist the Author of Scripture. You can use religious devotion itself as a shield against genuine relationship with the One to whom that devotion is supposedly directed.

The gospel narrative thus warns us that religious practice is not only non-equivalent to genuine relationship—it can become actively hazardous to our spiritual life when divorced from genuine revelation and responsive gratitude. The greatest threat to authentic faith may not be irreligion but religion itself when it becomes an end rather than a means.

This doesn't mean abandoning moral stances or doctrinal clarity. Rather, it means holding them with humility, recognizing that correct positions can coexist with hardened hearts. It means approaching Scripture not primarily as a source of positions to defend but as a narrative that reads us—exposing our tendency to substitute religious performance for genuine relationship.

When we read the gospels this way, the question is no longer primarily "What position should I take on this moral or doctrinal issue?" but "Is my heart truly open to God, even when He challenges my religious expectations and comfortable spiritual identity?" This question applies not just to ancient Pharisees but to everyone who claims to follow God—then and now.

The gospel narrative thus offers a profound warning against the very religiosity it inspired—reminding us that God is not contained by our theologies about Him, that His presence often disrupts rather than validates our religious systems, and that genuine devotion is marked not by correct positions but by open-hearted responsiveness to God Himself.

## "BUT WHAT DO I DO NOW"

Our knee-jerk desire to keep extracting "how-to" lessons that ends up re-centering the story on us rather than on Jesus. When we start treating every passage like a springboard for our personal "hero's journey," the Gospels end up sounding like moral fables—and we lose the cosmic weight of God Himself stepping into His covenant people's midst. **The narrative itself is the point**. It's the story of Yahweh incarnate, and it exposes hearts (including ours) simply by telling what happened when He showed up. Yes, there are times for explicit commandments and direct instructions, but the Gospels at their core are a theophany—God in the flesh among His people—and that drama is meant to stop us in our tracks, not just arm us with new tips for self-improvement. Instead of "over extracting" and parachuting back to ourselves right away, we're invited to remain in the tension and let the story shake us to the core. It's easy to rush past that uncomfortable dissonance by saying, "But what do I do now?"—However, that's exactly how we might inadvertently create distance from the One who should be the central player. The power is in **beholding** Jesus, not in turning the text into a self-centered action plan. In other words: * There's **no shortage** of moral implications in the story of Jesus. But trying to flatten the Gospel into bullet points risks missing the **narrative's deeper force**, which is that God walked among us and revealed our hearts by His very presence. * The irony is that the more we obsess over extracting applications and self-betterment, the more we can slip into making ourselves the focal point—and the story of Jesus slowly becomes another religious program rather than an invitation to wonder, worship, and reorientation around **Him**. It's less about skipping application entirely and more about **resisting the impulse** to reduce the Gospels to "me-focused steps," which can displace the radical, Jesus-centered drama. The very tension the Gospels create in us is often what we need to let ourselves feel before we jump to any "what's next?" --because that tension itself may be where Christ is doing His most transformative work. When we learn simply to *be*—to take in the story of Jesus on its own terms, to stand in wonder rather than rush to "implement"—something deeper happens. That uninterrupted vision of God awakens the exact humility, love, and obedience the moral approach tries (and often fails) to produce. Ironically, by refusing to turn the Gospels into a personal to-do list, we end up living the heart of the message more authentically.

# 64

# The Forest for the Trees on the Binary Outcome

Scripture presents a God who is both Savior and Judge—a reality many find unsettling. Why, people ask, must the outcome be so stark: **salvation or condemnation?** In truth, this binary is woven into the very nature of an "unavoidable" God. From Isaiah's depiction of the Lord enthroned above the nations to Jesus' claim that "all judgment" rests with Him (John 5:22), the Bible consistently teaches that we cannot sidestep God; we can either receive His sacrificial love or face His righteous judgment.

### 1. The Unavoidability of God

In Isaiah, God is portrayed as "high and lifted up" (Isaiah 6:1), beyond the reach of human power or manipulation. This unstoppable sovereignty continues into the New Testament, where Christ declares, "I am... the living One; I was dead, and now look, I am alive for ever and ever!" (Revelation 1:18). If **God** can be contained or ignored, He would cease to be God. Since He **is** God—unavoidable in love and authority—the final outcomes of encountering Him are necessarily momentous.

## Savior or Judge

- Isaiah's message: Those who repent find redemption; those who persist in rebellion face ruin.
- Jesus' message: "Whoever believes in the Son has eternal life, but whoever rejects the Son will not see life…" (John 3:36).
- No neutral space remains when dealing with infinite holiness.

### 2. A Paradox of Omnipotence and Sacrifice

- The mystery intensifies with the incarnation. The omnipotent Creator appears in vulnerable flesh, bearing humanity's sin. This paradox (Philippians 2:6–8) means that rejecting Christ isn't just declining a religious offer—it's dismissing the ultimate, sacrificial self-revelation of God.
- **Grace for the Unworthy**: Anyone, no matter how flawed or broken, can place faith in Him and receive forgiveness (Romans 10:13).
- **Judgment for the Defiant**: Spurning such grace, purchased at infinite cost, can't be a trivial act. As Jesus Himself says, "Whoever is not with me is against me…" (Luke 11:23). The stakes are necessarily high.

### 3. Love and Wrath Converge at the Cross

It's tempting to see love and wrath as incompatible—why can't there be a third, moderate path? But Scripture depicts them as two expressions of the same holy character:

### Love Displayed

> - Christ's crucifixion is God's self-giving love on full display: "God demonstrates his own love for us in this: While we were still sinners, Christ died for us" (Romans 5:8).
> - Such an act sets the bar for grace impossibly high—God withholds nothing, not even His own Son.

### Wrath Expressed

> - On the Cross, Jesus bears sin's penalty (Isaiah 53:4–6), satisfying divine justice. Rejecting that sacrifice is no mild snub; it's a direct stand against the only remedy for sin.
> - If one refuses the gift that is infinitely costly, the outcome cannot be a gentle shrug—so Scripture warns of condemnation (Mark 16:16).

**Thus**, in the same event (the Cross), love and judgment collide, showing no third way. We embrace the Son, or we reject Him; there's no middle ground.

### 4. Heightened Stakes: "No Response Is Neutral"

Because God stoops so low to save us—becoming human, enduring the Cross—**any** response to Him carries grave implications:

### Acceptance Leads to Unbounded Grace

> - "Whoever comes to me I will never drive away" (John 6:37). Faith unites us to Christ's resurrection life and secures eternal fellowship.

## Rejection Leads to Inescapable Judgment

- "They will go away to eternal punishment, but the righteous to eternal life" (Matthew 25:46).

- This is not divine pettiness; it's the logical consequence of turning from the One who alone holds life. For an "unavoidable God," refusal cannot be inconsequential.

### 5. Continuity from Old to New

Far from jettisoning Old Testament themes, Jesus amplifies them:

- **Isaiah** saw Yahweh as Redeemer and Judge, unstoppable and holy (Isaiah 13–23 for judgment on nations; Isaiah 40–55 for comfort and redemption).

- **Jesus** proclaims that He came "to seek and to save the lost" (Luke 19:10) yet also declares that rejecting Him leaves one "condemned already" (John 3:18).

Just as Isaiah encountered a glorious God no one can escape (Isaiah 6:5), so the Gospels present Christ as the same Lord, offering gracious salvation yet holding final authority to judge.

## GOD CANNOT BE INCONSEQUENTIAL AND STILL BE GOD

Throughout history, sovereign rulers left no "third path": you submitted or rebelled. A medieval peasant in England understood there was no neutral stance toward the king. A subject in an Egyptian dynasty recognized no middle option. This isn't overreach; it's simply the nature of sovereignty. A God who can be brushed aside is no God at all.

- **Not "Flexing" Authority**: This isn't about God "playing rent-a-cop" or a boss on a power trip. It's that true sovereignty—over life and death, time and eternity—cannot be inconsequential to human existence.

- **No Third Path**: Just as no nation's rule offers a partial loyalty plan, God's eternal kingship admits no half-measures. You can't truly sidestep the One "in whom we live and move and have our being" (Acts 17:28).

- **A "Black Hole" of Love and Judgment**: When you take all the weight of this unstoppable authority and channel it into the greatest act of self-sacrifice on the Cross, you create a pull so immense that nothing can escape its significance. The Cross demands a response—accept or reject. Indifference is ultimately a form of rejection when faced with infinite love on such display.

## CONCLUSION: THE LOGIC OF A BINARY CHOICE

A third option might seem more palatable—some neutral ground where one neither surrenders to God nor embraces total rejection. But the God of Scripture is too holy, too present, and too sacrificially loving for neutrality to make sense. **A small deity can be ignored or relegated; the God who created the universe and took on flesh demands a decisive response.**

- **Savior**: Trust in the Son, and you receive life beyond measure.
- **Judge**: Reject or feign belief, and you face the rightful King's condemnation.

Far from cruel, this binary outcome is the natural outflow of an "unavoidable" God. If He truly is the King, all must answer to Him. If He truly poured out His very life, then spurning such a gift is no inconsequential offense. Hence the "Yes or No" ultimatum: either embrace the saving love that cost heaven everything or face the just judgment of the One who refuses to be sidelined. The stakes are high precisely because His love is so great—and genuine love demands a wholehearted response.

# 65

# The Forest for the Trees – Progression

God's Word is perfect, timeless, and infallible. Yet the audience receiving it—humanity—is finite, flawed, and shaped by culture. Because of this, God, in His wisdom, has revealed His truth gradually. This unfolding approach doesn't make Scripture fallible; it makes it both accessible and transformational. If all truth were given at once, it would be like trying to pour an ocean into a cup.

Recognizing how God's revelation unfolds allows us to see Scripture as a cohesive story of redemption rather than a random collection of laws. The Law, though perfect, was a step on a path that leads us to a greater fulfillment in Christ.

## THE FOREST OF GRADUAL REVELATION

God's revelation doesn't change in substance, but it does build over time, reflecting our limited capacity to grasp His fullness. Scripture highlights this gradual process:

1. **Galatians 3:24 – The Law as a Tutor**

   - Paul describes the Law as a guardian or tutor, intended to guide us until Christ arrived. It provided moral boundaries for an ancient world rife with violence and disorder, laying down foundations of justice and holiness.

   - This doesn't imply that God's Word was incomplete; rather, it shows that humanity wasn't ready for the fullness of grace revealed in Jesus.

2. **John 16:12 – "You Cannot Bear Them Now"**

   - Jesus told His disciples there were things they weren't yet prepared to hear. He disclosed truth incrementally, giving them just enough to handle in that moment.

   - Later, the Holy Spirit would continue to illuminate further truths.

3. **Hebrews 1:1–2 – From Prophets to Jesus**

   - "In the past, God spoke to our ancestors through the prophets... but in these last days He has spoken to us by His Son."

   - God's message is consistent, but its clarity reached its apex in Christ, who revealed the fullness of God's character and purpose.

## THE TREES OF PROGRESSION: WHY THE LAW DIDN'T OUTLAW EVERYTHING

Modern readers often wonder why the Old Testament Law doesn't itemize every imaginable moral failing (e.g., drug abuse, road rage). The short answer is that these weren't issues in the ancient context, but there is a deeper reason as well.

1. **With God, Morality Is All-or-Nothing**

   - In James 2:10, we read that breaking one law is equivalent to breaking them all. Morality in Scripture is not a checklist; it reflects God's character.

   - One sinful act reveals a heart misaligned with God's holiness. Whether it's lying or something more severe, the root issue is the same: separation from His righteousness.

2. **Practical Guidance for a Brutal World**

   - The Law was delivered to a community navigating survival in a hostile environment. It didn't target future offenses like modern drug abuse because that wasn't part of their reality.

   - Commands like "Do not murder" set forth a timeless principle: human life is sacred. These principles endure, even if the specifics of cultural expression change over the centuries.

3. **God's Character as the Ultimate Standard**

   - Instead of listing every possible sin, the Law conveys the core attributes of holiness, justice, mercy, and love. These transcendent qualities apply to every generation.

   - Even if times and technologies evolve, the moral core remains the same because it's rooted in God's unchanging character.

## THE "OCEAN AND CUP" ANALOGY

Picture trying to pour an entire ocean into a single cup—it would overflow, break, or be wasted. That's how it would look if God revealed His entire plan to humanity in one instant. Instead, He pours out truth progressively, allowing us to grasp it step by step.

1. **The Law as a Starting Point**

   - Commands like "Do not commit adultery" set boundaries for a specific era, but Jesus took it further: "Anyone who looks at a woman lustfully has already committed adultery…" (Matthew 5:28).
   - Christ's teaching goes beyond external compliance, aiming at the state of our hearts.

2. **The Cross as the Fulfillment**

   - The Law could only do so much; Jesus, by fulfilling the Law, revealed the ultimate expressions of love, grace, and reconciliation.
   - "Do not think that I have come to abolish the Law or the Prophets; I have not come to abolish them but to fulfill them" (Matthew 5:17).

3. **The Spirit as Our Ongoing Guide**

   - Even after the resurrection, the revelation continued through the Holy Spirit, guiding believers into all truth (John 16:13).
   - This helps us apply eternal principles to ever-changing modern contexts, without losing sight of God's timeless character.

## WHY GRADUAL REVELATION MATTERS

1. **It Shows God's Patience**

   - God doesn't overwhelm us with knowledge we aren't prepared to handle. Step by step, He leads us into deeper understanding of His heart.

2. **It Makes Scripture Universal**

   - Since the Bible's moral truths rest on God's character rather than exhaustive lists of sins, its teachings remain relevant across history and cultures.

3. **It Leads Us to Christ**

   - Every stage of God's plan points to Jesus, who embodies the fullness of God's love, justice, and grace. This progressive unveiling guides us to the center of our faith.

## THE FOREST OF GOD'S MORALITY

To truly see God's overarching plan, we must recognize that the Law, while perfect, was never the end of the story—it was part of a journey culminating in Christ.

- **Morality Isn't a Simple Checklist**: God's standard is holistic, rooted in His nature.
- **Progressive Revelation**: Far from diminishing Scripture, it demonstrates God's loving adaptation to humanity's capacity.
- **Culmination in Jesus**: By fulfilling the Law and revealing God's character, Jesus brings the entire narrative into focus.

## CONCLUSION: EMBRACING THE BIGGER PICTURE

James reminds us that breaking one law amounts to breaking them all because God's morality is a unified whole. The Law doesn't list every sin—nor need it—because it was always pointing beyond itself to God's timeless nature. Recognizing the step-by-step unveiling of truth doesn't weaken Scripture's authority; it amplifies God's wisdom and love.

God's approach is relational rather than merely regulatory. He meets us where we are, adding "drops" of revelation until we can handle more. As you engage with Scripture, remember that behind each command and story stands a bigger narrative of redemption. Let that perspective draw you closer to the One who patiently guides us into the fullness of His plan.

# 66

# The Forest for the Trees— Divine Concessions and Adaptability

Scripture portrays God as unchanging in character yet remarkably adaptable in approach. While His nature remains consistent, His methods adjust to human frailty and historical context. This truth becomes evident when we examine the Bible's full story rather than isolating individual passages. The concept of divine concession—God working within human limitations without endorsing error—challenges both rigid fundamentalism and the assertion that Scripture contains mistakes.

## THE DIVINE BALANCE: UNCHANGING YET RESPONSIVE

Throughout Scripture, we see that God's flexibility reflects His wisdom rather than any deficiency in His revelation:

1. **Perfect Will vs. Permitted Will**

   ▸ God's perfect will often give way to His permitted will when confronted with human limitation or rebellion.

- This adaptation isn't compromise but strategic engagement with humanity in its fallen state.

2. **Concession Without Contradiction**

- When God makes a concession, He doesn't contradict His holiness—He reveals how His redemptive purpose works within our brokenness.
- These adaptations aren't errors in Scripture but deliberately recorded interactions showing God's divine pedagogy.

# THE TREES OF CONCESSION: BIBLICAL EXAMPLES OF DIVINE ADAPTATION

### 1. Marriage and Divorce – Adjusting to Hardness of Heart

"Moses permitted you to divorce your wives because of your hardness of heart, but from the beginning it was not so." (Matthew 19:8)

Jesus explicitly acknowledges that Moses' allowance of divorce wasn't God's original design but a concession to human stubbornness. This wasn't an error in the Law but a divine accommodation to Israel's condition. God permitted what He didn't prefer as a way of limiting damage while maintaining relationship with His people.

### 2. Kingship in Israel – Adapting to Israel's Demand

When Israel demanded a king "like all the nations," God told Samuel: "They have not rejected you, but they have rejected me from being king over them." (1 Samuel 8:7)

- Despite this representing a rejection of God's direct theocratic rule, He granted their request.

- God worked within their flawed desire, incorporating it into His larger redemptive plan that ultimately led to King David and eventually to Christ, the true King.
- The monarchy became both a concession to human desire and a vehicle for divine revelation.

### 3. Mosaic Mediation – Accommodating Fear

At Sinai, the people begged: "You speak to us, and we will listen; but do not let God speak to us, lest we die." (Exodus 20:19)

- God originally intended direct communion with His people yet adapted to their fear by speaking through Moses.
- This divine accommodation became a defining feature of the old covenant—God relating to Israel through mediators rather than directly.
- Rather than overriding their fear, God worked within it while pointing toward a future time when His Spirit would dwell within His people.

### 4. The Ark's Unexpected Dwelling – Beyond Prescribed Boundaries

Though the Ark of the Covenant was designed to rest exclusively in the Holy of Holies, we find it residing in Obed-Edom's house: "And the ark of the LORD remained in the house of Obed-Edom the Gittite three months, and the LORD blessed Obed-Edom and all his household." (2 Samuel 6:11)

- God worked outside His prescribed pattern, blessing a Gittite's home through the Ark's presence.

- This flexibility didn't compromise the Ark's holiness but demonstrated God's willingness to extend blessing beyond established boundaries.

## 5. Abraham's Negotiation – Divine Responsiveness

Genesis 18 records Abraham's remarkable negotiation with God over Sodom's fate, repeatedly lowering the threshold of righteous people needed to spare the city from fifty down to ten.

- God entertained each adjustment in Abraham's appeal, showing divine willingness to work within human intercession.
- This wasn't God changing His mind but revealing how He values relationship and incorporates human advocacy into His justice.

# INTERPRETING CONCESSIONS: WHAT THEY ARE AND AREN'T

What Divine Concessions Are Not:

### 1. Not Mistakes or Errors

- Concessions aren't flaws in earlier revelation that needed correction.
- They represent God's intentional strategy of meeting people where they were while moving them toward greater truth.

### 2. Not Contradictions

- Divine adaptations don't contradict God's character; they express His wisdom in relating to humanity at different stages.

- Each concession serves the larger redemptive narrative rather than undermining it.

### 3. Not Moral Relativism

- God's concessions don't mean truth changes or that morality is subjective.
- They show how God's unchanging truth interfaces with changing human contexts.

## WHAT DIVINE CONCESSIONS TRULY REVEAL:

### 1. God's Relational Nature

- Concessions show that God isn't a rigid force but a personal Being who engages with His creation responsively.
- They highlight relationship over rulebook, revealing a God who listens and adapts His approach.

### 2. The Reality of Progressive Revelation

- Each concession occurs within the larger story of God gradually revealing more of Himself and His ways.
- What appears as accommodation in one era often sets the stage for deeper truth in the next.

### 3. The Path to Christ

- Every divine concession ultimately points toward Jesus, who perfectly reveals God's heart.
- In Christ, we see the culmination of God's adaptability—He enters our broken world and accommodates to human form without compromising divine nature.

## THE FOREST PERSPECTIVE: GOD'S CONSISTENCY THROUGH ADAPTATION

When we examine individual concessions (trees), we might wonder about apparent inconsistencies in God's approach. But stepping back to see the entire forest reveals a coherent pattern:

1. **An Unwavering Destination**

   - Each divine accommodation moves history toward Christ and the redemption of humanity.
   - Though the path adjusts to human contingencies, the destination never changes.

2. **Unchanging Character, Flexible Methods**

   - God's adaptability flows from His consistent character—His love and commitment to relationship remain steady while His methods vary.
   - What might appear as inconsistency is the consistency of a wise parent adapting approaches for a child's changing needs.

3. **The Ultimate Concession: Incarnation**

   - In Christ, we see the greatest divine accommodation—God taking human form.
   - "The Word became flesh and dwelt among us" (John 1:14) is the ultimate example of God adapting to our limitations without error.

## HOW THIS RESHAPES OUR BIBLE READING

Understanding divine concessions transforms how we approach Scripture:

1. **Beyond All-or-Nothing Thinking**

   - We can affirm Scripture's inerrancy without demanding uniformity in every divine-human interaction.
   - God's word remains trustworthy even as it shows His ability to work within human constraints.

2. **Recognizing Multiple Voices Without Error**

   - The Bible records different covenantal stages and divine accommodations without contradiction.
   - Diverse biblical voices reflect God's intentional strategy, not mistakes needing correction.

3. **Appreciating Divine Pedagogy**

   - God teaches like a master educator—meeting learners where they are and gradually leading them deeper.
   - Early concessions often serve as object lessons preparing for fuller revelation later.

## CONCLUSION: THE BEAUTY OF DIVINE ADAPTABILITY

God's concessions throughout Scripture don't undermine biblical authority; they reveal the depth of His wisdom and commitment to relationship. He adapts His approach without compromising His character, accommodating human weakness while steadily moving history toward redemption in Christ.

This pattern of divine flexibility within unwavering purpose offers us a more textually faithful way to understand Scripture. We don't need to choose between rigid fundamentalism that denies these adaptations or liberal reinterpretation that sees them as errors.

Instead, we can embrace the biblical witness that God makes concessions without mistake, adapts without error, and relates to humanity in ways that honor both His unchanging nature and our changing needs.

The forest of God's story reveals a Creator who is both consistent and creative in His pursuit of relationship with humanity—a pursuit that finds its perfect expression in Jesus Christ, the ultimate divine accommodation who brings full revelation without compromise.

# 67

# The Forest for the Trees – The Kingdom

Much of Jesus' teaching centers on the **kingdom**—His role as King and people responding as subjects. While this overlaps with themes of God's law and Christ's pastoral care, it's still a unique framework. The King bears ultimate authority to bless or judge. When we grasp this relational dynamic, we see why Jesus' words about the kingdom can be so challenging, commanding devotion on one hand and threatening judgment on the other.

## A DISTINCT FRAMEWORK: KING AND SUBJECTS

1. **Promise of David's Throne**

    - The idea of a king ruling God's people was prophesied in the Old Testament, notably in God's promise to David: "Your throne will be established forever" (2 Samuel 7:16).
    - This sets up the future arrival of a Son of David who would reign eternally—a promise distinct from the old covenant law code or the relational metaphors of shepherd/sheep.

2. **Neither Old Covenant Nor New Covenant**

    - Under the **old covenant**, God related to Israel as Lawgiver and people bound by legal terms. This exposed Israel's unfaithfulness but didn't inherently produce intimate relationship (see *The Forest for the Trees on Sin*).

    - The **new covenant** speaks of believers as God's children or co-heirs with Christ, highlighting familial closeness (see *The Forest for the Trees on Intimacy*).

    - **Kingdom** stands in contrast: it's monarchy, with the King possessing legal and judicial authority over His subjects.

## THE KINGDOM'S BLESSING AND THREAT

In the Gospels, Jesus announces the "kingdom of God" (or "kingdom of heaven"). This arrival is good news for those who submit to the King but terrifying for those who reject Him.

1. **A Sword, Not Just Peace**

    - "Do not suppose that I have come to bring peace to the earth. I did not come to bring peace, but a sword" (Matthew 10:34). This statement, jarring at first, makes sense within a kingdom lens: a new King's claim often causes division among potential subjects.

    - "Son against father, daughter against mother" is stark kingdom language. Loyalty to the King outranks all else, so those who refuse His reign find themselves at odds with Him—and sometimes with each other.

2. **Judgment for the Subjects**

   - Jesus warns of outsiders being "thrown into the darkness, where there will be weeping and gnashing of teeth" (Matthew 8:12; Luke 13:28). In Matthew 13:42, He likens it to a fiery furnace.

   - Parables such as the **wheat and weeds** (Matthew 13:24–30, 36–43) or the **sheep and goats** (Matthew 25:31–46) illustrate a future separation of faithful vs. unfaithful subjects. The King's verdict is absolute; it's not the gentle tone we see with "shepherd and sheep," but a decisive, judicial role.

3. **Potential Opposition**

   - The kingdom concept can even turn adversarial if subjects reject the King. Mark 12:7 depicts tenants who plot against the landowner's son—an image of Israel's leaders plotting against Christ Himself.

   - This underscores the possibility of rebellion: monarchy cuts both ways. The King is benefactor to the loyal, but a threat to the rebellious.

## KINGDOM TEACHING IN THE SERMON ON THE MOUNT

Jesus' **Sermon on the Mount** (Matthew 5–7) often features commands and consequences that feel more exacting than the old Mosaic law:

- Benevolence of the King. "Your Father knows what you need," "The very hairs of your head are numbered," and "Seek first His kingdom and His righteousness" highlight God's care. The King genuinely wants to bless His subjects, meeting their needs.

- Severe Warnings. "If you don't forgive others, your Father will not forgive you" (Matthew 6:15). "Anyone who says, 'You fool!' will be in danger of hell fire" (Matthew 5:22). These stringent statements reveal the King's authoritative stance. This is not a new covenant "family" tone but a kingdom declaration: obey or face consequences. The King can pardon or punish. Like a benevolent monarch, He offers grace but reserves the right to judge unrepentant subjects.

## WHY THIS KING-SUBJECT FRAMEWORK DIFFERS

### 1. Different Than Lawgiver-People

- The **Law** was a code that Israel repeatedly broke. While God remained sovereign, the old covenant was more about commandments and national identity.
- The kingdom, by contrast, zeroes in on a **single King**—the Son of David—enacting His reign personally. He is the Law embodied, issuing judgments in real time, often through parables that separate loyal from disloyal.

### 2. Different Than Shepherd-Sheep

- Shepherd language emphasizes security and sacrifice: "I lay down my life for the sheep." The sheep never face threats like "weeping and gnashing of teeth."
- By contrast, the kingdom includes possibilities of defiance, treason, and punishment. The King has every right to expel or judge the rebels; ironically, the "sheep" framework never shows Jesus rejecting His flock in that way.

3. **Different Than Father-Children**

   - Under the new covenant, believers are children of God, co-heirs with Christ—an intimate familial bond.
   - Kingdom loyalty is less about inheritance by birth and more about submission to the monarch's authority. One can be a subject of the kingdom without necessarily sharing the closeness of a "child of God." Conversely, a child of God is not automatically in the same position as a kingdom subject. Distinct frameworks can overlap (one person can be both child and subject), but they aren't interchangeable.

## A DIVISIONAL STANCE

Jesus' repeated emphasis on separation—wheat vs. weeds, sheep vs. goats, loyal vs. disloyal—reflects how **kingdom** parables draw stark lines. Those who embrace the King will find blessing; those who reject Him will face ultimate judgment.

- **Matthew 8:12**: "Subjects of the kingdom will be thrown outside..." references covenant people who presumed safety but refused the King's reign.
- **Mark 12:7**: Subjects can even kill the heir, making themselves enemies of the throne.
- **Matthew 13:42**: The parable's "weeds" are burned, symbolizing rebellious subjects cast out of the kingdom.

## CONCLUSION: GRASPING THE KINGDOM "TREE" IN THE BIGGER "FOREST"

Within the Bible's grand narrative, **kingdom** stands as a crucial relational framework—a monarchy where Christ, the Son of David, rules. This dynamic can't be neatly equated with the old covenant's legal structure or the new covenant's familial adoption, nor is it the same gentleness as shepherd-and-sheep. Instead, it highlights:

- **Authority and Judgment**: The King has the power to bless or condemn.
- **Potential Conflict**: Subjects may rebel, receiving dire consequences.
- **Divine Benevolence**: His rule is beneficial for those who submit—He meets needs, provides, and establishes righteousness.

When we zoom out to see the entire "forest," we appreciate how the kingdom metaphor advances God's unfolding revelation, pointing to Christ's absolute sovereignty. When we zoom in on its unique "trees," we grasp the regal demands: absolute loyalty, willingness to accept His reign, and readiness to face either grace or judgment. Understanding **the kingdom** for what it is—neither purely old covenant law nor new covenant intimacy—helps us interpret Jesus' hard-hitting parables and the serious tone behind them. It is monarchy in the highest sense—eternal, unwavering, and inseparable from the King Himself.

# 68

# The Forest for the Trees on Sin

We often treat sin as a roster of wrongdoings— "don't lie," "don't cheat," "don't steal"—without recognizing the deeper scriptural portrait of sin as a reigning power. When Paul discusses sin in Romans 6, he goes beyond mere behavior management. He paints sin as a dominion into which we were born because of Adam. This distinction matters, because misunderstanding sin can keep us from the freedom Christ has already won.

## SIN: MORE THAN A LIST OF ACTIONS

If we reduce sin to a catalog of offenses, our faith becomes a relentless cycle of avoidance and guilt. But Romans shows us that sin is a spiritual reality. Once we grasp that its power was broken at the cross, we can shift our focus to the greater truth: our new position in righteousness.

### 1. Sin's Dominion Through Adam

> "Sin came into the world through one man, and death through sin..." (Romans 5:12)

From Adam onward, humanity lived under sin's authority before committing a single act. It defined our spiritual environment, much like a tree rooted in toxic soil inevitably produces bad fruit.

2. **Righteousness Through Christ**

*"For as by the one man's disobedience the many were made sinners, so by the one man's obedience the many will be made righteous." (Romans 5:19)*

Through Christ, we've been moved into new soil—righteousness. Just as sin once produced inevitable death, righteousness now brings life. Our actions flow from this reality.

## THE EFFECTS OF TWO REALITIES

### Sin Produces Death

*"The wages of sin is death." (Romans 6:23)*

This dominion led to inevitable consequences: brokenness, decay, and separation from God.

### Righteousness Produces Life

*"The free gift of God is eternal life in Christ Jesus our Lord." (Romans 6:23)*

Righteousness, likewise, carries inescapable results: life, freedom, and restoration.

## REALITY PRECEDES EXPERIENCE

Paul distinguishes these two domains—sin and righteousness—from the day-to-day experiences we often focus on. We slip into error when we let our day-to-day failings shape how we see ourselves, instead of letting our new position in Christ define us.

- **Sin was real before you ever "felt" it.** Its dominion came through Adam, so wrongdoing was a natural outflow.
- **Righteousness is likewise real before you fully experience it.** In Christ, righteous living will naturally emerge from your new identity.

*"Consider yourselves dead to sin and alive to God in Christ Jesus." (Romans 6:11)*

The Greek term "logizomai" (to reckon or account) encourages us to accept by faith what God says is already true.

## RIGHTEOUSNESS OVER "SIN MANAGEMENT"

Fixating on sin leads to exhaustion—an endless battle to stamp out bad behaviors. When we center on righteousness instead, we rest in Christ's completed work, trusting that His life within us fuels true transformation.

1. **Escaping the Guilt Cycle**

    - Constantly policing yourself for slips and stumbles reinforces a sense of failure.
    - Recognizing Christ's obedience credits you with righteousness, shifting the burden to Him.

2. **Christ Living Through You**

    *"It is no longer I who live, but Christ who lives in me." (Galatians 2:20)*
    - Righteous actions become an outflow of Jesus' life in you, rather than your own moral perfectionism.

3. **A New Inevitability**
   - If sin's dominion once made wrongdoing inevitable, Christ's dominion now makes godly fruit equally inevitable.
   - Though we may stumble, sin no longer defines us. We're governed by righteousness.

## PICKING UP RIGHTEOUSNESS

What does it look like to adopt a righteousness mindset each day?

- Present Yourself to God

*"Present yourselves to God as those who have been brought from death to life..." (Romans 6:13)*

Approach Him not as a guilty sinner begging for scraps, but as a beloved child living in His gift of righteousness.

- Embrace the Inevitable Fruit. Romans 5:21 notes that where sin once reigned in death, grace now reigns through righteousness. Let faith in your new position guide your thoughts and actions, rather than striving to "fix" yourself.

## CONCLUSION: THE BIGGER PICTURE IS LIFE

Sin's reality brought death; righteousness's reality brings life. Paul doesn't stop at describing our ruin—he unfolds the empowering truth that, through Christ, sin's dominion is over. You've been relocated into the realm of righteousness, where life naturally flourishes.

So, lift your eyes from the daily battles with wrongdoing to the overarching truth of who you are in Christ. You're not simply trying to avoid sin; you're called to live from His righteousness. Let that consciousness shape your identity, your behavior, and your peace with God.

*"The free gift of God is eternal life in Christ Jesus our Lord."*
*(Romans 6:23)*

That's the heart of the matter: sin no longer defines you. In Christ, the dominion of righteousness does. It's an unending source of life—eternal, abundant, and secure.

# 69

# The Forest for the Trees on Intimacy

Scripture reveals a gradual deepening of relationship between God and humanity. From Adam and Eve's creation in God's likeness, to believers becoming co-heirs with Christ, we see a **progression** of intimacy that cannot be flattened into a single model. Zooming in on each stage, we notice unique "trees"—distinct relational frameworks—but zooming out, we see one "forest": God's desire to draw us ever closer.

## FROM CREATION TO COVENANT

1. **Creator and Creation**

    - In **Genesis**, God breathes life into Adam and Eve. This is remarkable—human beings bear His image. Yet at this stage, the bond is simply "Maker and made."
    - There is a measure of dignity (likeness) but also distance. Humans steward the earth, reflecting God's authority, but the connection remains primarily that of a Creator and His handiwork.

2. **Abrahamic Covenant**
   - Moving beyond universal creation, God chooses Abraham's lineage to reveal Himself. Abraham and his descendants receive inheritance (the land) and a commission to bless all nations.
   - Here, God is not merely "Creator" but **Covenant Partner**—the One who grants promises and calls Abraham's seed (Israel) to steward His revelation among the nations.

## THE LAW: A STRAINED RELATIONSHIP

As discussed elsewhere (see *The Forest for the Trees on Morality*), the Law didn't transform hearts; it exposed sin and fractures in the covenant (Jeremiah 11). In terms of intimacy, the relationship was "God and people"—an arrangement often strained by Israel's unfaithfulness:

- **Distance Through Disobedience.** Israel's repeated covenant-breaking highlights how a purely legal structure doesn't foster closeness. The Law thus underscores our need for something deeper: a renewed heart, not merely external guardrails.

## KINGDOM: KING AND SUBJECTS

1. **A Benevolent, Yet Distant Framework**
   - From David onward, the dynamic of **"God as King"** and Israel as His people intensifies. This concept reemerges in the Gospels, where Christ proclaims the "kingdom of God."
   - A king can bring blessing and protection—or judgment. It's a hierarchical model: subjects obey, the king rules. While benevolent, it still implies subordination rather than family-like closeness.

2. **Parables as Judgment**

   - Jesus' parables about "subjects of the kingdom" frequently include warnings: "they will be cast out," or "there will be weeping and gnashing of teeth."

   - This judicial tone reflects the role of a monarch who enacts justice. If the King is received, the kingdom is a blessing; if rejected, it's condemnation. As Simeon prophesied, Jesus would cause the **falling and rising** of many in Israel (Luke 2:34).

## SHEPHERD AND SHEEP: A DIFFERENT KIND OF CARE

Contrasting the king-subject dynamic, Jesus also speaks of Himself as the **Good Shepherd** and believers as His sheep. Notice how the tone changes:

- **Unconditional Safety.** "They shall never perish; no one will snatch them out of my hand" (John 10:28). It's tender, protective language—no hints of "being cast out." The shepherd lays down His life for the sheep, highlighting sacrificial love rather than judicial authority.

---

**IMPORTANT DISTINCTION: We often lump kingdom parables and shepherd imagery together. Yet Jesus never blends them in the same parable. One deals with potential judgment on disloyal subjects; the other emphasizes secure belonging. Both are true views of God's reign, but they serve different relational pictures.**

---

## RABBI AND DISCIPLES: INSTRUCTION WITH PARTIAL REVELATION

Jesus also appears as a **Rabbi**, gathering disciples who follow His teachings:

1. **Learning from a Master**

    - Discipleship implies sitting under instruction, acknowledging a gap in knowledge. It's a more intimate form of mentorship than mere subjection to a king yet still retains some distance.

    - We see disciples who misunderstand or even walk away when the lessons are hard (John 6:66).

2. **Progressive Discovery**

    - Jesus often asks, "Who do you say I am?"—indicating that disciples must grow into fuller insight.

    - Even after years of teaching, they grapple with His identity until the resurrection unlocks a deeper awareness.

## FROM SERVANTS TO FRIENDS

In the Upper Room, Jesus declares, "No longer do I call you servants...but friends" (John 15:15). This shift is **significant**:

- **Friends Know the Master's Business.** Jesus reveals truths He once kept veiled, showcasing a deepening intimacy not found in an ordinary teacher-student or king-subject dynamic. Friendship here suggests shared confidences—He entrusts them with His mission, a level of closeness not enjoyed by earlier Israel.

## CHILDREN AND CO-HEIRS: THE HIGHEST INTIMACY

Finally, after the resurrection, the New Testament depicts an even closer union:

1. **Children of God**
   - Believers are born again into God's family (John 1:12–13). This is greater than merely being God's creation; it speaks of adoption, inheritance, and direct fellowship.
   - Romans 8:15–17 calls us co-heirs with Christ—sharing in His sonship, not just receiving orders or lessons from a superior.

2. **Shared Identity in Christ**
   - Paul frequently uses the phrase "in Christ," signaling a union that surpasses any earlier covenant form. We aren't just students or loyal subjects; we're made one with Him, participating in His life and kingdom from within.

## CONCLUSION: SEEING THE WHOLE PROGRESSION

Zooming in on each relational "tree," we see nuances: Creator/creation, covenant partner, Lawgiver/people, King/subjects, Shepherd/sheep, Rabbi/disciples, friends, and ultimately children and co-heirs. **Zooming out** reveals a grand design of growing intimacy—God drawing humanity closer, stage by stage:

- **Creator/creation** gives us dignity but leaves a natural gap.
- **Covenant** raises us to partners entrusted with inheritance.
- **Kingdom** reveals God's authority, offering blessing or judgment.

- **Shepherd** imagery reflects secure, sacrificial care.
- **Rabbi/disciples** introduce the dynamic of teaching and learning, with partial revelation.
- **Friends** share His confidences.
- **Children** and **co-heirs** enter the fullness of family and identity in Christ.

Each picture is valid, but they aren't interchangeable. Lumping them together may lead to confusion about God's intent. Instead, each stage highlights a unique aspect of His relationship with us. When we grasp that the "forest" is intimacy growing over time, we appreciate that the goal isn't mere obedience or knowledge, but a **oneness** with Him—heart, spirit, and destiny intertwined.

# 70

# The Forest for the Trees – Divine Communication Within Human Limitations

Scripture reveals a God who speaks to humans within the confines of our created limitations while simultaneously pointing beyond them. Like sunlight filtering through stained glass, divine truth passes through the medium of human understanding—illuminating without being diminished yet taking on shapes our minds can comprehend. When we fixate on isolated passages without recognizing this dynamic, we miss the magnificent interplay between God's transcendence and His loving accommodation to our finite capacity.

### THE NATURE OF HUMAN LIMITATIONS

Our limitations as created beings aren't simply intellectual—they're inherent to our very existence:

1. **Perceptual Boundaries**
   - We experience reality through five senses, creating a framework we cannot think outside of.

- As Jesus told the Sadducees regarding marriage in heaven: "You are in error because you do not know the Scriptures or the power of God" (Matthew 22:29). They couldn't imagine realities beyond their experiential framework.

2. **Cultural Embeddedness**
   - Every human is situated within a particular time, culture, and worldview that shapes their understanding.
   - We often fail to recognize our own cultural lenses—like fish unaware of the water they swim in.

3. **Conceptual Constraints**
   - Our very language and thought patterns limit what we can comprehend.
   - As Isaiah reminds us: "'For my thoughts are not your thoughts, neither are your ways my ways,' declares the LORD. 'As the heavens are higher than the earth, so are my ways higher than your ways and my thoughts than your thoughts'" (Isaiah 55:8-9).

The profound truth is that we cannot even perceive the full extent of our own limitations. Like a two-dimensional being trying to comprehend three dimensions, we have no frame of reference for what lies beyond our created boundaries.

## GOD'S SELF-DISCLOSURE WITHIN LIMITATIONS

If God desires relationship with humanity, He must communicate within frameworks we can perceive, or the revelation becomes meaningless. This isn't God being deceptive; it's God being relational:

1. **Divine Accommodation**
   - God speaks in human language with human concepts, not because He is limited to them, but because we are.
   - When Scripture uses anthropomorphic language (God's "hand" or "eyes"), it's not error but necessary accommodation.

2. **Progressive Unfolding**
   - God reveals truth gradually, not because earlier revelation was false, but because humans could only grasp certain concepts at certain stages.
   - Each revelation is truthful within its context while pointing toward fuller disclosure.

3. **Incarnational Communication**
   - The ultimate example is Christ Himself—divine truth wrapped in human form.
   - "The Word became flesh" (John 1:14) is God's most profound communication strategy, meeting us in our limitations.

God's revelation is like a parent explaining quantum physics to a young child—necessarily simplified but never false. The parent might use analogies and age-appropriate concepts, building understanding over time while never lying to the child, even when full comprehension isn't yet possible.

## BEYOND A "MORAL BOOK": SCRIPTURE AS GOD-TO-HUMAN COMMUNICATION

One of the most common misunderstandings is reducing Scripture to merely a "moral book"—a collection of ethical guidelines. This fundamentally misses the nature of biblical revelation:

1. **Relationship Over Rules**
    - The Bible is primarily "God-to-human communication" aimed at relationship, not simply behavior modification.
    - Its purpose is revealing who God is and how we can know Him; moral guidance flows from this revelation but isn't its primary purpose.

2. **Contextual Moral Expressions**
    - Moral directives in Scripture often address specific historical situations through concepts accessible to that audience.
    - God gives Israel laws about slavery not because slavery is His ideal, but because His revelation engages with humans in their historical context.

3. **Direction, Not Description**
    - The Law points toward perfect morality without capturing it exhaustively.
    - It's directionally perfect but not descriptively complete—as Jesus demonstrated by summarizing all law into love of God and neighbor.

When we demand that every biblical passage provide timeless, universal moral instruction applicable in exactly the same way across all cultures and eras, we misunderstand the purpose of divine revelation. We're asking Scripture to be something it never claimed to be.

## THE TEMPLE PRINCIPLE: GOD GIVES MEANING, NOT VICE VERSA

The Israelites in Jeremiah's day couldn't grasp how God could threaten to destroy His own temple. Their error reveals a profound truth about divine revelation:

1. **Derivative Significance**
   - The temple had meaning only because God assigned it meaning as a symbol of His relationship with Israel.
   - When that relationship was broken through persistent unfaithfulness, God could withdraw the meaning He had given.

2. **Morality's Foundation**
   - Like the temple, morality itself derives its meaning and authority from God's character.
   - God isn't subject to morality as some independent standard; morality is the expression of His nature within created order.

3. **Contextual Applications**
   - Just as temple worship changed across biblical history (tabernacle, temple, synagogue, church), moral expressions develop according to God's revelatory purpose.
   - The underlying truth remains consistent while the application adapts to human understanding and historical context.

This principle helps us understand why something permitted in one era (like divorce) could be presented differently in another. The foundation—God's character—never changes, but the expression adapts to human capacity and God's progressive revelation.

## THE SADDUCEES' ERROR: PROJECTING OUR FRAMEWORK ONTO GOD

The Sadducees' question about marriage in the resurrection (Matthew 22:23-33) perfectly illustrates how we project our limited frameworks onto divine realities:

1. **Assumption of Continuity**
   - They assumed heaven must operate according to earthly social structures.
   - Their "gotcha" question reveals how trapped they were within their own conceptual limitations.

2. **Jesus' Paradigm Shift**
   - Christ doesn't simply answer their question; He reframes the entire paradigm.
   - "At the resurrection people will neither marry nor be given in marriage; they will be like the angels in heaven."

3. **Beyond Our Categories**
   - Jesus points to a reality that transcends our social and moral categories rather than simply perfecting them.
   - God's ultimate reality often exceeds our conceptual frameworks rather than merely existing within them.

We commit the same error whenever we assume God must operate within our understanding of morality, justice, or relationship. Our moral intuitions and frameworks, shaped by our limited experience and cultural context, cannot fully contain divine reality.

# THE COMPLETION IN CHRIST: HEART TRANSFORMATION

Jesus solves the limitation dilemma not by providing an even more detailed law but by offering transformation:

1. **Internal Over External**

    - "I will put my law in their minds and write it on their hearts" (Jeremiah 31:33).

    - A transformed nature rather than a more comprehensive rulebook.

2. **Spirit Over Letter**

    - The Spirit guides believers into truth (John 16:13) that transcends written codes.

    - Paul notes that "the letter kills, but the Spirit gives life" (2 Corinthians 3:6).

3. **New Creation**

    - The ultimate solution isn't better moral instruction but regeneration.

    - "If anyone is in Christ, the new creation has come" (2 Corinthians 5:17).

Christ fulfills the Law not by abolishing it but by bringing its intended transformation—the alignment of human hearts with God's nature. This transcends mere behavior modification or updated ethical codes; it addresses the root limitation of humanity.

## IMPLICATIONS FOR READING SCRIPTURE

Understanding divine communication within human limitations transforms our approach to Scripture:

1. **Humility About Our Understanding**

   - Recognizing our own limitations should make us cautious about declaring exactly what God can or cannot have meant.

   - We approach difficult passages with both confidence in God's character and humility about our interpretive capacities.

2. **Purpose Over Proposition**

   - We ask not just "What does this passage say?" but "Why did God communicate this to these people in this way at this time?"

   - The intent behind the communication often transcends the specific form it takes.

3. **Christ as Interpretive Key**

   - Jesus becomes the lens through which we view all Scripture, not to negate earlier revelation but to fulfill it.

   - "All Scripture...makes you wise for salvation through faith in Christ Jesus" (2 Timothy 3:15).

This approach frees us from both rigid fundamentalism that ignores contexts and progressive revisionism that dismisses difficult passages. We can affirm Scripture's truthfulness at every stage while acknowledging its accommodation to human limitations.

## CONCLUSION: SEEING THE WHOLE FOREST

When we focus too narrowly on individual biblical commands or narratives (the trees), we risk missing how they function within God's overarching communication strategy (the forest). Scripture isn't primarily a moral handbook or systematic theology textbook—it's the record of God's progressive self-disclosure to limited human beings across history.

This forest perspective helps us see that:

1. God has always communicated truthfully, even when that truth was partial and adapted to human capacity.

2. Moral expressions in Scripture develop not because earlier expressions were "wrong" but because they represented what humans could grasp at that stage of revelation.

3. The Bible's purpose isn't to provide exhaustive moral instruction for all situations but to reveal God's character and draw us into relationship with Him.

By understanding this divine-human dynamic, we approach Scripture with greater wisdom—confident in God's truthfulness while humble about our own interpretive limitations. We trust that the God who accommodated His revelation to ancient human understanding continues to illuminate our limited minds today, drawing us ever closer to the full knowledge of Himself revealed in Christ.

# 71

# Forest for the Trees – All Things Fulfilled in Christ

Having explored how morality, cultural context, progressive revelation, sin, and authority weave through Scripture, we now come to the culmination: **Jesus Christ.** Far from discarding the Law or negating history, He fulfills them in a way that reveals God's heart like never before. In Christ, the "trees" of rules, cultural frameworks, and partial understandings find their place in the broader plan of redemption.

## CHRIST: THE FULFILLMENT OF MORALITY

Asked about the greatest commandment, Jesus responded with two proactive statements:

- **Love God with all your heart, soul, and mind.**
- **Love your neighbor as yourself.**

These weren't new commands; they came straight from the Torah (Deuteronomy 6:5; Leviticus 19:18). Yet by highlighting *active love* over mere prohibition, Jesus showed that *true morality* focuses on doing good rather than just avoiding evil.

1. **Doing Good over Avoiding Wrong**
   - Repeatedly, Jesus reframed questions of legality—like healing on the Sabbath—to emphasize the higher good of mercy.
   - In effect, He taught that love is the bedrock of God's moral law.

2. **The Cross as the Pinnacle of Love**
   - Christ's sacrifice on the cross was the ultimate expression of God's character, fulfilling every moral demand by offering Himself for sinners.
   - "Love does no harm," Paul writes, "thus love is the fulfillment of the law" (Romans 13:10). Jesus embodied this to perfection.

## CHRIST: THE FULFILLMENT OF PROGRESSIVE REVELATION

Throughout history, God unveiled truth in stages, giving people what they could handle at the time. In Jesus, we see the apex of that unfolding plan.

1. **From Shadows to Substance**
   - Old Testament sacrifices foreshadowed the need for atonement, but Jesus' death on the cross permanently dealt with sin, rendering those rituals complete (Hebrews 10:10).
   - He didn't annul earlier revelation—He brought it into clarity and completion.

2. **God's Patience and Jesus' Teachings**
   - Jesus said there were truths even His disciples couldn't bear yet (John 16:12), implying that revelation would continue.
   - The Holy Spirit, promised by Christ, guides believers further into the implications of His life and work.

## CHRIST: THE FULFILLMENT OF CULTURE

Jesus entered first-century Judea, adhering to Jewish festivals and customs, yet transcending cultural boundaries.

1. **Engaging with Culture**
   - Through parables about farming, marriage feasts, and daily life, Jesus contextualized eternal truths in familiar settings.
   - He honored the culture of His day without limiting His message to one people or era.

2. **Challenging Cultural Barriers**
   - Jesus ministered to women, Gentiles, and those deemed "unclean," thus breaking social taboos of His time.
   - His kingdom vision was never confined by ethnic or societal lines, affirming that "there is neither Jew nor Gentile... for you are all one in Christ Jesus" (Galatians 3:28).

## CHRIST: THE FULFILLMENT OF AUTHORITY

In Christ, we see authority defined not by coercion but by servant leadership.

1. **Redefining Power**
   - Jesus demonstrated authority by washing His disciples' feet (John 13:12–17) and teaching that the greatest should serve (Matthew 20:26–28).
   - The cross itself stands as the apex of authority exercised through self-giving love.

2. **Restoration over Domination**
   - God's rule in Christ isn't about controlling humanity; it's about restoring creation to its original purpose.
   - Believers, now reconciled to God, share in Christ's authority as co-heirs (Romans 8:17), living out a redemptive role in the world.

## SEEING THE WHOLE PICTURE IN CHRIST

With Jesus at the center, the diverse "trees" of Scripture—morality, culture, law, authority—compose a unified narrative pointing to God's redemptive plan.

- **Morality**: Not a list of prohibitions, but a call to active love perfectly modeled by Christ.
- **Progression**: Each biblical stage points to Jesus, who completes every hint of redemption given before.
- **Culture**: God works through real historical contexts, yet Christ's message spans every culture.
- **Authority**: Jesus reveals authority as a vehicle for restoration, rooted in love rather than force.

This synthesis shows how the Bible remains relevant to each generation. It's not an outmoded legal manual or cultural artifact; rather, it's a living testament of God's love, culminating in Jesus.

## CONCLUSION: CHRIST IS THE UNIFYING WHOLE

Jesus doesn't just stand among the "trees"—He embodies the entire "forest." In Him, all the threads of Scripture converge, revealing God's character and purpose in a way humanity had never fully grasped. Instead of defending every historical nuance or clinging to fragmented rules, we can rest in the truth that all is fulfilled in Christ.

When we read Scripture through the lens of Jesus' life, death, and resurrection, we see a coherent portrait of God's love unfolding across centuries. The invitation is to enter that story, letting Christ's fulfillment reshape our view of morality, culture, progression, and authority. In this grand forest of God's redemptive work, Christ stands as both the root and the crown—the One who ties it all together and brings it to fruition.

# 72

# The Menu Was Only the Beginning

*Conclusion*

You've navigated through five distinct sections—**clearing up misconceptions, practical Bible engagement, theological depth and transformation, Bible study mechanics,** and **seeing the big picture**. Think of them as different "dishes" that have hopefully expanded your palate. But here's the crucial truth:

**A menu is never the meal.** You can read the descriptions, pick your favorites, and form opinions, yet the real satisfaction only comes when you **taste**. Likewise, these chapters are just words unless you **encounter** the God behind them.

### Section 1: Misconceptions → Breaking Down Barriers

In the first section, you looked at common confusions—like "the Bible contradicts itself" or "the Old Testament God differs from the New." If these were roadblocks, you've now seen how Scripture stands firm under honest scrutiny. But smashing misconceptions isn't the end goal; it's an open door to **confidence**—so you can step forward and read the Bible **without fear** or doubt.

### Section 2: Practical Engagement → Building Real Habits

When the basics of Scripture feel overwhelming, it helps to have strategies—**when** to read, **how** to approach it, and **what** to do when confusion strikes. This section aimed to demystify the process so you could form a meaningful rhythm. Yet be clear: **habits** alone aren't enough. You're not just checking off boxes. You're showing up for a **relationship** that transforms you in subtle, everyday ways.

### Section 3: Theological Depth & Transformation → Encounter Over Knowledge

In the third section, we explored how **Bible reading** isn't about filling your head with theological facts—it's about **heart transformation**. If you only gather insights, you might impress people or win debates but miss the ultimate prize: **meeting Jesus** in the text. This part of the book reminded you that the Scriptures come alive most powerfully when they point you to the living Christ who still speaks, guides, and changes hearts today.

### Section 4: Mechanics of Bible Study → Learning to Fish

This section taught you **how** to read Scripture well—context, interpretation principles, avoiding common mistakes. Consider it your biblical "toolkit." Why does this matter? Because if your method is flawed, you might misunderstand or overlook the treasure right before you. But good tools are meant to **empower** you, not weigh you down with academic chores. The goal is to handle God's Word responsibly **so** you can see His story clearly and let it shape your life.

### Section 5: The Big Picture → Seeing the Grand Narrative

Finally, we took a step back to see how the Bible is a **unified story** of redemption—from Genesis to Revelation, pointing to Jesus as the central figure. Recognizing that overarching narrative stops you from cherry-picking verses or missing how each part connects. It's like stepping onto a mountaintop to view the entire forest, not just the individual trees. Once you grasp the scope, your appreciation deepens—and your sense of awe grows.

## READING IS NOT ENOUGH— ENCOUNTER IS EVERYTHING

All five sections had one consistent message: **the Bible is meant to draw you into relationship** with the Author. If you merely "study" Scripture as an academic exercise, or treat it like a mental puzzle, you risk missing out on the ocean you're meant to dive into.

Remember that metaphor from the introduction? Going out to the ocean but not getting wet. That's what it's like to read the Bible superficially—**you're near** the water, but you're not letting it **saturate** you. Real transformation comes when you step in—**feel** the waves, experience the mystery, and invite the living God to speak personally.

## AN INVITATION TO TASTE AND SEE

**Our bias** in writing this book has always been that you'd **encounter** the God of the Bible—far beyond words on a page. That's why we called it *The Menu*. You can scan the chapters, pick what resonates, dig in at your own pace—but never forget that the **encounter** is what truly matters.

- **Don't just read**—respond.
- **Don't just highlight**—ask questions, pray, let the text shape your choices.
- **Don't just admire**—obey. Put it into action, because God's Word is meant to be lived, not just studied.

## A FINAL ENCOURAGEMENT

Regardless of where you started—skeptic, seeker, or hungry student—God is big enough to meet you in your questions, your routine, your curiosity, and even your doubts. He's not waiting for you to become an expert in "spiritual discipline." He's simply extending an invitation: **"Come to Me. Know My heart. Let Me be the One who satisfies your soul."**

Let this book be a nudge, a spark, a door-opener—but let **Jesus** be your ultimate destination. If that's your takeaway—**that He Himself wants to guide you, speak to you, and transform you through Scripture**—then all the pages you've read have done their job.

May your Bible reading become less of a duty and more of a **delight**. May you move from secondhand spiritual "chewing" to directly tasting and seeing that the Lord is good (Psalm 34:8).

Bon appétit indeed.

**Closing Prayer:**

**Lord,**
*Thank You for how You speak through Scripture, revealing Your heart and truth. As we close this book, let us not close our hearts. Stir in us a fresh hunger for Your Word—one that leads to genuine encounter. Help us see beyond the pages to the Person who loves us. Transform our reading into a life-changing relationship with You. May every passage become an invitation to know You more deeply.
In Jesus' name,*
**Amen.**

# WORKS CITED

## Primary Sources

Holy Bible, English Standard Version. Wheaton, IL: Crossway, 2001.

Holy Bible, King James Version. 1769 Oxford Standard Text.

Holy Bible, New International Version. Grand Rapids, MI: Zondervan, 1973, 1978, 1984, 2011.

Holy Bible, New Living Translation. Carol Stream, IL: Tyndale House Publishers, 1996, 2004, 2015.

## Secondary Sources

Ehrman, Bart D. Misquoting Jesus: The Story Behind Who Changed the Bible and Why. San Francisco: HarperSanFrancisco, 2005.

Institut für neutestamentliche Textforschung. Kurzgefasste Liste der griechischen Handschriften des Neuen Testaments. University of Münster, 2012.

Jones, Clay. "The Bibliographical Test Updated." Christian Research Journal 35, no. 3 (2012): 32-37.

## Historical References

Dead Sea Scrolls. Qumran Caves, 3rd century BCE–1st century CE.

Josephus, Flavius. Antiquities of the Jews. c. 94 CE.

## Note on Biblical Citations

Unless otherwise indicated, Scripture quotations are taken from the Holy Bible, New International Version®, NIV®. Copyright © 1973, 1978, 1984, 2011 by Biblica, Inc.™ Used by permission of Zondervan. All rights reserved worldwide.

Scripture quotations marked ESV are from the ESV® Bible (The Holy Bible, English Standard Version®), copyright © 2001 by Crossway, a publishing ministry of Good News Publishers. Used by permission. All rights reserved.

Scripture quotations marked NLT are taken from the Holy Bible, New Living Translation, copyright © 1996, 2004, 2015 by Tyndale House Foundation. Used by permission of Tyndale House Publishers, Carol Stream, Illinois 60188. All rights reserved.

Scripture quotations marked KJV are from the King James Version of the Bible, which is in the public domain.

www.ingramcontent.com/pod-product-compliance
Lightning Source LLC
Chambersburg PA
CBHW070135100426
42743CB00013B/2710